THE WORLD'S MOST
MYSTERIOUS OBJECTS

This book is dedicated with great affection to our (unofficially!) adopted son in the USA, Rick Seidita, who shares our fascination with all things mysterious and unexplained phenomena in general.

THE WORLD'S MOST
MYSTERIOUS
OBJECTS

Very Best Wishes

Lionel and Patricia Fanthorpe

Lionel Fanthorpe

Patricia Fanthorpe

A HOUNSLOW BOOK
A MEMBER OF THE DUNDURN GROUP
TORONTO · OXFORD

Copy-Editor: Andrea Pruss
Design: Jennifer Scott
Printer: Transcontinental

National Library of Canada Cataloguing in Publication Data

Fanthorpe, R. Lionel
    The world's most mysterious objects / Lionel and Patricia Fanthorpe.

ISBN 1-55002-403-5

1. Curiosities and wonders. I. Fanthorpe, Patricia II. Title.

AG243.F358 2002   001.94   C2002-902289-4

1 2 3 4 5   06 05 04 03 02

Canada

THE CANADA COUNCIL | LE CONSEIL DES ARTS
FOR THE ARTS | DU CANADA
SINCE 1957 | DEPUIS 1957

ONTARIO ARTS COUNCIL
CONSEIL DES ARTS DE L'ONTARIO

We acknowledge the support of the **Canada Council for the Arts** and the **Ontario Arts Council** for our publishing program. We also acknowledge the financial support of the **Government of Canada** through the **Book Publishing Industry Development Program** and **The Association for the Export of Canadian Books,** and the **Government of Ontario** through the **Ontario Book Publishers Tax Credit** program.

Care has been taken to trace the ownership of copyright material used in this book. The author and the publisher welcome any information enabling them to rectify any references or credit in subsequent editions.

J. Kirk Howard, President

Printed and bound in Canada.⊛
Printed on recycled paper.
www.dundurn.com

Dundurn Press
8 Market Street
Suite 200
Toronto, Ontario, Canada
M5E 1M6

Dundurn Press
73 Lime Walk
Headington, Oxford,
England
OX3 7AD

Dundurn Press
2250 Military Road
Tonawanda NY
U.S.A. 14150

TABLE OF CONTENTS

FOREWORD
by Canon Stanley Mogford, MA

We live in an ordered universe. There is a pattern to it, a regularity, a system so coordinated and complete that we can base our lives on it. We know, accurately, when darkness is due to fall and the sun to rise. The movement of planets can be predicted long years ahead, and no eclipse of moon or sun now takes us by surprise. The force of gravity is constant and will always make walking on the street safe and falling off a skyscraper dangerous. The tidal system is so regulated that we know when to dock a ship and when not. We have times for planting and times to harvest what we grow. Generations long ago came to appreciate the consistency and order of their world. As the Book of Ecclesiastes, the Preacher, put it, centuries before Christ: "There is a time to be born and a time to die. A time to plant, and a time to pluck up what is planted." The universe is, in truth, like the mechanism of a great clock, each piece designed for a purpose and each fitting accurately into the whole.

Into this established order and consistency, human beings like ourselves are born and seek to make the best of our lives. A disordered life on an ordered background would seem a hazardous way to live. Those who set out to "buck the system" will clearly do so at their peril.

The Reverend Lionel Fanthorpe and his wife, Patricia, in the course of a long writing career, have recently completed a trilogy of books, both fascinating in their content and challenging in their interpretations. They have extracted from the orderliness of the world around them, and from its long history of people and events, the disordered, the abnormal, the mysterious — and have found much to leave us wondering.

In the first of these books, they singled out people who conformed to no order, system, or established patterns of behaviour. They found for us, to use the modern jargon, "one off" people, eccentric to a fault.

Shakespeare said of Julius Caesar that he "Bestrode the narrow world like a Colossus." He stood out from all the others around him. This book introduced us to some weird and wonderful people, and it is a fascinating read.

The second of their books moved away from people and concentrated on areas, places, and houses — which, in their turn, looked like all other places and houses, but certainly weren't. There are many grand houses in the land, but few like Bowden House, Llancaiach Fawr, or Borley Rectory, with their experiences of poltergeists and ghostly apparitions. There are many feared passages at sea where lives have been lost, but few as feared as the Bermuda Triangle, where whole ships and crews have disappeared without a trace. Only the intrepid and the foolish would venture casually and uncaringly into some of the places the authors outlined for us.

This book is the third of that trilogy. It identifies for us, this time, strange and mysterious objects. Most objects are commonplace. They are around us in millions, their purpose known and easy to understand. Those researched for us in this book are certainly neither ordinary nor commonplace. A box, for example, is by no means something out of the ordinary. The world is full of them, of all shapes and sizes, made of wood, cardboard, iron, or even silver. You will read in this book of boxes more sinister, with strange locking devices so made that if the unwary, or the unwelcome, dared open them the consequences could be fatal. There is another box, which — if any truth can be attached to the claim — contains within it the secrets of the future. A diamond, by legend, is a girl's best friend, but not the great diamond the authors have singled out for us, possession of which over generations has caused misery and death. The curse that was believed to have brought disaster to those who opened the tomb of Tutankhamen was as nothing compared to what appears to have happened to most of those who bought or inherited the Hope Diamond.

The authors have identified for us, in this, their latest work, machines, mazes, steeples, wells, precious stones, and more — and all of them have stories to tell. Some of what they describe for us seems almost beyond belief. Often, they will admit themselves baffled by what they have found. Sometimes they venture into interpretations. For many years, scholars were left baffled by the great mass of Egyptian writing that had been found but could not be read. The picture-based hieroglyphic language was like none other, and it could well have remained a mystery forever had not a stone been unearthed at Rosetta bearing a like inscription in three languages: two known, and one, the Egyptian, unknown. From the known it was possible to decipher the unknown, and thus were released the secrets of that picture language, so long hidden from us.

What mysteries, if any, could these objects explain? The secret of perpetual motion might have become known if only the paranoid Orffyreus had not taken an axe to his machine. The authors leave us in no doubt that *things* — as well as people — have a tale to tell.

The pursuit of the strange, the mysterious, the unknown, and the paranormal has exercised a fascination on many people for countless years. It has been a lifelong interest for our two authors. We owe them much for their long and careful researches, and for sharing their knowledge and expertise with us.

CANON STANLEY MOGFORD, MA,
CARDIFF, WALES 2002

(Canon Mogford is rightly regarded as one of the most brilliant scholars in Wales, and the authors are again deeply indebted to him for his great kindness in providing this foreword.)

INTRODUCTION

In a universe filled with the mysterious, the anomalous, and the unexplained, it is helpful to examine these mysteries by categories, rather than trying to take in their dazzling panoramic totality.

Lecturing on the theme of "The World's Most Fortean Object" at the 2002 Fortean Times *UnConvention* in the Commonwealth Institute in London, co-author Lionel concluded — after a wide survey of all the other mysterious objects that have intrigued researchers for so long — that the winner had to be the human mind. He said, "The human mind uses a physical brain that contains 10^{14} neurones and its electro-chemical synapse processes enable it to think as many separate thoughts as there are atoms in the known universe. There is nothing that it cannot do for us — if only we have the courage and imagination to unleash its amazing powers."

In this book, we have surveyed and analyzed a wide and varied range of other mysterious objects. They have taken us on a lengthy but intriguing research journey through history and the contemporary world. Can a diamond carry a curse — and, in any case, what exactly is a curse and how does it work? Back to the mystery of the mind again: a magician points a bone at a victim who believes in the magician's powers — and the victim promptly drops dead. He points the same bone at an agnostic Cordon Bleu chef, who thanks him politely and makes it into soup! The difference between death and culinary excellence lies in the minds of the chef and the man who thought the magician had strange powers.

From magical mysteries we have proceeded to look at pseudo-scientific ones: what exactly is ball lightning? Did Orffyreus really make a perpetual motion machine? What weird inventions of the brilliant but eccentric Tesla could we advantageously use today?

Locked rooms and locked boxes (like Joanna Southcott's) are

another great source of mystery — as are mazes and labyrinths. We've investigated several of those recently!

Curious codes, shrouded symbols, and anomalous alphabets bring their own special atmosphere of mystery with them. It's a very human response to want to find out what's written there.

Did the Golem of Prague really exist? Did the weird clay monster come to life and fight against its people's enemies? If so, the great question is *how?*

The quest for power and the fascination of mysterious objects often walk side by side. Did Charlemagne and Hitler have access to the mysterious Lance of Longinus — and did it affect the outcome of their battles? Did alchemists like James Price really succeed in making gold? What were the Emerald Tablets of Hermes Trismegistus (alias Thoth, scribe of the Egyptian gods) and where did they go? Could they possibly have become the mysterious and powerful Urim and Thummim of biblical times?

We've found these investigations both intriguing and fascinating, and we have great pleasure in sharing the research data — and a few of our theories — with our readers.

Lionel & Patricia Fanthorpe
Cardiff, Wales, U.K. 2002

CHAPTER ONE:
The Curse of the Hope Diamond

The history of the Hope Diamond is shrouded in strange Indian mythology. According to one Hindu legend, Bali fell by the hand of Indra during the great battle between Indra and the demons led by Jalandhara. From Bali's body came a flood of jewels — diamond from his bone, sapphire from his eyes, ruby from his blood, emeralds from the marrow within his bones, pearls from his teeth, and crystal from his flesh. Another Hindu demon, Ravana, abducted Sita, the wife of Rama. Rama, wild with grief, pursued her to the enemy's stronghold, destroyed Ravana, and rescued his bride.

The Hindu religion is rightly famous for its amazing artwork and statuary. The uniquely magnificent Hope Diamond probably came originally from the Kollur Mine in Golconda, India. The diamond initially formed one of the eyes of a beautiful statue of the goddess Sita. According to tradition, which seems reasonably historically accurate, the diamond, originally well over 112 carats, was stolen from the Hindu temple in which the statue of Sita stood. The tradition identifies the location as a temple of Rama-Sitra situated near Mandalay. A French diamond trader, Jean-Baptiste Tavernier, bought it from the thief, took it back with him to France, and sold it to King Louis XIV in 1668. Louis also purchased fourteen more large diamonds from Tavernier, as well as a number of smaller ones. The stone was re-cut by the court jeweller, Sieur Pitau, in 1673. The result was a 67-carat diamond described in the royal records as "steely blue." It was known at the time as the French Blue or "The Blue Crown Diamond." The King had it set in gold and wore it on a ribbon around his neck on ceremonial occasions.

The first indication that there was a curse on the diamond was the death of Tavernier. According to one account, having lost all his money, Tavernier returned to India to try to recoup his fortune. One account says he was savaged, killed, and partially eaten by wild dogs.

During the reign of Louis XIV, the stone apparently passed for a time into the ownership of Nicolas Fouquet, who during the early years of that reign was the last Surintendant des Finances. (The post was later changed to Controleur General des Finances). Son of a royal administrator who was also a wealthy ship owner, young Nicolas supported Cardinal Mazarin during the Fronde Period, 1648–1653. In an age when government posts were purchased, Nicolas bought the job of Procureur General to the Parliament of Paris in 1650, and his appointment as Surintendant des Finances came in 1653. He and Mazarin loyally supported each other, and Fouquet lent money to the French Treasury, thus becoming in all practical terms banker to the King. He conducted a number of intricate financial operations in somewhat irregular ways and became incredibly rich in the process. Unfortunately for Fouquet, Mazarin died in 1661, and Colbert struggled to oust Fouquet and become finance minister himself. On December 20, 1664, Fouquet was condemned to be banished from France, but Louis XIV changed the sentence to life imprisonment, and Fouquet was incarcerated in the fortress of Pignerol. This was under the command of Monsieur de Saint Mars, a trusted servant of the King and the man who had custody of the "Man in the Iron Mask." Fouquet was *said* to have died on March 23, 1680, but there are a number of serious researchers who believe him to have been the mysterious masked prisoner who lived on for many more years, and he was probably the custodian of some very strange secrets indeed. As one small example of just how much power and money Nicolas Fouquet controlled at the height of his career, we need look no further than Vaux-le-Vicomte. This incredibly luxurious structure occupied eighteen thousand workers and took over five years to build at a cost of millions of dollars. The great architect Louis le Vau designed the building. Charles le Brun, assisted by Andre le Notre, did the landscaping.

The most significant and interesting thing about Fouquet, apart from the source of his wealth and whether or not he became the Man in the Iron Mask, was the activity of his secretive younger brother, who was engaged in a great deal of seventeenth-century European espionage. This mysterious young man paid a visit to Rome, where he encountered Nicholas Poussin, the enigmatic painter closely associated with the mystery of the treasure of Rennes-le-Château — and more. A letter from the younger Fouquet to his immensely powerful and

14

The Hope Diamond.

wealthy elder brother makes it clear that Poussin had a secret that was worth a great deal more than money could buy and that he was more than willing to place that secret at the disposal of the Fouquet team.

After Fouquet fell from power, the stone went back under Louis's direct control. So Tavernier was apparently the first victim, Fouquet the second. When Fouquet was succeeded by Colbert, there is some evidence that one of Colbert's first tasks was to send a powerful and well-equipped expedition to Rennes-le-Château, where they proceeded to excavate the ancient tomb of Arques — the one said to have been a perfect facsimile of that in Poussin's most famous painting, *The Shepherds of Arcadia*. Whether Fouquet's fall from power was connected in any way with the Poussin and Rennes-le-Château mysteries or with the curse allegedly attached to the Hope Diamond is a matter of conjecture. Fouquet's fall was dramatic and indisputable.

Madame de Montespan, one of Louis XIV's mistresses, was allowed to wear the famous diamond. She was implicated in a widespread black magic and poisoning conspiracy, and, although she was lucky enough to survive, a great many of her co-conspirators were executed, and she herself fell heavily from royal favour.

The stone was part of the legacy of the hapless Louis XVI, who gave it to Marie Antoinette: both King and Queen ended on the guillotine, and the Princess de Lamballe, who had once borrowed the stone from Marie Antoinette, was murdered by the mob. The unlucky blue diamond then disappeared for a while. It actually vanished from the Gard-Meuble along with the rest of the French crown jewels around 1792.

15

Some of the pieces taken in this robbery were later recovered, but the Blue Crown Diamond was not. Surprisingly, one of Goya's portraits showing Queen Maria Louisa of Spain depicts her wearing a remarkable diamond closely resembling the one that disappeared in 1792.

Another strong tradition connects the mysterious Hope Diamond and its run of ill fortune with a Dutch diamond cutter named Wilhelm Fals. His son, Hendrick, whom he loved and trusted, stole the stone from him. Wilhelm died of grief, and Hendrick, overcome by remorse, committed suicide shortly afterwards. Around 1830, a deep blue diamond of some forty-four and a half carats appeared in London. Experts agreed that it was none other than the famous French Blue, or Blue Crown Diamond, carefully re-cut in an attempt to conceal its identity. The very wealthy Henry Hope bought it, and since that date it has been known as the Hope Diamond. Surprisingly, Hope himself does not seem to have suffered any ill effects from his purchase, and there is no record of anything untoward happening to any members of his immediate family. However, the diamond passed into the hands of a singer named May Yohe, who was married to Lord Francis Hope. Their marriage was markedly unhappy, and May believed that the diamond would ever after bring misfortune to any who owned it. Before dying in great misery and poverty, she laid the blame completely on what she thought was the unlucky stone. Her husband, who had also had severe financial problems, sold the diamond some time before the First World War to Jacques Colot, who had once been a prosperous broker. After buying the stone from Francis Hope, Colot lost his mind and committed suicide. Before his death, he had disposed of the diamond to Kanitovsky, a rather obscure Russian prince who was greatly attracted to a French dancer at the Folies Bergères. Kanitovsky then appears to have become as mentally disturbed as the unfortunate Colot: he shot his dancer friend, whose name was Ladrue, from his box in the theatre. He himself died not long afterwards — a victim of the Russian Revolution.

The diamond's next owner was Simon Mantharides. He was either thrown over a precipice by his enemies or simply fell over accidentally. Abdul Hamid II, who was Sultan of Turkey at the time and known to those who did not admire him as Abdul the Damned, was deposed and became mentally ill within a year of acquiring the diamond.

The next owner, Habib Bey, was drowned.

The diamond passed swiftly through the hands of a French jeweller named Pierre Cartier and went from him to Edward Beale Maclean, who was the owner of the *Washington Post*. Almost immediately after it came into Maclean's household, his mother and two of their servants died. Ten-year-old Vincent (or Vinson), his son, was run over and killed in a traffic accident. Maclean himself was involved in a notorious scandal case and died an alcoholic. His widow, Evalyn, had no apparent fear of the diamond and wore it on many occasions. Tragically, her daughter committed suicide in 1946 by taking an overdose, and someone remembered that she had worn the diamond on her wedding day. When Evalyn died a year later, Harry Winston, a prosperous New York jeweller, bought the whole collection for around a million dollars. He prudently presented the Hope Diamond to the famous Smithsonian Institution.

The problem with legends of curses is that they tend to grow in the telling. If something like the Hope Diamond is said to bring misfortune, all deaths, accidents, ruined careers, and other tragic disasters will be remembered and clearly associated with the stone — or whatever the accursed object is said to be. On the other hand, the thousands of hands that touched the stone and went on to prosperity and happiness are conveniently overlooked because they detract from the melodrama of the tale. It cannot be said that the diamond has not travelled. In 1962, the Smithsonian lent it to the Louvre in Paris, where it formed part of an exhibit entitled "Ten Centuries of French Jewellery." In 1965, it was exhibited at the Rand Easter Show in Johannesburg. In 1984, it went on exhibition at Harry Winston's in New York as part of their fiftieth anniversary celebrations. It went there again in 1996 in order to be cleaned and refurbished in its setting. In December of 1998, experts from the Gemmological Institute of America made a modern study of the stone. They reported on its very strong phosphorescence and recorded its colour as a dark greyish blue. A very sensitive colorimeter picked up a minute violet component within the deep blue colour, so slight as to be invisible to the unaided eye, but it is odd that Tavernier, who brought it from India in the first place, referred to it as having a beautiful violet colour. Its current weight is 45.52 carats, its length 25.6 millimetres, its width 21.78 millimetres, and its depth 12 millimetres.

Other famous diamonds — which can also be classified among the world's most mysterious objects — have followed trails of high adventure rather than downhill paths of ill fortune. The famous Millennium Star provides an example. Daringly taken from the war-ravished interior of the Democratic Republic of Congo by two fearless Britons working for De Beers, the 777-carat stone was found to be flawless when it reached London. Expert cutting brought it down to a mere 203 carats, but it remains a masterpiece of the diamond cutter's art.

Eight years after it was first found in Africa, it became the target of the most daring attempted jewel robbery of modern times. Using a JCB (a big earth-moving machine) to break in and a motor launch on the Thames for their intended getaway, the gang of diamond thieves was stopped by an ambush involving well over one hundred police officers. Perhaps it was the "lucky" number 777 that fended off tragedy, but allowed high adventure to surround the Millennium Star.

Yet another famous stone, the Koh-i-Noor, or Mountain of Light, left a trail of death and destruction behind it through centuries of Asian conquest and bloodshed. Nadir Shah took it from his defeated rival after the Battle of Karnal in 1736 and was duly murdered by a rival for the coveted throne. It finally came to rest in the late Queen Mother's crown, worn at the coronation of her husband, King George VI, and very appropriately laid in state with her.

There is an ancient and mysterious prehistoric passage tomb at Knowth, in County Meath, Ireland, and the strangest thing within it is a weird rock carving. At first glance, the researcher might be inclined to think that it was one of the familiar hunting pictures, designed, perhaps, to bring in the game by means of sympathetic magic. Is it a group of aurochs, running to escape the spears and arrows of the huntsmen? These strangely carved curves might represent their great flexed spines as they strain every sinew to escape.

Each curve is smaller than its outer neighbour — might they be incomplete circles? Is this the remains of yet another of the popular circular maze patterns that our Stone Age ancestors left in such abundance to intrigue today's historians? Some experts might see the three main curves as having religious symbolism, as representations of a mystical bridge, like the rainbow, linking the mortal world with the world to come. The Vikings believed the rainbow was called "Bifrost" and was the way the gods from Asgard reached the Earth. Yet another interpretation is a cornucopia.

Some researchers might interpret it as the all-seeing eye, the pupil in the centre of the lowest curve, the higher curves representing the brow and bone ridges of the upper part of the socket.

The carvings may be intended to be a fertility design, the newborn being discharged from the womb into the world. Yet another perspective suggests three fingers of the hand of a flint knapper, like those who worked in the mines in Grimes Graves in East Anglia in the United Kingdom. The knapper holds a flint instrument from which flakes are being chipped as he works to produce hand-axes, scrapers, and arrowheads. Or, the design might well be a plan of passage tombs similar to that in which it was found.

Every one of these conjectures has a reasonable level of probability — but what about the possibility of this old carving from Knowth representing the features of the lunar surface? It is only recognisable when these strange old marks are placed over a diagram of the moon's surface *as it appears to the naked eye*. Placing the carved design over the map produces a remarkably close fit. That piece of evidence on its own is admittedly interesting, but far from conclusive. It is only when some additional data about the Knowth burial site is added into the equation that the strange arcs and dots strengthen their claim to be a map of the moon. It has been known for over twenty years that at certain times it is possible for moonlight to shine along the eastern corridor of the

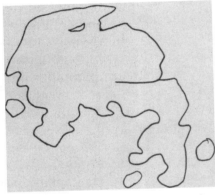
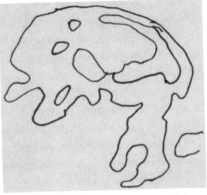

Dark area of the moon from actual photographs.

Dark areas of the moon adjusted for comparison with carving.

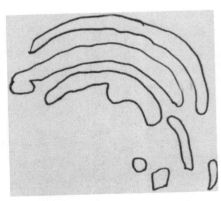
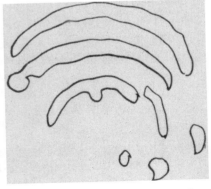

Original carving in ancient tomb.

Carving slightly adjusted to coincide with lunar surface.

Knowth tomb. It is also possible for moonlight to illuminate the Knowth "map" from time to time. Dr. Philip Stooke of the University of Western Ontario in Canada is an acknowledged world authority on maps of asteroids based on observational data obtained from spacecraft. He is convinced that the enigmatic carvings at Knowth form the earliest known lunar map.

This raises a great many intriguing questions. The tomb at Knowth is at least five thousand years old — the last earthly resting place of at least a hundred Stone Age kings and rulers. The moon map — if that's what it really is — is still comparatively modern when compared with an ancient map discovered at Mezhirich in the Ukraine in 1996. This one, showing a river and houses built beside it, was carved some twelve thousand years ago on a mammoth tusk. The ancient Egyptians, Babylonians, Assyrians, and Romans all made and used maps. Some of the earliest of these were on clay tablets, but it was the versatile seafaring Greeks who made the first truly scientific maps. In fact, it was Herodotus, the historian, who first referred to maps in his early writings. It was among followers of the great Greek mathematician Pythagoras that the theory of the Earth being spherical was first developed. Did those same pioneers see the moon as spherical too? Or did the idea of a spherical moon give them the related concept of a spherical Earth? There was certainly no lack of mathematical thought in those days: Eratosthenes — best remembered for his famous work on prime numbers — managed to work out the circumference of the Earth to within eighty kilometres.

The exciting work on Atlantis, which owes a great deal to Rand and Rose Flem-Ath, Charles H. Hapgood, and Colin Wilson, suggests that Antarctica was once Atlantis and that, far from sinking, it was swept south by a movement of the Earth's crust floating loosely on the magma below. Many of the ancient maps show a detailed knowledge of the coast of Antarctica that could not have been available to map makers in relatively recent times, but might have been preserved in very ancient libraries like the ones at Alexandria and Constantinople (Istanbul). The Piri Re'is Map in particular causes a great deal of controversy. Piri, nephew of a notorious pirate named Kemal, was beheaded in 1554, having held a highly responsible post in the sixteenth-century Arab world. Piri claimed that his map was based on twenty or more ancient maps from the library at Alexandria.

Where did all this ancient knowledge originate? Did Pythagoras, Eratosthenes, and their disciples have access to information from a highly advanced maritime culture that had flourished in Atlantis before the disastrous shift of the Earth's crust, about which Hapgood has speculated with such good evidence and such clear reasoning?

Was the mysterious lunar map in the ancient tomb at Knowth in County Meath, Ireland the product of knowledge from Atlantis?

CHAPTER THREE:
The Shroud of Turin, the Mandylion, and Veronica's Handkerchief

The greater the potential religious and historical importance of a mysterious object, the more controversy is likely to centre on it. There are three alleged, but semi-legendary, images of Christ on cloth that need to be considered together if maximum information is to be gleaned from them. They are almost certainly one and the same thing; their seemingly different origin stories have simply been mythologized, diversified, and embroidered over the centuries. This adds to the importance of the original mystery rather than reducing it. When something is considered important enough to have stories woven around it as the years pass, it's a safe bet to suggest that the historical original was something really significant.

To start with, there is a touching legend to the effect that a humane and pious woman named Veronica was moved with pity for Christ as the Roman executioners took him to Calvary to be crucified. She showed her sympathy in a practical and merciful way by moving through the crowd, defying the Roman soldiers, and wiping his face for him. According to legend, she was rewarded with a perfect picture of the divine countenance on the cloth she had used. Consequently, this became known as Saint Veronica's Hankerchief. However, the name Veronica, it has been suggested, actually came from Icon Veritas — meaning the true, real, or accurate picture. Moving away from the legend of the saint's kindness, was it possible that a Christian artist among the early disciples had painted a picture of his beloved master on cloth, a picture that later became known as the true or authentic likeness of Christ and around which the Veronica legend grew?

The best known — and the most controversial — image is undoubtedly the Turin Shroud. Saint Luke and Saint John both record that grave wrappings were seen in the empty tomb after the Resurrection of Jesus. There is an early Christian tradition that Thaddaeus, who was one of the

Early portrait of Christ, possibly based on St. Veronica's Handkerchief, the Shroud of Turin, or the Mandylion. St. Veronica (perhaps alias Icon Veritas — "The True Likeness") wiped the face of Christ.

seventy disciples mentioned in the Gospel of Saint Luke, chapter 10, verse 1, took the shroud with him for safekeeping. Thaddaeus was said to have gone as a missionary to Edessa, which is now known as Urfa and is situated in eastern Turkey.

Mannu the Sixth persecuted the Edessan Christians, and the precious shroud was carefully concealed in a secret hiding place among the stones above the west gate. Hermetically sealed there for two or three hundred years, it came to light again in the early sixth century. A disastrous flood had made it necessary to rebuild much of the Edessan city walls, including the critical area containing the west gate. Contemporary witnesses declared without hesitation that they believed it to be the Holy Cloth, or Holy Image, that Thaddaeus had brought to the city. (Might it not have been one and the same thing as Saint Veronica's Hankerchief — the Icon Veritas?) The Emperor Justinian also accepted its authenticity and promptly arranged for the Hagia Sophia Cathedral to be built to house it in Constantinople (later re-named Istanbul).

The mysterious image-bearing cloth (Veronica's or Thaddaeus's?) was from then on referred to as the Mandylion — and so the third version of the same legend was born. The Arabic term *mandylion* refers simply to a veil, a small cloth, or even a handkerchief — but the Shroud of Turin is well over three metres long. How is the apparent paradox resolved? Researchers have suggested that it was folded very carefully and framed in such a way that only the face was visible.

One reason for this folding may well have been the Jewish laws relating to what was considered to be ritually clean or unclean. A shroud was technically unclean, and was therefore an object to be scrupulously avoided by any law-abiding Jew.

Religious art historians have noticed that after the recovery of the Mandylion from its niche in the wall above the West Gate, all representations of Christ seem to have been based on it. Byzantine mosaics, frescoes, and paintings dating from the sixth century have shown more than a dozen significant points of similarity with the image on the shroud.

Beginning in the middle of the tenth century, the Mandylion was taken on a series of religious journeys. Art historians and icon experts again provided valuable supporting evidence for the apparent influence the Mandylion had had on religious art at this time. It would seem that during its tenth-century journeys, and right up until the start of the thirteenth century, the Mandylion, or Holy Shroud (originally called the Image of Edessa) was exhibited in its full, unfolded form. Earlier pictures of the dead Christ being laid reverently in the tomb had shown grave wrappings swathed around His body in the traditional funerary style. Pictures from the second half of the tenth century onwards, however, show the dead Christ lying in a position that would correspond to the image on the shroud.

The cataclysmic tragedy of 1204, when the misdirected Fourth Crusade destroyed Constantinople, led to the disappearance of the Mandylion for a century and a half. It seems probable that the mysterious sacred cloth was rediscovered by the valiant and indomitable Knights Templar, who had been founded in 1119, only eighty-five years before the overthrow of Constantinople. One of the central mysteries of this noble order of warrior-priests was a secret ceremony in which a sacred face, or head, was venerated. Prior to the malicious negative propaganda that Philip IV, ironically known as Philip le Bel, circulated about the Templars before his treacherous attack on them in 1307, the Templars had always enjoyed a reputation as men of total honesty and integrity. They were exactly the type of people to whom the Mandylion could have been safely entrusted.

Approximately half a century after Philip's attack, Geoffrey de Charny seems to have had possession of the Mandylion. When he died, his widow exhibited it, charging pilgrims a small entrance fee because Geoffrey's death had left her almost penniless. The querulous local bishop interfered and the widow's fund-raising exhibition of the Mandylion ceased. It seems ironic that the great Templar Order (which at the height of its power had ignored petty local bishops and jealous parish clergies with the contempt they deserved) should have had the exhibition of their most sacred relic inhibited by the whim of an unimportant rural bishop.

Although this discreditable episode apparently occurred in Lirey, a little French village over a hundred miles from Paris, it nevertheless brought the Mandylion back into the limelight. Research into accounts of this 1357 exhibition seems to suggest that the Mandylion was already a very old relic when Madame de Charny put it on exhibition. After her death, her son, also called Geoffrey, took charge of the Holy Shroud. This second Geoffrey of Charny also died impoverished, and his widow gave the shroud to Louis of Savoy.

In 1464, Pope Sixtus IV gave his support to the authenticity of the shroud, but it was over a century before it was sent to Turin. Borromeo saw it there in 1578, and Francis de Sales, who was then an assistant bishop, was one of those who were privileged to hold it during an exhibition in 1639.

Controversy continues to rage fiercely around the Mandylion as one piece of data continually seems to contradict another. In 1973, for example, threads from the Mandylion were scientifically examined at the Belgian Institute of Textile Technology in Ghent. Professor Gilbert Raes was in charge at the time. Rather surprisingly, traces of cotton were identified among the linen from which the shroud was largely woven, and this suggested to Raes and his colleagues that the linen had been made on a loom that was also used for weaving cotton. Cotton was apparently grown and used in Egypt and most of the Middle East in those days, but not in Europe. Raes also discerned herringbone patterns in the weave. These were characteristic of work done in Egypt and the Middle East two thousand years ago. The Associate Professor of Egyptology at Turin University in the 1970s was Silvio Curto, and it was his considered professional opinion that the cloth could indeed be two thousand years old.

Additional supporting evidence comes from Max Frei, a Swiss forensic scientist. Frei had had considerable botanical experience and was intrigued by the tiny pollen grains adhering to the shroud. In 1973, he categorized almost fifty different varieties of pollen clinging to the fibres of the Mandylion. More than thirty of the varieties he identified were found only in Palestine, the Turkish Steppes, and the area around Constantinople. Fifteen or sixteen varieties of pollen were identified as European, and some researchers argued that these grains could have become embedded in the Mandylion while it was being exhibited between 944 and 1204. As far as can be ascertained, it is highly unlikely that the shroud left European Christendom after being shown at Lirey by Geoffrey Senior's widow in 1357.

Members of an organization known as "The Shroud of Turin Research Project" were allowed to make a close and detailed examination of it in 1978. Their report included comments about the precise size and structure of the Mandylion. It felt silky to the touch; the colour was like that of mature ivory; and the whole thing felt surprisingly light. The cloth, as they measured it, was approximately four and a half metres long and just over a metre wide. There is a distinct strip roughly ten centimetres wide on the left side; otherwise, the cloth looks as through it was woven as one single piece. The mysterious image on the Mandylion dispels the pale Victorian Sunday School image of "Gentle Jesus." The man of the shroud was almost six feet tall and powerfully built. In life he probably weighed about one hundred and eighty pounds. As far as expert opinion can go based on so faint an image, he would have been around thirty-five years old.

The image on the shroud is very difficult to make out. Its details become much clearer in photographs and it is more easily understood at a distance than close up. The pigment — whatever it is — that is responsible for the image seems to touch only the outer fibres of each individual thread. The marking penetrates only three or four fibres down into the thread itself. Most experts are convinced that the more densely coloured areas give that appearance, not because the colour is deeper, but because the coloured fibres are more numerous in those darker areas.

In 1532, there was a disastrous fire in the Chambéry Chapel, where the shroud was kept inside a silver case. The heat was sufficient to melt the silver, and consequently the molten metal dripped through, leaving scorch marks on the shroud. The nuns of the Poor Claire Order devoutly repaired it. They sewed some fourteen large triangular patches, along with seven or eight smaller ones, to repair the holes that the fire had caused. There is much to commend in the courage of the two Franciscan priests who risked their lives saving the Mandylion and who preserved it from further damage by soaking the silver case with water as soon as they were clear of the fire. The aftermath of that trauma is still visible on the Mandylion today. Scorch marks, small holes caused by the molten silver, and what are presumably water stains after the silver box was doused are still visible. Another attempt — this time deliberate — to destroy the Mandylion took place in 1972, when an intruder burst into the chapel and tried to set fire to the holy relic. The asbestos inside the shrine saved it.

In 1898, the shroud was photographed for the first time by Secondo Pia. In his mid-forties, Secondo was a lawyer by profession but had won a number of prizes as a photographer. In 1898, electric lighting was still something of a novelty, and its results for an amateur photographer were likely to be uncertain. Pia first tried an exposure of fourteen minutes, and then with a later picture gave it twenty. It was about midnight, while he was working in his darkroom, that Pia was totally dumbfounded (his own description of his feelings) as the face of the shroud began to appear. Only then was it realized that the image on the shroud was a *negative*. The discovery that Secondo made was so impressive that the old box camera he used for that photograph is still to be seen in the Holy Shroud Museum in Turin.

In 1931, some exceptionally good exposures were made by Giuseppe Enrie, accompanied by Secondo Pia, who was by then well into his seventies. A young priest who was present with the two photographers went on to become Pope Paul VI.

Doctor Pierre Barbet and Professor Yves Delage brought their special knowledge to bear on the mystery of the Mandylion almost a hundred years ago. Both medical experts agreed that the man who had been laid to rest in the shroud was one who had well-developed muscles and had been used to hard work. They detected unmistakable signs of rigor mortis but maintained that there was no evidence of corruption. Again, in the opinion of these two medical examiners and others, the wounds as shown on the Mandylion were anatomically accurate. The lacerations of the scalp and above the brow suggested to them that the crown of thorns, unlike the circlet that religious artists normally portrayed, was more like a *cap*. Medical experts estimated the lance wound that penetrated the heart as being approximately five centimetres long by just over a centimetre wide. In the opinion of the experts, the wound had been made posthumously. The blood flow had simply run downward with gravity and had not spurted as it would have done if a living body had been penetrated in that way. Additional medical evidence would indicate death from asphyxiation, which is concomitant with crucifixion, as the victim is unable to breathe. The man of the shroud had bruises and cuts on the knees, which would indicate at least one heavy fall, and further marks on the back indicate, or suggest, that something heavy had been carried. Again, the medical evidence points to these back injuries having been inflicted after the scourging, because the whip marks had been modified and distended by this later, larger injury. Medical evidence in connection with the scourging suggested that well over a hundred blows had been inflicted, that two executioners had been involved, and that the wounds were of a type that would have been inflicted by the notorious Roman flagellum.

More recent — but equally controversial — evidence has suggested a completely different theory: the shroud probably originated in 1307, and was used to cover the tortured body of Jacques de Molay, the Grand Master of the Knights Templar. According to this theory, the fearless Templar leader was nailed to a door by his depraved interrogators, and the door was then slammed repeatedly. De Molay was then wrapped in the cloth that later became the Mandylion, or Holy Shroud of Turin. The medical evidence pointed to the man in the shroud as being tall and muscular. That description would fit a powerful fourteenth-century warrior-priest like Jacques. The theory is fascinating, but inconclusive. The mystery of the Mandylion remains unsolved, but it is one of the most mysterious objects on the planet. As a special stop-press item, it is relevant to note that archaeologist Dr. Shimon Gibson has recently discovered a shroud in a tomb near Jerusalem dating from the first century A.D. It may provide vital comparative evidence for accurately dating the Turin Shroud.

CHAPTER FOUR:
Alexander of Abonoteichous

The curious alleged miracles and mysteries and the strange artifacts and mysterious objects that were the property of Alexander of Abonoteichous (one of the weirdest miracle mongers of the second century A.D.) were recorded for posterity by Lucian of Samosata. Had he been alive today, Lucian would have been a satirical cartoonist, or maybe the presenter of one of those TV or radio shows that set out to expose charlatans. It would be the understatement of the millennium to say that Lucian was definitely not one of Alexander's supporters. Lucian describes him as "a thoroughgoing villain . . . god-like, handsome and tall with long hair that was partly artificial. He was intelligent and not without talent but he used his gifts wrongly. . . He was a blend of lies and trickery camouflaged as someone kindly and respectable . . . He loved to appear magnificent."

Alexander was apprenticed to a wizard-cum-doctor who sold mysterious healing potions and amulets. At an early age, he went into partnership with Coconnas, another young man who had similar interests. Financed by a rich Macedonian lady, Alexander and Coconnas went into business as travelling magicians. They settled not long after in Abonoteichous, which was Alexander's hometown. It is proverbial and almost invariably true in practice that "A prophet is not without honour except in his own land and in his own country." Alexander was the exception that tested that rule, but he survived. He attracted wealthy crowds and prospered like the metaphorical green bay tree.

When it suited him, he would pretend to be insane. In the second century, epilepsy was often looked at as being the result of a visit from one of the many gods. It was thought to give the epileptic the power to prophesy. Alexander discovered that by chewing soapwort he could produce some pretty realistic frothing at the mouth. (Soapwort is an herb that grows up to three feet high and carries attractive pink flowers, and the dark green leaves are very smooth to touch. It was used in the past as a cleaning agent for clothes because when boiled up it produced lather. It has also been used for treating itchy, flaky skin. It has many colourful local names, including "Bouncing Bet.")

Perhaps one of the main secrets of Alexander's success was careful preparation. He had noticed that a temple not far from his house was under construction. Water had formed a pool among the excavations the builders were making, and this gave Alexander an idea. He carefully blew a goose egg and inserted a minute live snake into it. The following day, suitably attired as a wild prophet with hair and beard flying characteristically in the wind, he made a public announcement that the god would shortly appear at the temple that was being built in his honour. Not surprisingly, this attracted a large crowd. Alexander offered loud prayers to Aesculapius and Apollo: "O Great Ones, give me evidence of your presence that I may show the people that you are indeed in your temple." He then took one of the libation vessels from the temple, slid the egg that he had prepared carefully underneath it, and covered the whole thing with mud. When the crowd was pressing around him sufficiently closely, he produced the little snake. The great majority of those present regarded it as a miracle and shouted accordingly. The symbol of Aesculapius, god of healing, was the well-known serpent coiled around a staff, a symbol that was also associated with Apollo. The appearance of their own symbolic snake in the temple that was being built to the gods was enough to convince the crowd watching Alexander that Apollo and Aesculapius were indeed present.

If preparation was part of Alexander's secret, timing was another. He knew when to act and when to wait quietly and unobtrusively, allowing things to happen. He disappeared for several days, mainly to allow the report of the snake miracle to grow and spread on its own. He then reappeared, lying artistically on a settee with a large snake coiled at his feet, its head tucked underneath one of his arms. He had, needless to say, recently bought a harmless tame serpent from a snake charmer who lived at a safe distance from Abonoteichous so that he could use it as an essential part of his show. He then created his artistic puppet masterpiece. This was a large snake's head made of painted linen and adorned with a human face. He kept the head of the real snake hidden and made the model look as though it were the genuine article. With a little well-placed horsehair, Alexander managed to open and close the linen snake's

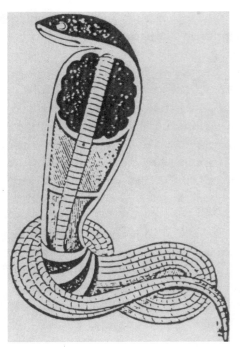

Weird ancient serpent similar to the one called Glycon, created by Alexander of Abonoteichous.

mouth to make it look as if it was speaking — and he also added an impressive forked black tongue.

As the cynical Lucian described the scene, Alexander performed in a small, dimly lit room in front of a very excited mixed crowd who had convinced themselves in advance that they were going to see gods and miracles. From what they had heard of the amazing appearance of the tiny snake in the temple, they were doubly amazed to find it had grown so fast and had been transformed into this vast serpent with a human face — totally under the control of the miraculous prophet Alexander.

Many centuries after Alexander's time, the famous Barnum and Bailey freak shows used to have a sign that said, "This way to the Egress." It was Barnum's way of moving the crowd along before they had time to look at anything in too much detail and begin asking awkward and embarrassing questions. Alexander used a similar technique: in his case, a number of accomplices moved people towards the exit before they could spend too much time looking at the linen snake's head with its horsehair control mechanism.

This great snake that Alexander had made answered to the name of "Glycon." It began the performance by crying out, "I am Glycon, bright light to mortal man and Grandson of Zeus himself." The prophecies cost two copper coins for each prediction — which was roughly equivalent to a day's wages.

Alexander had devised an interesting technique whereby those who wanted questions answered or specific prophecies spoken on their behalf would write their questions or particular areas of concern on a scroll, which would then be sealed and passed to Alexander. He would promptly disappear into his inner room and return in due time with the seals on the scrolls still — *apparently* — intact.

Shakespeare's Hamlet used a similar technique when disposing of the treacherous Rosencrantz and Guildenstern, who were trying to assist his wicked uncle in disposing of him. He found the letter that his usurping uncle, King Claudius, had written to the King of England requesting the recently defeated monarch kill Hamlet, well away from Denmark.

The worthy prince, who was sufficient of a scholar to be adept at such matters, *unsealed the murderous letter,* erased his own name, and inserted the names of Rosencrantz and Guildenstern instead. A little careful resealing with a hot knife or needle, and the fates of his two so-called friends were sealed as effectively as the letter.

Many of Alexander's answers were as ambiguous as those of Nostradamus or the Delphic Oracle. One popular format consisted of: "It shall come to pass when I will it — and when Alexander, my great prophet, has been given a generous gift so that he will ask it from me in his prayers."

Again like the Delphic Oracle's priests, Alexander knew a considerable amount about the political and social currents of his place and time. Like a skilled political commentator on radio, television, or in the press today, Alexander could often make a shrewd guess as to which way events were likely to develop.

The cruellest of the old rogue's deceptions concerned the health of the wealthy and credulous patrons who flocked to him. He had invented an ointment referred to as "cymides," which, according to Alexander, was capable of curing every complaint from housemaid's knee to myxomatosis. There was actually very little in it apart from bear's grease and a few spices.

Alexander invariably made the most of his mechanical skills. He was, in his way, quite an artificer. Perhaps the most mysterious object in all of his weird collection was a long speaking tube, which he had made by the simple method of neatly sewing together a number of windpipes from slaughtered cranes and herons. This artfully designed tube led into another room, where one of his accomplices spoke into it like the captain of an old-fashioned ship booming orders down to the engine room. The voice of the "god" that the clients heard — and only the very richest clients could afford it — came down this tube.

One of Alexander's greatest successes came when he moved to Rome and lured the wealthy and influential Rutilinus into his power. Surprisingly, the mysterious oracle told Rutilinus that he ought to marry Alexander's daughter, which he promptly did. In consequence of their union, vast amounts of Rutilinus's wealth made their way into Alexander's purse.

The problem with this investigation, as with all others of so-called seers and prophets, is that honest men like Lucian, acting from the highest of motives and doing everything within their power to expose the deceptions of cheats and charlatans, may, in their absolute certainty that it is trickery, *all* trickery, and *nothing but* trickery, miss the odd occasion — however rare — on which even characters as unscrupulous and amoral as Alexander sometimes stumble unwittingly upon a genuine, deep, mystical truth.

There is a strange parallel between Alexander of Abonoteichous and Harry Price of Borley Rectory. It might be suggested that at the very start of his career Alexander at least half-believed in the mysterious potions that he was distributing and prescribing. When Price first investigated Borley, there were a number of extraordinary phenomena that were very difficult to explain by rational means. When accompanied by journalists — but unaccompanied by the phenomena he desperately wanted to show them — Price seems to have yielded to the temptation to manufacture what would not demonstrate itself spontaneously when he most wanted it.

It has to be asked in all fairness whether Alexander of Abonoteichous had begun by experiencing some genuine paranormal or anomalous phenomena, and whether it was only when these failed to turn up on cue that he resorted to speaking tubes for gods made from the necks of luckless cranes and herons.

Harry Price was caught surreptitiously flicking a stone from his greatcoat pocket over a wall at Borley to produce what would seem like a poltergeist phenomenon. When Aesculapius and Apollo failed to come in person at their prophet's summons, perhaps Alexander decided to summon their facsimiles via his "autophone" engineered from cranes' windpipes. Our common sense and rational thought chuckle with Lucian at the exposure of a fraud, yet Lucian himself portrays a rigidity of mind that is not totally admirable. He strongly advises all his readers and investigators of the paranormal to begin with the inflexible premise that the paranormal does not exist and that anomalous phenomena never occur and cannot occur.

"Even if you cannot detect the mechanism by which the trick is perpetrated," says Lucian, "you must never waver from your absolute certainty that it is merely a trick." This attitude of Lucian's reveals a grim determination on his part to disprove the paranormal, whether it exists or not — just as grave an error in its way as Alexander's determination to bend the facts in order to prove it. Between two such diametrically opposed intellectual grindstones, the corn of truth is certain to be ground, not into fine flour, but out of any semblance of existence at all. What is needed in life is to keep a completely open mind and to study all phenomena objectively, including those that are anomalous or apparently paranormal.

It may well be, of course, that Lucian is right and that Alexander is no better than the lowest kind of trickster and the worst kind of charlatan, duping a gullible public and harming many of them in the process. Conversely, it may be that under a mountain of chaff and charlatanry, one or two grains of esoteric proof of the paranormal actually existed somewhere in Alexander's bizarre work.

CHAPTER FIVE:
The Nuggets from the Lost Dutchman Mine

Somewhere in the very aptly named Superstition Mountains in Arizona, well to the east of Phoenix, the Lost Dutchman Mine is believed to be situated. In 1887, Jacob Walz, also known as Jacob Walzer, was continually found in the saloons and drinking dens of the wild pioneer town that was Phoenix then.

Walzer invariably paid for his drinks with gold nuggets. When asked where they had come from, he always maintained that they were his own. He said that he had extracted them from a secret mine, the location of which only he knew and in which none but he had ever dug.

Most of those who heard his version of the origin of the nuggets tended not to believe him; the general opinion was that he had stolen them from other miners whom he had probably killed in the course of the theft. A few suspicious people spied on Walzer and followed him everywhere, but it brought them no closer to the mysterious Lost Dutchman Mine allegedly hidden away *somewhere* in the sinister Superstition Mountains.

In 1891, Walzer died, but not before telling everyone that he had hidden the tracks to his mine and camouflaged its location so effectively that after his death no one would ever be able to find it. For well over a century, prospectors have traced the trail from Phoenix to the Superstition Mountains, trying their best to get on the track of Walzer's legendary Lost Dutchman Mine.

As far back as 1965, the great Erle Stanley Gardner, the author who created Perry Mason, produced a fascinating book entitled *Hunting Lost Mines by Helicopter*. Most of that excellent book refers to the Superstition Mountains and Walzer's lost mine.

A very old Hollywood western, *Lust For Gold*, starred Glen Ford and Ida Lupino. Much of the filming was set against a rock formation, which in reality was a part of the Superstition Mountains. The film shows an enormous boulder and a natural opening in the rock that looks particularly atmospheric when the moon's rays stream through it. There is also, at this point, a weird inscription that has been cut into the stone. It is generally believed that the Lost Dutchman Mine is somewhere below this inscription. Erle Stanley Gardner had a theory that the mine was first discovered, worked, and then hidden by the indigenous Amerindians of the Superstition Mountains. They preferred not to have their territory invaded by prospectors hungry for gold. Gardner also believed that every clue to the mine's whereabouts was wiped out by earthquake devastation a century ago.

Even without earthquakes, the Superstition Mountains are not the healthiest of places for innocent and honest prospectors and treasure hunters. At the end of the nineteenth century, while Walzer was spending his nuggets in Arizona, nearly four hundred men met violent and untimely deaths in that area.

Arizona at that time was technically Mexican territory; in practice, however, it was controlled by the indigenous Apaches. According to tradition, the Peralta family from Mexico discovered the original location of the mine. They set up camps at Sonora and Chihuahua, and then despatched their Mexican drivers with mule trains to pick up the nuggets from the Lost Dutchman Mine and pack them on to their mules.

The ancient Romano-Welsh goldmines in Dolaucothi, Wales are as mysterious as the Lost Dutchman Mine in the Superstition Mountains, USA.

*Mysterious bag of gold nuggets from the church mural at
Rennes-le-Château in France — close-up.*

*Mysterious bag of gold nuggets on the church mural at Rennes-le-Château in
France — wide view of complete picture.*

38

One such group was on its way back when the Apaches attacked them. The mule drivers were slaughtered, the gold was unloaded, and the mules were taken away. This was not a happy event for the mules, as the Apaches in those days were alleged to have regarded mule meat as something of a delicacy.

According to more of the ancient legends and traditions that surround the weird history of the Lost Dutchman Mine, a prospector accidentally discovered one of the heaps of gold that the Apaches had unloaded from the mules. He took as much as he could carry and went to Tucson; instead of having the good sense to enjoy it there, he got himself into a gun fight, which he lost. The Tucson undertaker was the main beneficiary of the gold that had been found.

Probing such information as exists as carefully and as thoroughly as possible places a big question mark over Jacob Walz, or Walzer, from whom the mine eventually took its name. Opinions of Walzer range from his being an innocuous old prospector who had just stumbled by chance on the incredible treasure lying within the mine, to his being one of the most callous and ruthless serial killers in that part of Arizona. Was he a man who, like the notorious Charles Peace of Victorian England, camouflaged his ruthless homicidal tendencies behind a convincing veneer of respectability and harmless semi-senility?

Treasures of many types and in many locations seem to attract sinister hazards. Those who have spent any length of time researching the mysteries of Rennes-le-Château at first hand will be swift to agree that Rennes has a number of sinister secrets attached to it and that it is by no means a safe place to explore. Just as the semi-legendary Oak Island, Nova Scotia treasure has already claimed at least six treasure hunters' lives, so the Lost Dutchman Mine has claimed a series of victims over the years.

One set out way back in the 1930s. A treasure hunter named Adolph Ruth made his way towards a strange, isolated peak known as Weaver's Needle. Ruth said that he had obtained an accurate map of the location of the Lost Dutchman Mine from certain confidential papers that had come from the Peralta family. When Ruth's skeleton was finally discovered, the head had been removed and the body shot through by two rounds from a nineteenth-century Colt Peacemaker, or a similar type of heavy-calibre hand gun.

As recently as 1947, James Cravey also believed that he had an accurate map. He hired a helicopter and asked the pilot to set him down — by himself — at a point that he indicated. He also gave the pilot orders to pick him up again two weeks later. The pilot kept the rendezvous faithfully and went to find his charter client as planned — but there was no sign of James Cravey. He had vanished as surely as Benjamin Bathurst vanished when he walked around the horses at Perleberg and was never seen again. Cravey vanished as finally and mysteriously as the three lighthouse keepers from the Flannans, or the captain and crew of the *Mary Celeste*.

Almost a year later, however, a skeleton that was almost certainly Cravey's was found near the sinister Weaver's Needle. He had suffered the same fate as Adolph Ruth had fifteen or sixteen years before — Cravey's head was missing. Insofar as a mine or its location can be broadly defined as an object, the Lost Dutchman Mine — or the gold allegedly taken from it — is among the most mysterious objects on Earth. *Something* in the Superstition Mountains produced a supply of gold far greater than most other workings in Arizona. How much did the Peralta family really know about it? What did Walz the Dutchman discover? Who killed Adolph Ruth and James Cravey — and had the two succeeded in finding the Lost Dutchman Mine before its mysterious guardians found them?

CHAPTER SIX:
The Statuette of Yemanja

The oldest spells and enchantments often seem to depend upon a picture or three-dimensional image of the subject who is to be healed or hunted, protected or punished. Our earliest ancestors painted remarkably lifelike aurochs on the walls of their dimly lit caves, presumably in the hope of attracting prey into the path of their hunting party. Models of wood or clay representing women, men, and beasts were prominent features of early magic. Sometimes these effigies were burnt, impaled, or crushed underfoot. At other times they were blessed and protected by amulets and talismans in order to keep the subject whom they represented safe.

Today, the territory of the Yoruba nation is located towards the south of modern Nigeria, and the traditional African beliefs in a universe inhabited by spirits are still strong there. Animals and birds, rocks, rivers, and waterfalls, and trees and plant life — especially "healing" and "magical" herbs — are all regarded as the dwelling places of spirits with varying degrees of power. The most powerful spirit of all in the minds of the Yoruba was their great goddess Yemanja. They believed she was the mother of the sun and moon, and one of a dozen gods and goddesses who made up the ancient Yoruba pantheon. The making of small figurines as votive offerings to Yemanja became an integral part of Yoruba worship.

Some four centuries ago, the Portuguese were searching for slave labour to run their new South American plantations, and it was the Yoruba's tragedy to be in the wrong place at the wrong time. Thousands of them were shipped out as slaves. The only (very minor) redeeming feature was that the Portuguese tended on the whole to be less cruel and more tolerant than most other slave owners of that era. Unlike certain more rigidly fanatical Christian slave owners, the Portuguese allowed their captives to practise their own African religion. As the centuries passed, however, well-meaning but theologically blinkered Christian missionaries tried to force their rigid and exclusive ideas about faith on to the Yemanja-worshipping Yoruba descendants. Their attempts to persuade the Yoruba of the importance of Mary the Virgin, however, met with success beyond their wildest dreams — or their worst nightmares. To the Yoruba, this new "Queen of Heaven" figure was simply their beloved Yemanja wearing a thin Christian disguise, so Yemanja's Feast Day on August 15 became Mary's as well — or vice versa.

Statuettes of Yemanja — perhaps as a kind of "Black Madonna" figure — are ubiquitous throughout Brazil. It is also common practice for offerings to be left out in Brazilian streets for Yemanja, and even the hungriest and most desperate beggars will not touch them; such is the power of Yemanja's grip on the hearts and minds of her people.

Apart from the large-scale celebrations to honour Mary and Yemanja on August 15, there is an even more spectacular event on Copacabana Beach in Rio de Janeiro on December 31. An enormous crowd of Yemanja worshippers wearing white and carrying candles wade into the sea chanting her praises and throwing flowers into the water.

The true identity of the central character of this strange Yemanja narrative has to be protected, but the records are all in the rigorously kept scholarly archives of the Society for Psychical Research in London. An eminent and trustworthy SPR investigator was working in Brazil a few years ago when the subject (whom we shall refer to simply as "Belinda" to protect her real identity) was brought to his attention. She had studied psychology at the University of Sao Pâolo, and this may have led her into a scientific, pragmatic, and, perhaps, rather materialistic paradigm.

One day, however, Belinda accompanied some other members of her family to an attractive beach near Santos, less than one hundred kilometres from Sao Pâolo. Here she found a small statuette of Yemanja that had apparently been thrown up by the sea. Very little paint was left on the tiny figurine after its exposure to the action of the sea for so long, but such paint as was left was highly significant when studied in detail in the light of later developments. The jaw and neck still retained some pigment, as did the arms, together with a little more between the shoulder blades. In addition, one eye still retained its bright blue colour. Belinda took the curious little statuette home, despite the remonstrance of the more superstitious members of her family, who believed that it was a votive offering to Yemanja and, as such, should be left severely alone. Within days, Belinda became so ill that she was taken to a hospital and tested for tuberculosis. The test was positive, but she was lucky, and, following some excellent medical treatment, she was cured. The X-ray had revealed what looked like a sinister patch on her right lung, just below the equivalent spot where the statuette had been painted between its shoulder blades.

Her doctor ordered her to take a long rest, and she stayed with her parents for several months, a long way from Sao Pâolo — too far away, some psychic practitioners might suggest, for the Yemanja figurine to influence her. During the time that there were several hundred kilometres between them, the sinister figurine seemed powerless to injure Belinda.

As soon as she returned home, however, her pressure cooker exploded and severely scalded her arms, face, and neck — precisely where the flecks of paint still adhered to the Yemanja figurine. A few days later, her gas oven exploded, much as the pressure cooker had done. But worst of all, she began to feel continual urges to commit suicide — to throw herself into the road in front of a bus or heavy lorry, or to jump from her apartment window, which was more than a dozen storeys above the street.

For Belinda, the most loathsome and mysterious part of her prolonged ordeal was a sensation of being raped repeatedly by something invisible that nevertheless felt totally solid and real. She knew, of course, about the medieval legends of incubi and succubi — the sexually-oriented demons and demonesses who ravished human victims — but this was the twentieth century, and Belinda was a pragmatic university graduate. Scarcely able to believe the evidence of her own senses, she now felt in desperate need of help.

This, she decided, was a problem that her orthodox scientific paradigm could not adequately contend with. Terrified and reluctant, Belinda went to the nearest Umbanda Centre.

Umbanda was the traditional spirit-based religion that had crossed the sea with Belinda's distant Yoruba ancestors. In the opinion of the local Umbanda leaders, Belinda should take the statuette of Yemanja as close as she could to the spot where it had been found. It was also explained to her that the run of "bad luck" leading to one injury or illness after another coincided in a quite remarkable way to the areas of pigment that still remained on the model of Yemanja. The tuberculosis was in an area of her lung that corresponded to where the pigment remained between the shoulder blades of the tiny statue. The marks on the arms, the jaw, and throat corresponded, closely enough, to the burns she had received when the pressure cooker had exploded.

Once the strange statuette had been returned to the beach and then — presumably — carried away again by the waves, Belinda's life settled down to a safe, normal, routine existence once more.

The Yemanja statuette certainly qualifies as an extremely mysterious object — but it is as nothing compared to the mysteries that lurk within the darker recesses of the human mind. There is no doubt that every reader will have in his or her own experience at least one memory of an occasion when sheer willpower and determination brought him or her through a difficult, dangerous, or unbearably tedious and monotonous situation that nevertheless had to be endured somehow.

We have all heard of spectacular examples of the power of a determined mind to control a body that is sick, injured, or exhausted. The massively determined Ray Kroc, founder of the multi-million-dollar MacDonald's restaurant chain, is on record as saying that persistence is the key to success; and a famous oil millionaire is also on record as saying that the secret of his vast fortune was to carry on drilling when his rivals had all given up. If the power of the mind can be with us on such benign occasions, it is perfectly logical to assume that it can also work against us on other occasions.

Stress in the mind can all too often lead to physical problems in the body. The woman or man who is blissfully happy, fulfilled, and contented is likely to enjoy radiant health and to be filled with dynamic energy combined with practically limitless stamina. The mind that is listless, with no interests, hobbies, or goals that it wants to pursue is likely to find itself — sooner rather than later — as the skipper of a leaking, listing, unseaworthy hulk of a body.

One of the most deleterious things that can happen to any of us mentally is to have ambivalent feelings about the same object, person, or set of ideas. In Iris Murdoch's brilliant novel *A Severed Head*, the title was chosen to indicate just such ambivalent feelings. The cryptic meaning was that the severed head hanging from the belt of a traditional witch doctor, medicine man, or priest both attracted *and* repelled the group with whom he or she worked. When the human mind is confronted by such ambivalent objects, it experiences severe stress and tension.

Belinda, the subject of the encounter with the Yemanja statuette, was, in a sense, a woman of two cultures — two sets of ideas that were almost diametrically opposed. The modern university education from which she had benefitted had made her open minded, investigative, and rational. The deeper cultural strains of her people and the spirit-beliefs of her ancestors went back for centuries prior to their being brought to the Portuguese colonies in South America. Although the conflict in Belinda's mind lay far below the surface, her logical, scientific university paradigm and the old Yoruba belief that spirits inhabited everything were in serious conflict.

Her insistence — despite the warnings of her family — on taking the strange Yemanja statuette back to her apartment may have been the work of her rational, scientific, college-educated component, whereas her final acceptance of the Umbanda counsellor's advice to return the statuette to the sea represented a resurgence of a much older mental substratum that still lingered vestigially within her: the spirit-culture of her Yoruba ancestors.

Much is reported in medical literature of problems arising from so-called psychosomatic illness. From the earliest centuries A.D., devout, mystical saints contemplating the wounds and sufferings of Christ have been able to produce in their own bodies the *stigmata* — marks that look very much like the injuries to hands and feet resulting from crucifixion. There are many recorded cases of phantom pregnancies, in which the abdomen swells and other physiological symptoms of pregnancy, like lactation, are presented by the patient. Husbands have also been known to experience "sympathy pains" with their pregnant wives. Some back pains and certain forms of paralysis seem to be psychosomatic in origin rather than to have any strictly physiological cause.

Belinda had noticed very particularly where the pigment was still visible on the Yemanja statuette. It is, therefore, conceivable that she subconsciously "arranged" the series of accidents and the apparent tubercular lung lesions to correspond with the pigment still adhering to the figurine.

We all have friends and acquaintances who could well be described as "accident prone," but their clumsiness, carelessness, and apparent inability to relate cause and effect accurately and rationally may be more than a simple behavioural characteristic. A clinical psychologist might suppose that the accident-prone patient was working against him- or herself at a very deep and powerful subconscious level. The accident-prone subject may, however, be trying to attract attention, in which case the pain of the injury caused by the accident, or the pain or discomfort from the psychosomatic illness, may be regarded by the subject as a price which he or she is perfectly willing to pay in exchange for the much craved attention. Another theory is that the subject believes him- or herself to have committed some fault or sin that needs to be punished, and the series of accidents or psychosomatically induced illnesses, disabilities, and discomforts may be understood at a level beyond the patient's conscious control as the "appropriate punishments" for what he or she believes has been done amiss.

The jury has four apparent options in this case study. The first is to accept the possibility that some strange, conscious, and purposeful psychic forces caused the accidents and illnesses that Belinda suffered. This need not necessarily be an external spirit force, but could be the product of many minds *believing* in such a force and — by their belief — actually producing it. The experience of the Toronto psychical researchers who managed to produce psychic phenomena from a "ghost" that they knew perfectly well existed only in their own minds may shed some light upon this possibility. The Tibetan idea of *tulpas* of the kind that Alexandra David-Neel thought that she had manufactured is also worth bringing into the discussion. At a better known and more popular level there is the phenomenon of a football or baseball team winning more often on its home ground, where it is surrounded by the goodwill and enthusiasm of thousands of fans and supporters who are *willing* their team to win.

If it was not a genuine disembodied spirit force focusing through the Yemanja image, and if it was not the power of external minds over matter, then was it something that had its origins and found its dynamism *exclusively inside Belinda's own mind?* Was it her ambivalent feelings and the culture clash that brought about her accident proneness, her illness, and her feelings of suicidal despair?

The fourth possibility is that the whole thing was no more than a series of remarkable coincidences, but this theory, of course, raises the far larger question of just what coincidence (or synchronicity) *really* is.

CHAPTER SEVEN:
The Relics of Saint Anthony of Padua

Born in Lisbon towards the end of the twelfth century, Anthony spent most of the last years of his life in the Italian city of Padua. Portuguese by birth, Anthony became one of the canons of St. Augustine at Coimbra when he was barely twenty-five years old. While he was there, the relics of five Franciscan martyrs were brought across from Morocco. In an emotional surge of dangerous and irrational religious enthusiasm, Anthony was filled with a desire to follow the example of the five dead Franciscans.

Not long afterwards, a group of travelling Franciscans visited the Augustinian canons at Coimbra. Anthony expressed his deep desire for martyrdom to these Franciscan visitors and was so impressed by them that he decided to join their order instead of the Augustinians. There was a little difficulty over this to begin with, but after a while Anthony overcame it and began his new life as a Franciscan.

He had been baptized originally as Ferdinand, but now took on the new name of Anthony in order to venerate the memory of Saint Anthony of Egypt, who was the hero of the Franciscans whom he had just joined. This Anthony of Egypt was born in A.D. 251 and died in A.D. 356 at the advanced age of 105. He had been born in Coma, which was part of Upper Egypt, and, when only twenty years of age, had sold everything he possessed and gone to live among a local religious community. From A.D. 286 until 306, he lived in a deserted fortress at Pispir. While he was there, he underwent a series of well-publicized temptations. Curiously enough, similar temptations, associated with one of the multiple Saint Anthonys, featured prominently in the mystery of the priest's treasure of Rennes-le-Château. One theory of this Rennes-le-Château mystery was that Bérenger Saunière, the priest of Rennes who became immensely, but inexplicably, rich towards the end of the nineteenth century, had discovered some ancient coded manuscripts that led him to the treasure. According to this particular Rennes theory, which may well prove to be totally inaccurate, when these mysterious manuscripts were allegedly decoded, part of the message that came from them concerned one of the Saint Anthonys.

The first part of that cryptic Rennes record referred to a painting by Nicholas Poussin showing a shepherdess, three shepherds, and a tomb. The reference to Saint Anthony is simply "No temptation." The message then goes on to mention the names of three painters — the two Teniers and Poussin — who were said in the coded manuscript to collectively "hold the key" to the Rennes treasure mystery.

If the Poussin painting referred to the shepherdess and the shepherds of Arcadia with their sinister, inscribed table-top tomb, then the "no temptation" message was believed by these researchers to apply to one of the many versions of Saint Anthony painted by one of the Teniers.

It was alleged in quaint medieval phrasing that many of Saint Anthony's temptations consisted of "demons who came to torment him in the guise of lewd wenches." Several early painters found that it was rather easier to sell their "religious" paintings if there was an attractive "lewd wench" or two somewhere on the canvas! In several pictures of Saint Anthony he was shown with what was tantamount to the modern cartoonist's "think bubble" coming out of his head and — within it — one of the alluring demonesses who was trying, unsuccessfully, to tempt him. Although strong-minded Anthony, reinforced by his ascetic lifestyle, was able to resist these delectable demonesses, the painters and their clients apparently were not!

By the year 306, however, Anthony of Egypt decided to give up the solitary life at Pispir and devote himself to teaching the disciples who had gathered around him. He went off to Alexandria in 355 in order to argue against the Arian heresy. Anthony was a profound philosopher and theologian, and soon became admired not only for his brilliant mind and rhetoric but also for his charisma and the miracles that he was reported to have been able to perform. This combination of miracles and charisma won him a great many disciples and converts, some of them very eminent. There is even a letter from him to the Roman Emperor Constantine, which has been preserved for posterity.

There was another famous hermit saint named Paul (nothing whatever to do with the famous Paul whose missionary work fills the Acts of the Apostles). This later Paul, who died around 350, was sometimes

Saint Anthony of Padua.

referred to as Paul of Thebes, sometimes as Paul the First Hermit. He had originally escaped to the desert to avoid the persecutions of Decius. Like the desert Anthony, who followed him in the tradition for several years, Paul was said to have lived to be well over a hundred.

Jerome wrote an account of Paul's life that was based on a very early original Greek text. According to Jerome's account, Anthony of Egypt encountered Paul of Thebes in the desert shortly before the ancient hermit died. Also in Jerome's account, a raven flew by and dropped some bread, in much the same way that the Old Testament prophet Elijah was fed miraculously by ravens. Two lions then appeared mysteriously and dug Paul's grave with their powerful paws. Anthony then buried the venerable hermit saint.

When Anthony himself died many years later he was — at his own request — buried in a place that no one knew. Within ten years, however, so great was his reputation that his remains were found and taken to the city of Alexandria. Rival locations inevitably competed for the saint's relics: Constantinople put in a bid for them, as did La Motte. It was here that the Order of Hospitallers of Saint Anthony was founded at the beginning of the twelfth century.

Not surprisingly, it soon became a centre of pilgrimage for victims of ergotism, which was also referred to by the folk name of "Saint Anthony's Fire." In the Middle Ages, ergotine was a deadly hallucino-

genic drug and an inducer of aetiological delirium. It was a sinister bio-
logical toxin derived from the ergot fungus, which frequently contam-
inated both bread and ale during the unhygienic Middle Ages.

Many rational theories to explain numerous apparently paranormal phenomena have laid the blame fair and square on ergotine poisoning. In addition to its *general* hallucinogenic effects, ergotine causes the victim to see *specific* aetiological visions. These aetiological delusions, in one form or another, set out to explain to the tormented mind
of the sufferer what is responsible for the agonizing pain that the ergotine is causing in his or her abdomen.

Those who have suffered from ergotine poisoning — and who have
been among the lucky few to have recovered from it — have given
clinical accounts of their horrific experiences.

To victims of ergotine, other people are seen as aliens, monsters, or
demons who are invariably attacking them, either biting at their stom-
achs or tearing at them with fiendish claws. Because those who go to
assist the victim are seen as enemies, the sufferer often strikes out at the
very people who are doing their best to help.

The ergotine poison theory has been put forward as an explanation
for what became of the ill-fated crew of the *Mary Celeste* in November
of 1872. Those who hold this theory have suggested that ergotine poisoning caused some of those aboard to hurl themselves into the sea to
escape from the agonizing abdominal pain and from the "monsters"
who they thought were pursuing them, while the remainder attacked
one another, believing, because of their hallucinations, that they were
attacking demons or monsters who were threatening them.

These Hospitallers of Saint Anthony wore black robes with a blue
tau-cross, and they soon spread across much of western Europe. A part
of their ritual consisted of ringing small bells to attract gifts for the
Order; these bells were given to those who had helped them and were
placed round the necks of their benefactors' animals with a view to
protecting them from disease.

The Hospitallers also had a rather strange privilege in that their
pigs roamed where they wished in the street. Consequently, in the symbols representing Anthony in the later iconography, bells and pigs featured prominently.

Anthony became widely known and was greatly venerated during
the Middle Ages. He became the patron saint of many monastic orders

and was believed to be a healer both of animals and human beings. The word "tantony" slipped into the language as a diminutive form of "Saint Anthony" and came to mean — by association with both iconographic bells and pigs — either the smallest bell or the smallest pig. The tantony was simply the tiniest one.

It was this Anthony of Egypt after whom Anthony of Padua named himself. The newly named Friar Anthony set out for Morocco, where it was his intention to preach Christianity to the Islamic Moors. He was taken ill, however, and was unable to complete the mission on which he had originally set his heart. More problems swiftly followed. The difficulty of the illness that had altered his plans in the first place was now augmented by strong winds blowing in a direction he did not want: they drove his vessel to Messina in Sicily.

Despite these setbacks, he made his way up to Assisi in 1221, where Francis and Elias were holding a special gathering of the chapter for all Franciscans. After this meeting, Anthony was sent to San Paolo, not far from Forli. Once there, he busied himself — like Martha, the industrious sister of Meditative Mary of Bethany — by washing the Order's simple cooking utensils after meals.

Up until this point in his career, it seemed that none of the senior members of the community recognized Anthony's great intellectual gifts. His remarkable abilities first came to light when he was one of the priests attending an ordination; it transpired that none of the others had been told to prepare the necessary special ordination sermon, due to a failure of communication and some general administrative misunderstandings. The senior priests having all declined because they had nothing ready, young Anthony offered to give the address. He did it with such fervent eloquence and such depth of spiritual knowledge that all who heard him were deeply impressed by the young man's great ability. He was immediately commissioned as a preacher and sent up to northern Italy and then to France.

Not only a preacher but also a teacher, he gave lessons in theology at Padua, Montpelier, Toulouse, and Bologna. Just as Saint Francis was said to have preached to the birds, so Saint Anthony of Padua was said to have attracted the fish from the Marecchia river. According to tradition, these remarkably perceptive fish were alleged to have popped their heads out of the water and to have remained in neat rows until he had finished his sermon. Anthony was only thirty-six when he died in Padua in 1231, in a building next to the convent of the Poor Clares at Arcella, just outside the city. An altar was put up at the place where he died, and the room was made into an oratory.

The cult of Saint Anthony has always been associated with the most extraordinary miracles. He is particularly credited with being the finder of lost articles. This may date back to an occasion when someone borrowed his Psalter without his permission. According to legend, the unauthorized borrower saw a terrifying apparition, which led to the immediate return of the book.

A far nobler and worthier memorial to him is Saint Anthony's Bread, a very special charitable fund that helps the necessitous and starving, especially in the developing nations. Just as Anthony of Egypt has pigs and bells for his emblems, so Anthony of Padua has a book and a lily, often with the infant Christ seated on his book. The basis of the inclusion of the infant Christ on Anthony's book is a remarkable report made by Count Tiso.

The Count had given the Franciscans a hermitage on property that he owned. When Tiso called to visit them one day, he saw a brilliant light around the edges of the hermitage door. His first thought was that the new building had caught fire and that the Franciscans whom he honoured and revered were in serious danger. Running fearlessly inside to see if he could offer them assistance, Tiso halted in amazement when he saw Anthony sitting in ecstatic rapture with the Holy Child in his arms — just as though he were one of the Magi or shepherds at Bethlehem.

Within a year of Anthony's death, the traditional rigorous ecclesiastical examination of his life and works was carried out with meticulous thoroughness, and as a result he was raised to sainthood. It was not until 1946, however, that he was declared to be a Doctor of the Church as well.

In addition to his special reputation as a recoverer of lost property and missing objects, Anthony is also the patron saint of the poor, the imprisoned, and all who have become despised social outcasts. It was to such people in particular that he gave help during his all too short earthly life.

Elbart of Temeswar believed that God had given the saint's relics the power to bring back lost objects because during Anthony's earthly life he had done everything he could to bring back people who had gone astray.

Those who had known and admired Anthony during his lifetime were assisted by the citizens of Padua in building a great basilica to him, which was begun within just one year of his death. In 1263, when Bonaventure was in charge of the Franciscans, Anthony's body was transferred to this new basilica.

It was for his preaching and teaching in particular that Anthony was so admired, and, according to contemporary records, when the sarcophagus was opened during the transfer, his *tongue was found to be uncorrupted*. The thoughts of those who performed the transfer were that this was a special sign of the validity and truth of his preaching and teaching.

His tomb, which nowadays is referred to as the Ark of Saint Anthony, is constructed of fine marble with distinctive green veins, and it is so placed that pilgrims are able to walk all around it. As many as two thousand visitors an hour pass the tomb on peak days. These devout pilgrims usually try to touch the sacred green-veined marble, and the contact of reverent pilgrim hands over the years has worn the back of the tomb completely smooth. Hundreds of letters arrive at the basilica from all over the world each day. Anthony's original home, Lisbon, Portugal, did not forget him either, and an impressive church was built over the site of his birthplace.

In 1981, on the 750th anniversary of Saint Anthony's death, John Paul II gave permission for the tomb to be opened on the sixth of January. In addition to high ranking members of the Church, anthropologists, anatomists, and doctors of medicine attached to the University of Padua were present. Anthony's remains were found to be enclosed inside two concentric wooden caskets. These sturdy old caskets contained three significant bundles wrapped in red damask and trimmed with gold. In the first bundle was the robe in which Anthony had been buried. The second contained an assortment of his bones, and the third contained his skull.

The thirteenth-century records of his tongue having been perfectly preserved were augmented by a report from this 1981 ceremony. It was recorded that the pathologists and anatomists present at this 750th anniversary examination commented that Anthony's *vocal cords* could still be identified and were as well preserved as the tongue had been centuries before. The same symbolic conclusions were drawn. The vocal cords were removed from their red damask containers and placed in the reliquary chapel alongside the still uncorrupted tongue.

This reliquary for the tongue and vocal cords is itself a unique and mysterious object. It is fashioned in the form of a silver book with golden letters. Representations of flames made of the same precious metal are constructed so that they seem to be coming up from the book, and the sheath of golden flame supports a hand-shaped crystal container inside which the relics can be seen. The symbolism is plain enough as a memorial for a man whose preaching and teaching were so effective and so well remembered.

But what of the miracles surrounding Saint Anthony's remains? The finding of lost objects is itself something of a mystery. Like the authors, most readers will have experienced episodes similar to the classic tale of the absent-minded professor who looked everywhere for his glasses, only to find that they were already resting on the bridge of his nose.

Writers, publishers, and proof readers — even with the aid of the latest computerized spell-checkers — also know only too well that it is possible for the keenest eye and the sharpest mind to look through a proof a dozen times and *still* miss something that a keen-eyed reader will report within an hour of opening the book!

A great deal could be said at this point about the psychological phenomenon of "mental set," and Edward de Bono, whose theories and interesting experimental work have contributed enormously not only to our understanding of human thinking processes but to practical improvements in them, always emphazises the importance of lateral thinking.

One type of mind focuses in on a problem and hammers away at it relentlessly until a solution is found. The second type of mind, which belongs to the lateral thinker, whose technique may either be instinctive or learnt, goes *outside* the problem and attempts to solve it by methods that may seem impossibly tangential, wild, and imaginative, but which nevertheless lead to satisfactory, if unexpected, solutions on most occasions.

Idea teams in the media and creative arts worlds, as well as advertisers, inventors, and designers, frequently meet in "brainstorming" think-tank sessions in which new ideas are hurled uncritically in all directions, recorded, and then analyzed and critically evaluated at later sessions. This type of work frequently leads to quantum-leap progress. Could it be that when we are experiencing difficulties in locating lost objects, we need to get outside the immediate focus of our own particular mind set and to look in the least likely place that the object we're hoping to recover might have gone?

A visit to the tomb of Saint Anthony, or a prayer invoking his help, might be just the mental nudge that the searcher needs in order to escape from his or her current ineffectual mind set and begin looking somewhere else.

It is, of course, equally possible that a man who devoted so much of his time and energy to thinking, doing, and saying good things during his short earthly life had not finished the excellent work he began. Is Anthony still helping others despite the interruption called death?

One well-known theory that goes the rounds among psychical researchers is that the fabric of a building in which extreme emotion was once experienced has *absorbed* those emotions, and, in a sense, *recorded* them, in much the same way that magnetic tape can record pictures and sounds. A man with Anthony's spiritual power and charisma would have been a very impressive recording agent. It is reasonable to assume that, despite the joy he is experiencing in the abundant and eternal life of Heaven, Anthony's characteristic concern for those whom he loved and helped on earth still takes up part of his time, in so far as "time" can have any meaning in Eternity.

In this context, we need to consider the real possibility that Anthony of Padua is still very much alive, active, and interested in our physical world as well as in his own spiritual one, and that he does genuinely intervene when his help is sought. So many posthumous miracles have been credited to him that they cannot lightly be ignored.

Anthony once lived a very good and positive life. His relics survive. The miracles associated with them are well documented. That is Anthony's part; the conclusions we draw from that evidence are our own responsibility, but his mortal remains are among the world's most mysterious objects.

Chapter Eight:
Orffyreus's Perpetual Motion Engine

Every science student studying for his or her school or college examinations knows perfectly well that even the most efficient machine loses some of the energy that is put into it. Friction, air resistance, and a host of other "energy leakages" prevent the full force of what went in from performing one hundred percent of its optimum work before it comes out. Energy, like matter, cannot, theoretically, be created or destroyed, and only through Einstein's famous $E = mc^2$ formula can matter and energy be exchanged one for the other. Once this basic scientific principle is firmly grasped, it seems that a perpetual motion machine is a contradiction in terms.

It has been said, however, by some of those who are expert in such matters, that the design of a bumblebee's body and wings is aerodynamically unstable and, theoretically at least, the bumblebee ought not to be able to fly. Fortunately for the bumblebee, it does not know this, so it goes on flying contentedly despite all scientific theories to the contrary.

The inventive eighteenth-century wildman who gave himself the strange pseudo-Greek name of Orffyreus had no knowledge of the scientific principle of the conservation of energy. His early years are clouded in mystery. He led what seems to have been a stormy, lonely, and unhappy life, feared and hated as an enchanter, warlock, or wizard. He was regarded as an enemy of both traditional revealed religion and the "new religion" of orthodox science. There is evidence that, while still a very young man, Orffyreus constructed at least three machines that he believed capable of perpetual motion. One of these was built at Zittau in Saxony. If he had hoped that his amazing machines would make him rich, famous, respected, and popular, Orffyreus was sadly mistaken. Regarded as a dangerous loner who fought obdurately against the received wisdoms of both religion and science, Orffyreus was undoubtedly something of a rebel. He became a social outcast, and his savage, unkempt appearance did not help him back into acceptability. His eyes were wild and hostile, his long black hair flew out in the wind behind him like the hair of an Old Testament prophet. His beard was shaggy and dishevelled. He was a great wild bear of a man who seemed to have the ability to inspire a mixture of fear and loathing in most people who met him.

He turned up in Hesse-Cassel and was promptly thrown into the dungeons of Weissenstein castle, home of Prince Karl, the Landgrave of Hesse-Cassel. Like a condemned man being taken before the judge to be sentenced, Orffyreus was marched by the guards into Karl's presence. His clothes were filthy, his hair as wildly disarranged as river bank rushes in a thunderstorm, and his eyes red from exhaustion and lack of sleep. Orffyreus expected to be sentenced to further imprisonment: a flogging, a few days in the stocks, and, finally, ignominious expulsion from Hesse-Cassel. What happened was the precise opposite of his worst and darkest fears.

Karl of Hesse-Cassel was one of the few men in Europe who was prepared to welcome Orffyreus and offer him genuine protection and friendship. Although he himself was a complete amateur in terms of engineering science and mathematical knowledge, Karl was very interested in mechanical things. Unlike those who had more orthodox scientific knowledge than he had, Karl believed that a perpetual motion machine *was* a genuine possibility. He had heard about Orffyreus's work in Zittau and believed that his unpromising-looking guest had actually succeeded where orthodox scientists and engineers had failed.

Under Karl's patronage, Orffyreus regained his enthusiasm, dignity, and self-respect. The Landgrave of Hesse-Cassel treated the eccentric inventor with great kindness and understanding. He gave him good food, clothes, comfortable quarters, money to spend on equipment that he needed, and as good a workshop as the early eighteenth century was capable of providing. The problem, however, was that all Karl's kindness and toleration were not able to undo the harm that had been done by the years of persecution and derision. Orffyreus was still basically hostile, aggressive, and unbelievably suspicious. Karl, as Landgrave of Hesse-Cassel, knew all the right people. He managed to persuade two of the early eighteenth century's most eminent scientists — Baron Fischer, who was the official architect to the Austrian Emperor, and Willem s'Gravesande, a friend of Sir Isaac Newton and a member of the academic staff at Leiden University in Holland — to look at the machine Orffyreus had built.

Although ostensibly objective in their approach and with the expressed intention of examining the strange machine without prejudice, there was no doubt that Fischer and s'Gravesande both considered Orffyreus to be an impostor. They were convinced that his so-called perpetual motion engine had to be a deception of some kind. Orffyreus himself, although eccentric, was by no means a fool, and he quickly assessed the hostile attitude of the two visiting scientists. Their approach to life, with all its challenges and problems, was totally different from his.

There can be little doubt that Orffyreus was paranoid about his machine. He felt it was worth a vast amount of money, and he also believed that his enemies, the orthodox scientists, were untrustworthy and that their intention was to steal the secret from him and pay him nothing in return.

Prince Karl acted as his intermediary and did everything he could to persuade Orffyreus that the scientists were honourable and trustworthy men and that he should take them fully into his confidence. Orffyreus refused absolutely. Although he liked and trusted the Landgrave of Hesse-Cassel, he had the gravest doubts about Fischer and s'Gravesande.

He laid down stringently rigorous conditions for their examination of his machine. So far as he was concerned, they could study the room in which it was situated and all its external parts and supports as thoroughly and penetratingly as they wished. Orffyreus would not allow them to see the mechanism inside until he had been paid for his secret.

The room that Orffyreus was using as a workshop had at one time served as a last-ditch defence, a sort of infra-keep, or stronghold, should the castle be attacked. Its walls were thick and stout and it was protected by a ponderous door reinforced with iron.

The records and documentation from the period indicated that what Orffyreus showed the two scientists was rather like a miniature Ferris wheel or the wheel of a watermill. It stood between three and four metres from the floor and was just under a metre wide. The supports held it comfortably clear of the flagstones of the floor, and two wooden uprights supported the axle on which it rotated. Each of those upright supports held another piece of wood perpendicular to it, and from this crosspiece a pendulum was suspended. That was all there was visible.

With the aid of the powerful lamps they had brought with them, the two visiting scientists examined the exterior of the machine, the chamber, and the walls for any signs of rope or slim wires that might be attached to the great revolving wheel. Their reports indicate that they found nothing suspicious at all. When they were totally satisfied that the exterior of the machine and the chamber in which it was situated contained no hidden tricks, they asked Orffyreus to start the machine.

He did this by giving it a gentle push with one hand. It began to move smoothly and then actually accelerated to a precise twenty-six revolutions a minute. It was Baron Fischer, architect to the Austrian Emperor, who timed it with his own accurate watch. Twenty-six revolutions a minute seemed to be its maximum speed. As the wheel rotated, the long pendulums hanging from the wooden supports swung slowly to and fro, and those who were present described a strange thumping and a buzzing, whirring sound apparently coming from *inside* the wheel. The mechanism was hidden from view by the wheel's covering of oiled cloth.

"How do you stop it?" asked s'Gravesande.

"With your hands," replied Orffyreus. It seemed impossible. Very cautiously, he stretched one gloved hand towards the machine and brought it into contact with the edge of the rim. The machine began to slow down, rotating less and less quickly, and then it stopped, almost like one of the landing wheels of an aeroplane when it has completed a perfect three-point landing. S'Gravesande raised the problem of whether the machine would be capable of performing work of any value if it could be stopped and started with such little difficulty. Orffyreus did his best to explain that the energy within the machine could be used for all kinds of industrial work. It could, for example, operate a loom or be used to pump water. The next objection that the two inspecting scientists raised was the possibility that so large a wheel could easily conceal a human accomplice and that its magic and mystery were nothing more unusual than a pair of human legs on a treadmill.

S'Gravesande told Fischer that investigating a similar machine in London he had put that theory to the test by dropping snuff into it, whereupon the "machine" sneezed loudly and repeatedly. Fischer and s'Gravesande continued to examine the outside of the machine. They took the supports to pieces and replaced them. They moved the wheel to another point on the floor. They looked for secret passages in the room, tunnels, trapdoors, and loose stones. They found absolutely no trace of any kind of trickery. Neither could they find any trace of the secret power that made the great wheel of Orffyreus behave as it did.

After three days of intensive examination of the inexplicable mechanism, the two scientists proposed a test. They asked Orffyreus to set the machine in motion and then seal up the room. They would want the right to re-enter at short notice after a delay of hours, days, weeks, or months. Orffyreus was more than willing to accept the conditions of their test.

"The machine," he exclaimed, "will run for centuries. It will run until it falls to pieces."

It was on the twelfth of November, 1717, that the machine was set in motion for the test. Once more, according to the scientist's watch, it reached twenty-six revolutions per minute exactly. The Landgrave gave orders for the room to be locked and sealed. The whole situation was very similar to the sealing of the sinister Barbados Tomb ordered by Lord Combermere, the governor, in the early years of the nineteenth century, while he was investigating the mystery of the moving coffins.

Some of Karl's administrative officers used their official seals and the two visiting scientists added their own. Time passed.

On January 4, 1718, Fischer, s'Gravesande, and the Landgrave, along with a party of his attendants and officials, broke open the seals, which had previously been inspected and accepted by all concerned as intact and inviolate.

It was Prince Karl himself who led the procession into the test room. The sound of the great wheel halted them in their tracks. The whizzing, whirring noise and the regular thudding were unmistakable. The machine was running exactly as it had been when they sealed it two months before: it was rotating at precisely twenty-six turns every sixty seconds. One touch of a hand on the rim and the machine slowed down and stopped as smoothly and as gently as it had done before. Not understanding the basic principle, but accepting now that it undoubtedly *worked*, the two visiting scientists asked Orffyreus how much he wanted for the invention. It was Prince Karl who spoke for him.

"I am acting as Orffyreus's agent in this," he said quietly, "and the price is twenty thousand English pounds." S'Gravesande looked at Orffyreus with a new respect and promised to write to Amsterdam and to send a personal letter to his friend Sir Isaac Newton.

As great as the mystery of the wheel and its secret mechanism was the mystery of the strange psychological convolutions taking place inside the mind of Orffyreus. There are no extant records that would explain his incomprehensible behaviour. The two previously sceptical scientists had sent out reports stating that, although they did not understand how it was done, they accepted that the wheel of Orffyreus really possessed some strange, inexplicable energy, power, or dynamism that had enabled it to pass their strict sealed-room test. Perhaps if Orffyreus could have read the contents of the reports that Fischer and s'Gravesande had sent to the scientific world of 1718, he might have acted very differently. Perhaps it was diagnosable clinical paranoia that drove him to his next desperate move.

He locked himself in the workroom and smashed the machine to pieces with a great forester's axe. Then he flung open the door and, with his axe raised threateningly, stormed out of the castle like a madman. The guards observed him running into the woods. No one was anxious to pursue the wild-eyed inventor as he raced away through the trees until he was lost in the darkness of the night. What became of him after that no one knows. The wheel and its precious mechanism had been destroyed so effectively that none of those who studied the wreckage were able to reconstruct it. The secret, like its inventor, had disappeared forever. Those are the simple, basic facts in the case of Orffyreus, Karl of Hesse-Cassel, the architect, Fischer, and the learned university man, s'Gravesande.

What may be added by way of explanation or speculation? The two visiting scientists were highly intelligent and were totally in tune with the scientific attitudes of their day. At the beginning of the eighteenth century, although science was more or less in its infancy, certain pragmatic principles were known, shared, and understood by the scientific community (such as it was). Despite the prejudice that they displayed on occasion against unorthodox and, by their lights, unqualified people like Orffyreus, there was, to give the scientists their due, a certain objectivity and fairness in their ethos. They certainly did not like what they found, but they were not so intellectually dishonest that they would lie about it or attempt to deny its existence.

Fischer and s'Gravesande were convinced by their sealed-room test that Orffyreus's wheel was still running smoothly and effectively two months after they had sealed it into the extremely secure laboratory.

Of their integrity and their intelligence there can be no doubt. Their scientific training, although limited by the narrow borders of eighteenth-century knowledge, was enough to ensure that what they thought they had heard and seen formed the substance of a report that has left scientists and researchers wondering about Orffyreus's wheel for close to three centuries.

Is it sometimes necessary for us to unlearn an incorrect fact before we can make any further progress? Orffyreus was not encumbered by the "knowledge" that perpetual motion was impossible, and, because he did not believe it to be impossible, he produced a mechanism, a mysterious wheel, that seemed to contradict all the known laws of eighteenth-century science.

No matter how closely the facts are examined, we come up again and again against the insurmountable obstacle of two sceptical, prag-matic scientists like Fischer and s'Gravesande, who reported sealing an oilcloth-covered wheel inside a very secure laboratory, then checking on it two months later and finding that it was still running.

There are a number of conjectures that can be suggested. If we re-examine the case, remaining open minded to the possibilities of mind over matter, was Orffyreus cranking the wheel around with some strange mental power of the sort that also expresses itself in poltergeist phenomena? Had Orffyreus discovered the electric motor a century and more before it was rediscovered? If he had, and if it was an electric motor that whirred away at the centre of his wheel, then where did it draw its power from?

Is it possible that Orffyreus had stumbled by accident upon what-ever weird power — some sort of natural gravity shield, perhaps — had hurled the Barbados Coffins around that sinister tomb in Oistins Bay in Barbados in the early nineteenth century?

Something moved the wheel — Orffyreus did not deceive Fischer and s'Gravesande. The wheel moved. It moved for eight weeks! If only Orffyreus's secret could be rediscovered, we could be on the verge of an ecological bonanza.

CHAPTER NINE:
Did the Eldridge Travel Through Hyperspace?

The story of the Philadelphia Experiment is so well known to researchers of paranormal and anomalous phenomena that only the briefest outline is needed here.

According to the "legend" of the Philadelphia Experiment, the American warship *Eldridge* dematerialized mysteriously in Philadelphia in 1943 and reappeared in Norfolk a short while afterwards. If that legend is true, then the *Eldridge* becomes one of the most mysterious objects of all time. Again in the barest and most simplified outline, the ship was supposed to have been surrounded by a very powerful electromagnetic field, and it was this mysterious field that caused its "invisibility" and its "transfer through the dimensions."

According to these strange, semi-legendary accounts of the *Eldridge* and the whole Philadelphia Experiment, a number of horrendous things happened to the officers and crew of the ship. Some found themselves "locked," their bodies somehow *interwoven* into the steel structure of the ship. Others were reported to have burnt to death as a result of some strange type of spontaneous human combustion.

In September 1989, the mysterious Alfred Bielek turned up in Phoenix, Arizona, as a lecturer at a UFO Conference. He told the audience that he had been part of the Philadelphia Experiment and that he had miraculously survived it. He said that he had been through time warps, that he had experienced invisibility, and that electromagnetic attacks on his mind had not been completely successful. He felt sure that he had survived, and this was his story.

He believed that the background to the Philadelphia Experiment went back at least to 1931. In Bielek's view, John Hutchinson, who was then the dean of Chicago University, the outstanding electrical genius Nicola Tesla, and Albert Einstein had all been involved. Again according to Bielek's evidence, the eminent Austrian physicist, Dr. Emil

Kurtenauer, was also part of this pioneering stage. Bielek also testified that Tesla had become involved because of his association with President Franklin D. Roosevelt. Bielek alleged that Tesla was also concerned with a death-ray machine that was tested in New Mexico just before the start of World War II.

Like so much other material connected with the Philadelphia Experiment and the mystery of what — if anything — really happened to the *Eldridge*, there are so many episodes told by "friends of a friend" or "people who knew someone who said" that the truth is very difficult indeed to reach. Certainly, it was alleged that Tesla's hypothetical death-ray machine was so terrifyingly effective that the military commanders who had seen it in action decided that it was far too horrifying to be used in actual warfare. It is alleged that the machine, its design plans, and all information associated with it were destroyed. The argument was that should such a machine ever fall into enemy hands as a result of espionage, the consequences for the world would be unthinkable. Within this same "cloud of unknowing," it was also alleged that Tesla designed another very similar system that he offered to the British in the dark days of 1940, when it would have seemed reasonable to take advantage of *any* weapon at all, no matter how horrendous, in view of the reverses in France and the evacuation of Dunkirk. Tesla's particle beam weapon system was said to have been declined — even in warfare, the bureaucratic mind is harder to open than a giant clam. Undoubtedly, a number of wild and impractical schemes *were* offered to the British War Office during those dark days. It could well have been that a harassed, overworked junior somewhere in a blitzed office in Whitehall gave half a glance at Tesla's design, did not know who Tesla was, and dismissed his particle beam weapon as something from Jules Verne or H.G. Wells! Supposing that the weapon had really existed and worked effectively, supposing also that the civil servant concerned had been alert, receptive, and imaginative, it is possible that the war would have ended within a month with the total defeat of Nazi Germany and the saving of millions of lives. Human history is often balanced on such delicate fulcra. Again according to Bielek's evidence, it is alleged that Tesla became the first director of the Philadelphia Experiment. Bielek also paid tribute to the brilliance of Dr. John von Neumann. Von Neumann, according to Bielek, was a Hungarian mathematical genius who had studied at both Berlin and

Hamburg before immigrating to the United States in the late 1920s or early 1930s. He began as a Visiting Professor at Princeton but shortly transferred to the Philadelphia Experiment group.

The mystery deepens and thickens over the profound question of Bielek's alleged *dual identities*. In one set of life experiences he understood himself to be Alfred Bielek, but in another he was Edward A. Cameron. Under this other name, Bielek believed that he had obtained a doctorate in physics from Harvard and in 1939 had attended the Naval Officers' Training School at Providence on Rhode Island.

Bielek then said that he remembered an experiment conducted with a mine-sweeper in 1940. The vessel was unmanned, and when the necessary arrangement of coils and current were employed, the ship became invisible. America had not yet entered the war, and Bielek explained that it was not until the attack on Pearl Harbour that full attention was given to the Philadelphia Experiment. Another of Bielek's fascinating theories was that Tesla had certain strange extra-terrestrial connections. Bielek alleged that a friend who used to work with both him and Tesla was convinced that Tesla had daily conversations with at least one alien.

According to Bielek, Tesla was a good and responsible man who did not want to run the risk of putting human lives at stake in the project. There was, said Bielek, an experiment conducted in March of 1942, which failed. The test ship on this occasion was a huge battleship — but nothing happened. Bielek was of the opinion that Tesla himself had deliberately made the experiment fail because he did not want to put so many human lives at risk. In Bielek's view, Tesla's main concern at that point was to find a polite, but adequate, excuse to tell the government that, as the experiment had not worked and as he had a lot of other projects that he wanted to get on with, he was severing his connection with them. It is perhaps only a sinister coincidence that on January 7, 1943, less than a year after the failed experiment with the battleship, Tesla's body was discovered in his hotel room in New York.

The great mystery about all of Bielek's evidence was that the things he alleged were so remarkably accurate and detailed that, if he was simply imagining the amazing evidence that he was putting forward, his powers of creative imagination vastly exceeded those of the best science fiction and fantasy writers — and even those of the legendary Baron von Munchausen. Bielek alleges that with von Neumann in charge of the mysterious project, there was a significant change of direction. Von Neumann ordered one of the forward turrets of the *Eldridge* to be removed in order to position two huge generators below decks. As many as four transmitters were located on the deck itself. Another went down in the hold, and a huge antenna was erected. Vast generators were brought on board to provide the necessary power to make the complicated system work. Bielek said that he and his brother were down in the hold of the *Eldridge* during the notorious test. Bielek maintains that at precisely 9:00 A.M. on July 22, 1943, he and his brother were responsible for switching on the power. Bielek also testifies that for a full twenty minutes, the *Eldridge* could not be detected visually or by radar. Bielek then told how many of the crew became clinically insane. He thought that he and his half-brother had been shielded from the worst of the side effects of the experiment because most of the power was leaping around or on the deck, whereas they were in the control unit deep in the hold.

Again according to Bielek's account, the experiment was to be repeated on the twelfth of August. This time, in order to try to limit damage to personnel, they would attempt to take the ship out of a field where it would be perceptible to radar without going the whole hog and aiming for *complete invisibility*, as they were alleged to have done on July 22, when so many of the crew members were traumatized.

Bielek's account says that the *Eldridge* was off radar screens for just over a minute; after that there was an unparalleled blue flash and the ship vanished entirely. There was not so much as a line in the water to show where the invisible hull lay. Bielek's report stated that on this occasion, the *Eldridge* was invisible for a total of four hours.

He said that with the crew going insane all around them, he and his half-brother leapt off the ship. Naturally, they had expected to land in the sea. To their amazement, they landed on the ground by the Montauk Military Base on Long Island, New York.

From this point onwards, Bielek's story becomes even more amazing. Somehow he and his brother had been sucked into a vortex in hyperspace and *dragged into the future*. They had leapt from 1943 to 1983 — and waiting to meet them on the grassy plain of the Montauk Military Base was Dr. von Neumann. As von Neumann was supposed to have died in 1957 it was, to say the least, very surprising to find him welcoming his time-travelling colleagues in 1983! Bielek also reported that one of the UFOs that had been hovering over the *Eldridge* had been drawn into hyperspace with them. He maintained that it was dismantled and examined in Montauk. When the *Eldridge* returned to normality it was found, according to Bielek, that just as on the previous occasion several members of the crew were embedded in the ship, some were glowing, and most were clinically insane.

Where thick steel walls or decking had offered a degree of insulation or protection, damage was relatively minor to the personnel. After the experiments, the *Eldridge* was returned to normal, active naval service, but was mothballed in 1946. Five years later she was sold to the Greek navy.

Bielek then added the most mysterious comment of all: he claimed that his brother Duncan had died of old age — and that he had aged at the rate of about a year an hour as a result of his having been sucked into hyperspace. Not content with this rapid ageing process, Bielek's report contained further theories about secret government activities.

He maintained that the government did not wish him or his brother to die and claimed that there were secret government agencies that had the necessary technology to prevent, or at least to circumvent, death. Bielek (formerly Cameron) said that he had been given the body and life history of Alfred Bielek, allegedly born in 1927. He maintained throughout his remarkable narrative that both the CIA and NSA had access to very advanced technology that could switch minds into other bodies and create age regression or progression.

Bielek says he was finally able to contact his half-brother again and they remembered collectively that they had both been involved in the Philadelphia Experiment *almost as though it were part of another life.*

So much for the outline story of the Philadelphia Experiment and Alfred Bielek's astounding evidence about it. What conclusions is it possible to draw?

The most useful place to begin is with the concept of visual and radar invisibility. From the moment when a baby first begins to get its eyes into focus and distinguish something of the colour and shape of the external world in which he or she is living, the brain, or the mind behind it, has more to do with perception than the eyes and the optic nerve have.

The existence of dozens of clever optical illusions and psychological test diagrams that very quickly illustrate the fallibility of perception ought to make all observers — especially those who aim for scientific objectivity — extremely careful. The mind detests a vacuum. It will do all it can to provide rational explanations to account for the stimuli that reach it via the sensory organs. There is a very good illustration of this in the case of two Victorian cyclists who were travelling in line behind each other as they cycled home along a village street as dusk was falling. The second rider was absolutely convinced that he saw his friend collide with some obstacle or other on the road surface and fall heavily from his machine. The second man increased his pace in a hurry to catch up with and help the friend whom he assumed would be quite seriously injured. He was very relieved — but even more surprised — to find his friend riding safely and steadily just around the next bend. When he asked anxiously if his companion was hurt, or had been hurt, by the fall, his friend looked at him in astonishment and they both dismounted to discuss what might have happened. They then retraced their ride for a few yards. A large sheet of metal, formerly part of an advertising billboard, had fallen into the road some time before, and this metal sheet had clattered loudly as the first cyclist went over it. It was only a flat sheet, albeit a rather noisy one, presenting no hazard at all to an experienced cyclist with a good sense of balance and strong wrists.

The first man remembered going over it and hearing the clatter, but he had not been inconvenienced by the metal obstruction because the sheet was so thin. Evidently the second cyclist, not being able to see what was really going on, had conjured up in his imagination a picture of his friend falling heavily in order to explain the clattering metallic crash, which he had heard, but could not identify optically.

As has been noted, the mind dislikes a vacuum and will do all in its power to supply an explanation for the missing cause of any sight or sound which may have reached it. Hallucination and/or a vivid imagination can supply the observer with the impression that something that is not there, is there; but it is somewhat rarer for the imagination to make something that is there *invisible*.

A number of competent and highly entertaining stage hypnotists can suggest to suitable subjects that a member of the group is missing, so that when, as part of the entertainment, sweets, drinks, or sandwiches are passed around on stage, the "missing" person is totally ignored. When asked later about such disappearances, those hypnotic subjects who have been able to recall something of their experience and their observations at the time in any degree of detail have said that they did not see an *empty* chair where the "invisible" person was sitting, but rather a black or white screen, or mask, that seemed to fit over the person whom the hypnotist had forbidden the subject to see. The "invisible" person did not so much vanish as become "censored" out of the mind of the observer.

So although suggestion and the mental aspect of the act of observation may well have had something to do with the apparent invisibility of the *Eldridge*, it seems unlikely that they could have accounted satisfactorily for the reports — if there is any truth in those reports — of the ship's disappearance. Although observation and perception are mental rather than physiological functions, depending upon the mind and the brain rather than upon the eye, there would nevertheless seem to be a great deal more truth in the *Eldridge* story than could reasonably be explained by optical illusions or mental error of that sort.

But if the rumours and legends of the disappearance of the *Eldridge* are to be taken at face value, and if only ten per cent of the reports are strictly accurate, then something very, very strange indeed took place during the Philadelphia Experiment. What we call sight depends upon photons of light bouncing off the object being viewed and being registered in the human eye and optical system. Unless there is something off which those photons of light can bounce, the thing will not be seen. That does not mean it cannot be observed: it is possible to observe perfect blackness in the sense that it *interrupts* the rest of the field of visibility.

For an object to exist and yet to either absorb or refuse to reflect photons from the light falling on it would create a black patch like a silhouette in the position occupied by that photon-free object in the middle of a visibility field. It would be as if a piece of black cardboard had been lowered in front of the *Mona Lisa* or Gainsborough's *Blue Boy*. The obstruction would not be visible and neither would the portion of the painting which it covered. This does not seem to have been the case with the Philadelphia Experiment. If the rumours are correct, the ship simply became invisible, and on the later occasion did not even leave a hull-shaped depression in the water to indicate where it was.

In an old but well-written piece of fiction about invisibility called "The Shadow and the Flash," two rival scientists had worked on invisibility from opposite directions. One was working on the line of trying to produce a substance so black that it would reflect no light. The other was working on a substance that would possess a transparency so perfect that, to all intents and purposes, wherever the transparent object was placed it would not be seen. The story was entitled "The Shadow and the Flash" because the two weaknesses of the opposing invisibility systems were that one cast a shadow and the other, at certain angles, produced a flash. The two rival invisibility experts fought each other on a sunlit lawn, and all that the observers could see of their conflict was an occasional shadow and a spasmodic surge of brightness when critical angles of refraction were reached.

Neither of these malfunctions was associated with the invisibility ascribed to the *Eldridge*. It is easy enough in a science fiction story to produce a piece of technology like an Elizabethan *deus ex machina*. The technology produced by futuristic science fiction authors is always capable of overcoming shadow and flash disadvantages, but the *real* science, however advanced, responsible for the invisibility of the *Eldridge* (if it took place at all) is qualitatively different from the "science" of the science fiction novel.

The universe works consistently. Advanced lubricants can get rid of a great deal of friction in bearings, but the greatest chemical advances in lubrication are unlikely to dispose of the laws of friction altogether. If the *Eldridge* really did seem to be invisible, leaving neither a shadow nor a flash behind her, then the conclusion has to be that she was not merely invisible — *she was not there*.

In the innermost recesses of sub-atomic physics there are some weird little particles that apparently vanish. Some physicists have suggested that these erratic little characters have so much energy that they exceed the speed of light (impossible?) and travel *backwards in time* until they slow down sufficiently to reappear. Other modern theoretical physicists have put forward the concept of extra dimensions in addition to the three dimensions of space and the fourth dimension of time that make up the Einsteinian space-time continuum. One physicist at least has suggested that there may be some seventeen or eighteen actual dimensions. If the universe is a thought in the mind of a supreme mathematician, then there could well be more than seventeen dimensions. Like eternity, the number of dimensions could be infinite. In a boundless universe there is more than enough space and time into which an experimental warship rigged with electromagnetic fields (whose designers understood only a fraction of what they were supposed to be doing) could very easily "disappear."

There is, of course, an even more mind-boggling alternative. Whatever strange forces were being exerted on the *Eldridge* and her hapless crew — if the disappearance *really* took place — may have held her stationary while Earth and the rest of the universe moved on! Einstein, himself, would be the first to remind us that movement is *relative*. It is like the old paradox of the two perfectly spherical spacecraft that approach each other (or, rather, that come into each other's proximity) somewhere in the vastness of space where there are no background landmarks or navigational points to which the captains can refer. It could be argued that they are going from opposite directions and meeting each other. It could be argued equally logically that a fast one is overtaking a slow one. Without a third frame of reference against which the two ships and their movements can be tested there is no real way of settling the argument.

Did the Philadelphia Experiment ever take place? Did the *Eldridge* move away from her place in the sea — *or did her place in the sea move away from her?* Alfred Bielek's amazing story takes us so far from the here and now, the common-sense, everyday world of burger bars, offices, factories, and shops, that its very *weirdness* tempts us to wonder if it could be true.

If it is, it takes us into a realm that is far stranger and more disturbing than anything in Alice's Wonderland. Those who dare to ship aboard the metaphorical *Eldridge*s of this strange old universe of ours need bodies like Hercules' and minds like Sir Isaac Newton's. If even a few of the legends of the Philadelphia Experiment are true, then the *Eldridge* must be a leading contender for the title of the most mysterious object of all.

CHAPTER TEN:
The Tarot

There are seventy-eight cards in the Tarot pack, and these are divided into the Major Arcana, which consists of twenty-two cards, and the Minor Arcana, with fifty-six. When the cards are used for games, the Major Arcana become the trumps. When used for fortune telling, or divination, they are normally regarded as being more significant than the Minor Arcana, which consists of four suits with fourteen cards in each.

The twenty-two cards of the Major Arcana are pictures that represent characters, vices, virtues, and what could loosely be described as "forces." The twenty-two cards of the Major Arcana are numbered from one to twenty-one; the Fool, or Jester, is not numbered.

Taking the cards in order, the first is the Juggler, sometimes referred to as the Magician or Thaumaturgist. The significance of this card is that it represents power behind the scenes. This is Mr. Fix-it. This is the power behind the throne, the Grey Eminence. Card number one is a politician or financier with enormous manipulative power in the context of the modern politico-economic world. The "magic" being performed on the card is to be understood metaphorically rather than literally. This is the man or woman at the centre of the web, the operator of the "old boy" or "old girl" network.

The second card, sometimes called the Goddess and sometimes called the Female Pope, is another symbol of power or influence. There is, however, a subtle difference between the "power" of card number one and the "power" of card number two. This Goddess or Female Pope works in secret. The Juggler/Magician does not often use his power in the open, but the Goddess card uses her power in a more discreet and concealed way still. There is in this card an element of the unexpected and the hidden. In stories of espionage, this card would represent the "sleeper": the type of espionage agent who is not called upon to do anything for several years, then is suddenly and unexpectedly at the very centre of the action with a vital role to play. The power of this Female Pope is the power of the dagger behind the tapestry on the castle wall. In a detective novel, this would be the card that represented the apparently faithful old cook/housekeeper who has been waiting to take revenge for the loss of a loved one some thirty or forty years ago and who can strike suddenly and unexpectedly. It could also represent the kind of character who actually owned a factory or building yard but, in order to find out what was really happening, dressed as a labourer and mingled unobtrusively with the other workers to try to obtain a clear and accurate picture of the real, grass-roots facts.

The third and fourth cards are the Empress and the Emperor, respectively. While the power of the Magician and the Female Pope is a power behind the scenes (to a greater or lesser extent), the power of the Empress and Emperor is an ostentatious power. They occupy front stage all the time. These are media tycoons, magnates, heads of commerce and industry, archbishops and cardinals, prime ministers, presidents, and royalty. Just as the first two figures had real manipulative power and concealed it, so the *apparent* power of cards three and four can be far greater than the reality. The Emperor and Empress have a *show* of power. The Female Pope and the Magician have something more significant and pragmatic.

Psychologically, these four characters could almost be seen to indicate the depth of difference between introverts and extroverts. The Female Pope and the Magician are introverts. The Emperor and Empress are extroverts. Empresses and Emperors could be show-business personalities, well known film and television faces. Female Popes and Magicians are directors, producers, and commissioning editors: people wielding real power.

The fifth card is the Pope, and here we have moved away from the consideration of power to a consideration of *holiness*. This fifth card, along with the ninth card, the Hermit (which is somewhat different from it), is power in the sense of the power of morality, the power of ethics, the power of true religion. This is power of the kind that was found in a man like Thomas Becket, who dared to stand against King Henry II. The character represented by this papal card is found in the kind of man or woman who has the inner strength to stand up for what

73

he or she believes to be true and not waver in the face of threat or bribe, to be moved neither by fear nor hope, but only by conscience.

The sixth card is yet another very strong contrast with those that have gone before and contains one of the deepest mysteries of the Tarot, even if the cards date only from the fourteenth century and not from the ancient mysteries of Egypt as is widely believed among Tarot enthusiasts.

One of the strangest things about the Tarot is the way that it seems to understand and reflect all the depths and all the movements and motivations of the human mind. If Freud had lived before the Tarot was created, it would have been a reasonable bet to have suggested that he was responsible for the cards and their meanings.

This would certainly have been especially appropriate in connection with the sixth card: the Lovers. What Freud called the "libido" can be expressed directly through sexual energy or in a thousand other positive patterns. Through these, that energy can (in Freudian terms) be "sublimated." It seems to be one of the most powerful motivators in the whole complicated human psyche. Perfect love, transcending basic physicality, exceeds fear — and exceeds even the powerfully rooted desire for self-preservation.

There are many cases on record of human beings who have risked their lives in an effort to save a much loved pet from a fire or a flood. There are even more cases on record of human lovers who would go through any pain barrier or feat of endurance in order to save the person they love. This is by no means restricted to a greatly loved and appreciated sexual partner, but can be seen in the risks and self-sacrifice demonstrated by a parent saving a child or a child saving a parent. The same affection can exist between brothers and sisters, cousins, grandparents — even between close friends who have neither blood nor sexual bonds.

The holy, spiritual love of God was expressed by Christ, whose knowledge and depth of understanding of the human beings whom He created is unsurpassed. He summed it up by saying that "perfect love casteth out fear" and that "no man hath greater love than this: to lay down his life for his friends."

By incorporating card six into the Tarot, the originator of this strangely probing pack has fathomed some of the profoundest depths of the mysterious reservoir of human motivation. This card refers to altruism and a process of going-outside-oneself, which is the only way to truly become oneself. To quote again from the words of Christ, "except a corn of wheat fall into the ground and die, it abideth alone." Academic Bible commentators and theologians generally regard this teaching as meaning that until a human being has found some much loved person or worthwhile cause that matters more than life itself, then existence will be lonely, unfulfilled, and lacking any real quality. By following this particular teaching of Jesus, it is possible for a person to find a level of altruism and a nobility of spirit that can best be described as a willingness to die to one's own selfishness. This seems to be the only way of finding a level of consciousness and a fulfilled state of being far beyond anything that the self-centred consciousness is able to experience. It is the difference between Scrooge *before* the supernatural Christmas visits and Scrooge *after* the supernatural Christmas visits.

In this Lovers card of the Tarot, the mystery of union with — and genuine altruistic love for — another human being, some great abstract cause, or even a much loved pet, is clearly and perfectly exemplified. In card six, the Tarot reveals the highly desirable and dynamic power of straightforward sexual attraction, but it also reveals the power of a love that is not necessarily sexually oriented. When the two great powers of love and sex are running parallel and pulling in the same direction, the consequences they can produce are the emotional equivalent of a hydrogen bomb.

In any Tarot reading, the sixth card can be an indication of indescribable pleasure or a warning of unparalleled disaster. Men and women at their noblest will die willingly for someone they love; at their worst they will stop at nothing — not even murder or suicide.

In considering the depth and importance of these first six cards, and the Lovers card in particular, two aspects of the mysterious Tarot need to be considered. There are two ways in which the enigma of the Tarot can be approached. A clue to these two approaches may be found in the wisdom of the nineteenth-century religious author George MacDonald. On being asked by readers about the meaning and symbolism of his intriguing fantasy stories, MacDonald replied that the creative power in the mind of the reader is at least equal to the creative power in the mind of an author. He said that if one of his readers sees a meaning, a depth, another dimension in a MacDonald story that George himself had *not* seen, then the power of that reader's creativity generates a meaning-structure that is just as valid as anything that MacDonald himself had thought of in his role as an author.

Does the Tarot reader, therefore, need to ask whether the cards are a masterpiece of *neutrality*? Do they, themselves, have no particular meaning other than that which the active human mind imposes upon them? Is the true genius of the Tarot its malleability and plasticity? Is it simply an extremely useful medium for the mysterious creative and perceptive power of the mind of the user?

An artist, a sculptor, a woodcarver, or an architect has to work with certain physical media. Most materials have their characteristic advantages and disadvantages: stone will serve one purpose, brick a different one. Iron, acrylic, and timber can all be used in different ways. Each presents a range of opportunities and a range of limitations. The more versatile the medium, the more versatile the craftsperson can be. So then, does the *real* power of the Tarot lie in a similar neutrality and versatility of its images and the mysterious concepts behind them?

Another view would put forward the proposition that there is some mysterious, arcane, and esoteric power in the symbols themselves. Far from being a neutral medium upon which the human mind can operate, is the hidden "magic" of the Tarot itself a stimulus to the human mind?

A third view would be that there is some kind of *synthesis,* and that the neutrality of the Tarot as a medium incorporates somehow a mysterious, esoteric stimulus that leads both the reader and subject to find a meaning in the cards. This would be close to the dialectic concept, which suggests that while a craftsperson is creating something, that same something is fashioning the craftsperson: "While I'm making something — something is making me." The blacksmith, the goldsmith, the diamond cutter, the racing driver, or the professional gangland killer are all fashioned to some extent by the environment in which they work. So perhaps reader and subject influence the cards while the cards reciprocally influence them.

The seventh card is the Chariot, believed by some to be the missing thirteenth sign of the Zodiac. Experts in the history of chess regard the rook, or castle, with its powerful, direct, lateral move, as representing a chariot in ancient warfare. It is, in fact, thought to have taken its name from the Persian *rukh,* which meant chariot. In the Tarot reading, the force of the Chariot can be a direct and physical one, something external, like the force of a river, waterfall, storm, hurricane, or perhaps a huge tidal wave, the power of electricity, or the power of the Internet. It can represent a forest fire, a volcano, or an earthquake. It can also represent social, religious, or political force, the desire for social change, a movement towards freedom for the oppressed or egalitarianism for the poor. It can represent conquering armies like those of Ghengis Khan or Alexander the Great. It could be Nazism or Communism. It could be the almost limitless power of the will that drives a woman or man to achieve, to endure, to take on the seemingly impossible and to overcome it. It could be the determination and strength of character of the escapees from Colditz Castle. Anything or anyone with force, power, and directness could be represented by the Tarot Chariot.

The eighth card is Justice. This does not merely represent its face value of honesty, fair play, and judgement in the legal sense (as personified in the wisdom of King Solomon), it also represents *balance*. The Justice card is the resolution of the mathematical parallelogram of forces. It is the compromise that is reached when a raging tide comes up against an immovable granite cliff. It is that moment of truth between two perfectly matched tug-of-war teams at the annual village fête. It is reason and logic; it is pragmatism and the art of the possible. It is the realization deep inside the mind that a human being has to be something more than love and hatred, hope and fear, feverish action and tranquillity. This card is the acknowledgement that fire and ice *can* both exist in the same universe.

The ninth card is the Hermit. Just as the Chariot shows the path of directness, dynamism, power, and action, so the Hermit shows the power of calm meditation. The Charioteer is the man or woman who drives onward and outward against all obstacles, determined to conquer or die. The Hermit is that aspect of the personality which seeks to conquer the *internal* world rather than the *external* world. For the Hermit, the truth of the old proverb "Greater are they who conquer themselves than those who conquer cities" is the quintessence of truth.

Human beings seem to be approximately mid-way in the universe's scale of size between the sub-atomic particles of the microcosm and the incalculable distances of intergalactic space in the macrocosm. From this vantage point between the infinitesimally small and the infinitely vast, humanity is able to achieve a realistic perspective of all that is observable.

The Hermit reminds us that there is just as much to explore inside our minds as there is in the external universe. Just as the Chariot beckons to conquest and adventure outside of ourselves, so the Hermit reminds us of the need to know who and what we really are in order to make sense of the internal conquest that we long for.

Card ten is the Wheel of Fortune, frequently represented on the Tarot illustrations as the Wheel of Misfortune. It is this Wheel of Fortune that is exemplified in the old wisdom of the horseshoe nail.

> For the want of a nail the shoe was lost;
> For the want of the shoe the horse was lost;
> For the want of the horse the rider was lost;
> For the want of the rider the message was lost;
> For the want of the message the battle was lost;
> For the want of the battle the kingdom was lost —
> And all for the want of a horseshoe nail!

It often looks as though the universe appears to run on the wheels of "if." This is what the tenth card, the Wheel of Fortune signifies. It says with Robert Burns:

> The best laid schemes o' mice an 'men
> Gang aft a-gley,
> An ' lea'e us nought but grief an' pain
> For promis'd joy.

It is the Wheel of Fortune in the Tarot cards that reminds us how much seems to depend upon the smallest details, like the horseshoe nail. Being in the right place at the right time, or in the wrong place at the wrong time, can have cataclysmic effects upon the remaining years of a person's life. The decision to go by sea rather than to fly, to use the Harley Davidson rather than the Volvo, to take the train rather than the bus (decisions that are trivial in themselves) can make a wealth of difference — even, on occasion, the difference between life and death. At any moment, disaster may strike the most prosperous and secure man or woman, and it may strike out of the proverbial clear blue sky. At the other extreme, the business tycoon on the verge of bankruptcy might suddenly win a ten-million-dollar lottery prize and recoup everything. Such is the Wheel of Fortune. Its purpose among the Tarot cards is to remind the reader and the subject that when we think we have covered every eventually and made allowance for every possibility, something may suddenly emerge that will turn victory into defeat — or ignominious defeat into brilliant, glorious, and totally unexpected victory.

The eleventh card is known as Strength or Fortitude. It conveys the idea of strength of both mind and body. There is a marvellous cartoon drawn by a brilliant (but anonymous) cartoonist that occasionally makes its way over fax machines and e-mails. It shows a rugged and muscular old bullfrog being swallowed by a heron. The frog, although a third of the way down the heron's beak, has not given up! His powerful front webs are locked in an unbreakable stranglehold around the heron's throat. It cannot swallow him as long as his grip does not weaken. This cartoon might well be used for card eleven of some new Tarot pack. The caption simply reads, "Never give up."

One important aspect of the Tarot is to teach, specifically to teach those aspects of personality and attitudes to life that will bring us through difficulties and dangers successfully. Strength of mind, spirit, and body are inextricably interlinked. A determined martial artist can defeat a stronger, heavier, and more skilful opponent, if he or she has greater determination than the opponent who has all the other advantages. This is sometimes referred to as sheer fighting spirit. During World War I, the German battle cruiser *Emden* fired a salvo at a small Russian gunboat called the *Jemchug*, which blew it practically in half. As it sank, the gunners in the rear turret of the *Jemchug* swung their gun around, and with a last defiant act of supreme courage and determination, managed to fire just one shell at the triumphant *Emden*, which had destroyed both them and their boat. It is that kind of strength and fortitude which this eleventh card exemplifies. It is the eternal spirit of Templarism: first to attack and last to retreat. During World War II, the Bavarian Gypsies survived in their mountain strongholds against all the depredations of crack Nazi storm-troopers because the Gypsy motto was, "Take one with you." From the youngest toddler to the oldest Romany chief, the determination not to die while your enemy lived was etched indelibly into the Gypsy soul — and a simple piece of broken glass concealed in a ragged sleeve was capable of severing the jugular vein of a heavily armed storm-trooper.

The greatest part of the legend of Hereward the Wake, the formidable anti-Norman freedom fighter of the East Anglian Fens a thousand years ago, tells of his ambush and final battle in a timber-built

Saxon long hall. Hereward had been lured into the trap to find a dozen Norman men-at-arms, their strongest and best, waiting to kill him. He made no attempt to escape, barred the door behind him, took his great Saxon axe in both hands, and said, "Come on! I'll take the lot of you!" — and he did. He had the ultimate satisfaction of seeing the last Norman would-be assassin dead on the floor in front of him before dying of his own wounds. Could any true-hearted warrior hope for a better death? It has about it an echo of the grand old Texan saying, "You can take my gun when you prise it from my cold, dead fingers."

In the Parable of the Sower, Christ spoke of the seed that fell on shallow ground where there was no worthwhile depth of earth. It sprang up and then very soon wilted and withered in the sun and achieved nothing because its roots were not deep enough. When He explained the meaning of the parable to the Disciples, He told them that the shallow ground represented people who had great enthusiasm for God's Word but no strength nor fortitude — no depth of character.

There is a sense in which card six, the Lovers, and card seven, the Chariot, both represent aspects of motivation. Card eleven reminds us that motivation without strength or fortitude to back it up is like an arrowhead with no arrow, or a spearhead with no heavy shaft to drive it through the enemy's chain mail. Card eleven reminds the most powerfully motivated man or woman that strength and fortitude are equally essential for success — motivation alone is not enough.

The twelfth card is the Hanged Man. It is a strange card, in which the victim is seen hanging upside down with a cord around one ankle and usually the right foot crossed over the left knee, which is straight because it is the left ankle that is secured by the rope from which the hanged man is suspended. This card represents those occasions when we feel nothing is moving. The hanged man is literally pending, waiting, because a decision somewhere beyond his control is held up; everything is in the balance, everything is delayed. The card refers to those occasions on which we have to wait for the answer to some important question: the start of a new personal relationship, the outcome of a job interview, the commissioning editor's decision about a proposal for a new radio or television show, a publisher's decision about an idea for a new book.

This card reminds us of the importance of waiting calmly for a decision that is outside our control. When we have done everything possible to produce a favourable result, and there is nothing to do now

except wait, it is card twelve that reminds us of the importance of waiting quietly. Any attempt to interfere with the Hanged Man is more
likely to produce a negative result than a positive one.

When the roulette wheel is spinning and the ball is bouncing from
number to number, a gambler can only wait. When you have bought
your lottery ticket, waiting is the only option until the draw is made.
How can we learn the best way to handle these log-jam situations?

Marjorie Copeman was the psychology lecturer at Keswick Hall
College near Norwich many years ago. She was a lady of great wisdom
and experience, what one might rightly term a practising psychologist
as well as an academically profound theoretical one. One of her wisest
and most relevant sayings was, "We are all familiar with the traditional flight or fight responses to a stimulus: but there is a third way — we
may simply ignore the stimulus and allow it to dissipate on its own."

The Hanged Man of the Tarot cards symbolizes Marjorie
Copeman's insight about the third way. There are occasions when it is
necessary to realize that time can be our greatest ally, but it is not a
weapon whose use is easily learnt. The purpose of the Hanged Man in
the Tarot is to remind us that effective waiting can be both an irre-
sistible attack and an impenetrable defence.

The thirteenth card is Death. It is one of the strange ironies of the
Tarot that things are not always what they seem. It appears at first
glance to be a grim and awesome card, one that most subjects would
not wish to turn up during a reading, but the Death card does not refer
to physical death at all. In the mind of the Tarot originator, death stood
for *change*, for moving from one kind of life to the next. It was not an
end, it was a new beginning. To an originator with such views about
survival, physical death simply became a change of environment. In his
view, the soul went on to a wider, brighter, and happier realm.

This is the meaning of the thirteenth card. It signifies some major
change: perhaps in a relationship — a subject will begin a new life with
a new partner — or in some other major sphere. It could signify a
change of job, a major promotion, or a change of political or religious
allegiance and the consequential new view of life from this paradigm.
Very often change is for the better, so that the thirteenth card is something to look forward to rather than something to dread.

The fourteenth card is usually called Temperance. This is similar in
some ways to the Justice card and represents balance, but it is balance

of the appetites, drawing back from dangerous and extreme attitudes. In terms of military tactics and strategy, it would represent Fabianism or the way that Russia defeated Napoleon's France simply by withdrawing and allowing Napoleon's Grand Army to over-extend itself until the Russian winter came. Temperance recommends to us a defence against fanaticism and obsession. Temperance is the flagship of common sense. All good and true religion draws people slowly and gently closer to the one true benign and loving God and to one another. This is true religion, blessed by the kind of Temperance that the fourteenth card of the Tarot is supposed to represent.

The dangerous, obsessive, fanatical, and frequently fundamentalist faith that drags people away from one another and into desperate situations where they feel an urge either to damage others or themselves is as far from true religion as a stomach ulcer is from a good healthy appetite after exercise.

If Temperance, the fourteenth card, was a person, she could well be nominated for the role of the Patron Saint of all True Religion. If only her wisdom could be universally heard and accepted, cults would wither and vanish and religious warfare and martyrdom would cease. The serious psychological malfunctions that convince their victims that God is calling them to do something uncomfortable, embarrassing, restrictive, misery-generating, or hazardous would be shown for the life-crippling errors that they are.

The fifteenth card is The Devil — as far from the wisdom of Temperance as it is possible to be. This is the symbol of temptation: the urge to neglect what is good and needs doing and to apply our energies instead to that which is mischievous, irritating, injurious to others, or downright evil. The demon symbol on the card refers not only to the dark psychic forces of personified evil (Satan, Lucifer, Mephistopheles, and the host of fallen angels), it also refers to the evil within us: selfishness, greed, and what C.S. Lewis would have referred to as those "inferior instincts and cravings which spring from visceral humanity." This fifteenth card is our Tarot warning that evil lurks frighteningly close to the surface of even the kindest and best-natured human being. If we think of human progress through life as being analogous to the flight of an aircraft, or the movement of a ship through the ocean, this card reminds us that on board the plane or ship of our own life there lurks an insane terrorist who is anxious to take over the controls and crash the plane, or drive the ship on to a dangerous shoal. This fifteenth Tarot card warns us that both external and internal danger are ever present. Goodness and sanity, rationality and kindness — these are not maintained without constant effort. Hobbes, the political philosopher, was right about one major plank in his otherwise questionable argument structure: there is always a danger that (in Hobbes's words) human life can all too easily become "solitary, poor, nasty, brutish, and short."

It is this fifteenth card that reminds us of the necessity of never-ending vigilance against the destructiveness that subsists both within our own minds and in the external universe.

The Lightning Struck Tower, which is the sixteenth card, is very well placed by the designer of the Major Arcana, as it follows the Devil. It is when a human being succumbs to those external or internal forces of evil, according to the apparent wisdom of the Tarot, that the tower is struck by lightning. The metaphor indicates — as does the Wheel of Fortune — the possibility of a sudden dramatic change of circumstance. Whereas the Wheel of Fortune can bring benign changes as it spins, the Lightning Struck Tower is the warning that fate can deal terrible blows. The Lightning Struck Tower is a constant reminder that security is an illusion and that life is fragile and precious. One purpose of the Lightning Struck Tower is to remind us of the wisdom of the old advice, "Eat, drink and be merry — for tomorrow we die." The ruined tower can represent the wrecking of a valued personal relationship, the end of a rewarding career, the loss of significant financial or political power and influence. The lightning can take the form of a successful rival, illness, accident, revolution, or unwelcome change of government. The turbulent and blood-stained history of the seventeenth century reminds us that those who were loyal to King Charles I fared badly when Cromwell won the war and, conversely, those who fared well as loyal followers of Cromwell found themselves in a very different world when King Charles II was restored.

The Star is the seventeenth card and it signifies hope. It is not only the light in the sky, it is the light at the end of the tunnel. It is the last and only worthwhile thing in Pandora's box. It is the Star card that tells the condemned prisoner that a stay of execution and a royal pardon may yet arrive. It is the Star that sends the unsold manuscript to the twenty-ninth publisher, and it is the Star that persuades that publisher to give it a chance and put it before the public. It is the Star that reminds the very sick of miracles of healing that have genuinely happened for others and could yet happen for them. It is the Star that keeps the ship-wrecked mariner swimming in an icy or shark-infested sea in the undying hope of rescue. It is the Star that lights the dark sky of the clinically depressed. Again, the Star is supposed to be one of the motivators of the strength and fortitude found on the eleventh card. It is the Star that shines on the Lovers of card six. However slim common sense and statistics suggest that our chances of success may be, it is the Star that enables us to reach our goal somehow at some distant future time.

Just as hope is an apparently distant and insubstantial thing, so to the primitive and medieval mind were the stars. Yet to those who believed that astrology worked, the planets and stars, despite their distance, were felt to have a massive effect on human life.

Card eighteen, the Moon, is the card of mystery. It could almost be set alongside the fist card, the Juggler or Magician. In Shakespeare's *Midsummer Night's Dream*, it is by moonlight that the magic happens when Oberon and Titania take over from the sunlit world of common sense and reason. It is the Moon card that reminds us that there is a mystical, half-visible side to our lives and to our universe. Taken in conjunction with the cards of Justice and Temperance, the Moon is supposed to tell a Tarot reader, or subject, that he or she needs to look carefully at this *balance* between faith and reason, between magic and materialism, between mysticism and machinery. We neglect the Moon at our peril. The moon world is the dream world. The sun world is the world of science, activity and technology.

This nineteenth card, the Sun, is our constant and necessary reminder that we do live in a world of glare and of harsh, practical realities. The dreamer cannot retreat to the Hermitage, the monastic cell, or the moonlit glade in the Forest of Arden. The telephone bill has to be paid, letters have to be written and posted, work has to be done, fuel has to be found, and fires must be lit. None of the everyday necessities of life happen by themselves. The input of human energy and activity is indispensable. The Sun card of the Tarot reminds us that no matter how good, how transcendental, or how beautiful our moonlight world may be, it cannot exist independently of the Sun. Food must be prepared, a bed must be made, wine and beer will not ferment or brew by themselves, the ship of life will only take us across the river if we set the sails. Taken together, the solar and lunar cards remind us of the vital importance and inescapable necessity of balancing our lives.

The twentieth card is the card of Judgement. Although the symbolism on many of the older Tarot packs portrayed it as a colourful scene of heaven and hell, or went back even further than the Judaeo-Christian ideas to the ancient Egyptian Book of the Dead, the Last Judgement is a card representing finality. The card suggests that there is a point, a goal, an objective to which all the thoughts, words, and deeds of our earthly life are directed. This Judgement card, the twentieth card, is the *card of accountability*.

When Cain murdered his brother, Abel, according to the account in the Book of Genesis, and was subsequently questioned by God about his dead brother's whereabouts, the guilty man responded with a question: "Am I my brother's keeper?" The definitive answer that Christ has taught us is "Yes." We *are* responsible. There is no escape from this liability, there is no turning back. Individually and collectively, we are most solemnly charged by God with the care and keeping of all those of our brothers and sisters who need our help when they cannot help themselves. Jesus clearly taught: "In as much as you have done it to the least of my brethren you have done it unto me."

Card twenty of the Tarot may well remind us of this responsibility. The twentieth card of the Tarot asks us over and over again whether we are doing *enough*, whether anyone ever *can* do enough, for the necessitous, the under-privileged, the sick and the starving, the homeless and the oppressed.

The twenty-first card is the Universe, or, perhaps, our one small planet within it. The idea of responsibility and judgement expressed in the twentieth card extends naturally to this twenty-first symbol. The same message comes across: we are all responsible for one another, and we are all responsible for the care and maintenance of the ecological systems within which we live. Just as we depend on the world for food, water, and oxygen, so the world depends upon us. It is the medieval village well writ large: no one is compelled to drink — but all are duty bound to preserve the water supply and keep it pure.

There is one more card in the Major Arcana, and it is not numbered. It is sometimes represented as a Fool (in the medieval sense) or as a Court Jester. This card represents an entertainer: a man or woman who is concealed behind a persona. The Fool is a wild card, and it represents the wild card within ourselves and within other people. It also reminds us of the concept of the *Holy* Fool: the simpleton in the eyes of the world who is wiser than the greatest sage at the most reputable university. The Fool represents freedom and the whimsical, autonomous, uncontrolled, and uncontrollable aspect of our own lives or the lives of those whom we meet in the world.

This last, unnumbered card serves to remind the Tarot reader and subject of the need for freedom. As the old text reminds us, "The wind bloweth where it listeth" — and so does the Fool within the human heart. It is our capriciousness that is represented by this strange, untamed card. It is frequently argued by theologians and philosophers that God-inspired, spiritual love — spontaneous and freely given — is the greatest good in the entire universe. Love cannot exist unless we are free to chose, which is why God gave us free will despite its incalculable dangers. The unnumbered Fool, last card of the Major Arcana, may well represent that *uncertainty principle* as far as human behaviour is concerned. If we do not have within our gamut of powers the capacity for irresponsible folly, then neither do we have the capacity for true love. The closest card to the Fool, therefore, may well be number six, the Lovers.

This study of the cards of the Major Arcana and their meaning encompasses the deeper and more significant part of the Tarot pack. By contrast, the Minor Arcana consists of fifty-six cards, which are made up of four suits, with fourteen cards in each. The suit that is referred to as rods, batons, or wands corresponds to clubs in a pack of ordinary playing cards. The cups of the Tarot are the hearts of the normal pack. The suit of swords in the Minor Arcana is related to that of spades in playing cards. The coins, discs, or pentacles are related to diamonds. The cards of the four suits of the Minor Arcana range from an ace to a ten, just as ordinary playing cards do, but there is one additional picture card. The Page, which is equivalent to the Knave, or Jack, is the lowest of the picture cards. Above him is a Knight, above him the Queen, and, at the top, the King. When the full Tarot pack is used for fortune telling, the four suits have their own specific aspects. The wands are linked with career and business. The coins are close to them in that they are also linked to money and material well-being. Whether we can afford a cottage, a castle, or a caravan is held to lie in the suit of coins. The cups, like the hearts of the ordinary playing cards, are the cards of love and personal relationships. The swords are the cards of war, of conflict and strife. The most experienced and expert Tarot readers are usually inclined to explain that the cards act for them mainly as focal points and that it is something deep and instinctive inside the reader that tends to give the most accurate apparent meanings of the cards that have been shuffled and perhaps dealt by the subject who has come for the reading. If Jung is right about group-mind and a vast, collective human subconscious — something akin to the mysterious "Force" in *Star Wars* — then it could well be that what a Tarot reader is actually doing is linking his or her psychic perceptions with something in the mind of the subject and the vast reservoir of the human subconscious. Some believe that the ultimate, esoteric truth is hidden down there somewhere in the depths of those psychic waters. The Tarot cards could then be thought of as a scuba diving outfit enabling the reader to seek out the mystical treasure from the bottom of the reservoir.

CHAPTER ELEVEN:
Ball Lightning

T
he authors' personal experience of ball lightning is limited to one occasion in 1952 when co-author Lionel was riding his Ariel 350 through a wooded area of Norfolk in England during a very heavy thunderstorm. It was a narrow country road, and the heavy rain on top of the summer dust had made the surface far from ideal for a biker. The storm seemed to be almost directly overhead, and lightning was darting among the trees on both sides of the road. Suddenly it seemed to Lionel that it was actually *rolling* in the form of two or three balls — not much larger than tennis balls — from his left to his right across the chromium-plated handlebars of the Ariel 350. There was no characteristic electrical-energy smell; neither was there any sound audible over the roar of the engine and the noise of the heavy rainstorm through the trees. The whole experience did not last more than thirty to forty seconds at most. After this "ball lightning" — if that is what it was — had left the bars, the storm seemed to ease considerably. The rain dwindled to a vestigial shower and the sun came through the storm clouds again. Although Lionel can identify the year accurately because of the particular bike that he was then riding, he cannot be accurate about the precise date other than to recall that it was definitely the summer of 1952 and that it was *probably* mid-June.

Ball lightning is an extremely strange phenomenon, and one that is only partially understood by meteorologists and scientists in allied disciplines. It may be described basically as a rare natural phenomenon that is almost invariably associated with thunderstorms. It has the appearance of a bright sphere of what *seems* to be electrical energy. Some witnesses say they have seen it moving fast, but others have described the ball lightning they saw as going relatively slowly. Ball lightning is reported by those who have witnessed it to be able to pass through windows and to disappear silently or with a loud report. Its colours have been noted as most frequently in the red/orange/yellow areas of the spectrum, although occasionally blue ball lightning has been reported. The example that co-author Lionel saw on the handle-bars of the Ariel 350 was yellowish white, the kind of colour that is associated with "normal" lightning. Some witnesses have reported a smell not unlike the smell of an electric storm, and on occasion it has been thought by observers that the smell was sulphurous. This may well account for certain medieval references to ball lightning being accompanied by imps or demons of some description who were tradi-tionally associated with the acrid smell of sulphur burning in hell! The sample that Lionel saw in 1952 did not seem to be hot although it was within just an inch or two of his gloved hands.

Other observers have occasionally reported great heat in the pres-ence of ball lightning. Some has been witnessed to melt glass and metal. Most reported movement is horizontal, only a metre or two above the ground, and the velocity is relatively slow. It took the light-ning several seconds to go from the left to the right of the handlebars of the Ariel 350. At least it was visible there for several seconds, but this could have been the result of an after-image in the observer's eyes. Some witnesses have reported the ball lightning remaining stationary, hovering in mid-air, while others have thought they saw it actually descending from a cloud. The spheres on the handlebars that Lionel saw were roughly the size of tennis balls, which would have been a diameter of approximately three inches (seven or eight centimetres). Several witnesses have seen ball lightning less than half this size and in other cases it has been up to a metre across. Most observers have reported that their encounter with ball lightning took place at the same time as familiar storm lightning from cloud to ground.

Another interesting factor about ball lightning reports is that most of these seem to have come from southern or northern hemi-spheres rather than the equatorial tropics. It could be argued that this is because a greater number of observers would be likely to be in those latitudes. A similar phenomenon seems to have occurred with sightings of the Loch Ness monster. Early in the 1930s, a great many trees were felled near the Loch so that a new road could be con-structed. It was after the trees were felled and the new road opened that a great many reported sightings took place. The more populous an area is and the clearer the viewing zone, the more likely it is that *numerous sightings* will take place, irrespective of the *actual recurrence* of the phenomena.

In 1753, in the city of St. Petersburg in Russia, Professor Georg Richmannin was apparently killed by ball lightning when he was in the vicinity of a lightning rod.

An interesting legend from Japan regards ball lightning as the soul of a Samurai warrior; the Japanese phrase for ball lightning is *hito dama*, which roughly translates as Samurai soul. If Japanese bank notes are held up to a strong light, it is possible to see that the late Emperor Hiro Hito is surrounded by what looks like a ball of fire, which may well be intended to represent ball lightning.

Physicists specializing in the ball lightning phenomenon have suggested that it might be some sort of plasmoid. When plasma is trapped within a magnetic field it becomes a plasma vortex, otherwise known as a plasmoid. The plasma itself is composed of ions, or charged particles, which travel along the lines of the magnetic field; these naturally close in upon themselves, and this makes it impossible for the plasma to escape. The vast numbers of negative and positive charges inside the plasma are always the same; they balance so that the plasma is electrically neutral. It has been theorized that in some cases an electrical charge derived from the neighbouring cloud-ground lightning is present and that produces the ball lightning effect. This, however, raises the question of why the ball should be so *luminous*. Certainly very high temperatures up to twenty thousand degrees, or perhaps even more, with pressures of fifteen atmospheres, or even higher, could be generated by the normal ground-cloud lightning associated with — and possibly responsible for — the ball lightning as a side effect. Such temperature and pressure could not help but lead to an explosion. But what happens when the ball lightning quietly disappears without the characteristic explosion, as it did in the Norfolk woods after traversing the handlebars of the Ariel 350?

Imagine a circle of very intense electric current. A globe of ball lightning could feasibly originate from the discharge of normal lightning, and if it did it is equally reasonable to suppose that it would result in a closed magnetic structure and so become a plasmoid. This then produces another scientific problem: when physicists construct magnetic bottles in laboratories, they find it extraordinarily difficult. Such magnetic bottles are extremely fragile and unstable. Their life spans are measured in micro-seconds. The problem is to explain *why* ball lightning in the natural environment can last as long as the thirty or forty seconds during which it seemed to roll along the handlebars, or the even longer appearances that other witnesses have reported. Why can that not be reproduced in the laboratory? If ball lightning is a plasmoid in its magnetic bottle, then what strengthens the magnetic bottles of nature to enable the plasmoid to exist for thousands of times its life span in the laboratory? Ball lightning seems to be able to escape the net of the theorizers as deftly as it escapes the observers who have been able to report some brief evidence of it.

Perhaps a clue to the real nature of ball lightning is worth following up in terms of strange phenomena occasionally reported in submarines. When a current of between one and two hundred thousand amps is discharged from a volt source of between two and three hundred volts across a circuit breaker, something like ball lightning is said to have been seen.

There has undoubtedly been some confusion over the years between ball lightning and St. Elmo's Fire. The St. Elmo's Fire phenomenon is a corona-like discharge from a conductor in a strong electric field, and it seems to depend upon the conductor having a pointed shape. St. Elmo's Fire can occasionally seem to be spherical, and in that aspect it does resemble ball lightning. Where it differs totally from ball lightning is that it cannot function unless it is attached to its conductor. It may move along the conductor as the display moved along the handlebars of the Ariel, so that the 1952 evidence could well have been St. Elmo's Fire rather than ball lightning. What is also relevant here is that St. Elmo's Fire can, without too much difficulty, last much longer than true ball lightning.

Some witnesses have reported that ball lightning is able to change both its size and its brightness during the period that they are observing it. The fact that ball lightning has been observed to hover or to apparently descend from clouds suggests that it might be hot air at atmospheric pressure rising in the way that a hot air balloon rises. The problem is that most reports describe ball lightning as remaining at the same level or *descending*. It would have seemed reasonable to assume that ball lightning that consisted of some sort of heated air would have been more inclined to rise than to hover or sink. Other reports have described the ball lightning as rotating or spinning. Certainly the ball lightning — if that is what it was — on the motorbike handlebars appeared to be rolling. It was rather like a string of intangible electric tennis balls rolling along one behind the other.

What is to be made of the nature of ball lightning, which, according to certain reports, appears to have the ability to rebound from solid barriers and to rebound from the ground itself? There are reports of ball lightning striking water: a pond, a lake, or a reservoir. Those who have sent in such reports have described an effect that sounds like sodium or potassium on a bowl of water in a laboratory. Others have described a sound as if a blacksmith had plunged a piece of white hot iron into water to temper it. In addition to the smell of sulphur, other smells similar to nitric oxide have also been reported in the literature.

Although accounts are varied, and occasionally paradoxical and contradictory, reputable witnesses have given accounts of ball lightning attracted to metallic objects: telephone lines, electric cables, or wire fences and grills. Once the ball lightning has actually reached such metallic objects it seems inclined to move along them. There have been reports of ball lightning running along in this way and then entering a house. Some witnesses have seen it going through a glass window pane as if there were nothing in the way at all. Reports also exist of ball lightning that seems to have started inside the building and is then associated with a piece of electrical equipment like a telephone or computer. There have even been reports of ball lightning existing inside a metallic closed space such as the interior of the fuselage of an aeroplane.

The general scientific explanations for ball lighting can probably be divided into two major categories, the first suggesting that some external power is responsible for the ball lightning, and the second suggesting that the ball lightning is somehow internally powered.

The external power theories include ideas about energy from thunderclouds being able to create and then maintain ball lightning, or a steady current connecting ground and cloud could perhaps shrink in cross section where there was a zone of extreme conductivity. It has been ingeniously argued that the extra energy input resulting from the shrinkage or constriction of the current at this point would be sufficient to preserve the ball. Well thought out and logical as this concept is, it does not account for ball lightning reports that have come from inside buildings and from metallic containers such as the fuselages of aircraft. Another scientist has come up with the idea that radioactive cosmic ray particles might possibly be focused by a thunderstorm's electrical fields. His case is that such focusing would possibly create discharges in the air at one specific point in space, which would produce the ball lightning phenomenon.

Theories concerning internally powered models include the idea that ball lightning is a sphere of gas or air that is somehow burning, or that there are chemical reactions taking place during high discharges in thunderstorms from soot or particles of pollutant in the air.

These theories, although far from untenable, do not seem very probable. The theory that ball lightning is caused by an odd configuration of a current flow operating in and around a closed loop and held in place by its own magnetic field is open to question. It has been shown by Finkelstein and Rubinstein that this does not seem to be possible in air under normal atmospheric conditions.

Another theory in the internally powered category suggests that ball lightning is a curious type of air vortex, which is able to act as a container for luminous gases. The type of air vortex envisaged by this researcher would be something resembling a smoke ring blown from behind a cigarette. Two expert experimenters, Dawson and Jones, put forward the theory almost thirty years ago that ball lightning is something like a microwave radiation field held inside a spherical plasma shell.

The strangest theories of all have suggested that ball lightning, far from being a scientific electronic phenomenon, is actually all that we can see from our three dimensional observation points of an intrusion from the fourth dimension — or even some other, far stranger, dimension beyond that. This theory would regard ball lightning as an act of interdimensional trespass made possible by the extreme conditions of the electrical storm with which it is associated. If a membrane separating the dimensions could be used as a model in the course of this particular argument, and if this hypothetical interdimensional membrane is kept in position by balanced forces on either side, then when an electrical storm takes place on *our* side of that membrane, energy is diverted into the storm and its effects reduce the pressure on the membrane, allowing *something* from the other side to penetrate our universe — the electrical equivalent of osmosis. Think of the theories regarding negative matter: the "intruder" is not capable of surviving in what — for it — is an alien part of its universe. It therefore either dissipates harmlessly or goes out with a loud report.

The most intriguing and whimsical theories of all suggest that ball lightning is some form of living, sentient being that is alien not only to our planet but to our entire spacetime continuum. It is then conjectured, by those who hold this particular theory, that it is either hoping to study and observe us or has been catapulted here from its own strange realm as the result of some weird accident. Its presence in and with the storm on our world may then by hypothesized as *causative*. In other words, the arrival of a being from another dimension, a being which as part of its body structure has massive electrical energy potential, may have *produced* the storm rather than being a product of it. The hypothesis suggests that it is the traumatic arrival of the visitor and the consequent rupturing of various fields between the two planes of existence that is likely — among its other side effects — to generate an electromagnetic storm.

It is always of great value to a researcher to be able to contact individual eyewitnesses to an unusual phenomenon and to invite them to give their own accounts in their own words. The authors are especially grateful to the following witnesses, who have very kindly given permission for their accounts to be reproduced in this way.

Tom Anderberg

"I was raised on a farm in the corn belt of Illinois until I was eighteen years old. The farm was four miles east of the village of Raymond, which was approximately forty miles south of the capital city of Springfield.

"One summer when I was roughly twelve to thirteen years old (circa 1960), I was driving one of our small tractors, a Ferguson or Ford, down our gravel lane from the farmhouse towards the road and saw a huge ball (sphere) which was approximately three feet in diameter and whose appearance was a radiantly brilliant silver white light source bristling with sparkling shimmering needlelike edges.

"I can attest to the size and description, because all this happened while I was driving directly towards it, dead centre in the middle of the lane. I was driving slowly, the day was moderately overcast, not sunny, and all of a sudden this brilliant shimmering ball, as I have described, was descending in slow motion as if someone were placing it down to rest very carefully and softly.

"I first noticed this brilliant shimmering sphere of silver white light when it was approximately three feet or so directly in front of me and roughly fifteen feet off the ground. As I continually drove towards it, it slowly descended, and after two to three seconds, when I was approximately twenty feet or so closer to it, it exploded when it was approximately three to four feet off the ground.

"When it exploded, it was as if the entire sphere were a glass beach ball being exploded by dynamite. It was unbelievable. Since my grandfather, Lester Foster, had mentioned the term 'ball lightning' before, I knew exactly what it was when I saw it and didn't think that much about it.

"A couple years ago on a radio station in northern California, I heard the announcer mention the term Ball Lightning. As I listened, I believe he said that there were probably only a half dozen or so people in the world, alive today, who have seen this event. I have no idea if this is true or not. Even if others have seen it, has anyone seen it as close as I have? I would really like to know and talk to them.

"I must admit, being roughly thirty feet in front of it and seeing it explode at head height right in front of me, it was just unbelievable at the time and more unbelievable as time goes by. Since the tractor motor was running, I could not hear if there was any associated low level hissing or hum to the event. I also do not recall hearing a loud boom or other associated noise other than the visual exploding and shattering of the sphere of light into what seemed to be millions of points of light."

By Tom Anderberg — anderberg.t@cwix.com

Bill Melfi

"While on vacation on a small farm in Tennessee, I was playing between the house and the barn about 5:00 P.M. on a clear day. I saw two balls of light, one about three feet and the other about four feet in diameter. They were glowing with a blue green light that was about as bright as a fifty watt light bulb and translucent as a balloon.

"They moved side by side, the larger one leading. They moved across the barnyard towards the woods. The movement was quick and somewhat zigzag. I chased after it with a stick in hand, but they were faster than me. I'm sure that I was lucky that I didn't catch up with them. They didn't break up, just disappeared in the woods.

"My Uncle had lived there all his life and never saw anything like that, but had heard of ball lightning in the area before."

By Bill Melfi — Melfi@gate.net

Bernard Wieszczyk

"During the summer of '68 me and my brother (Joe) were working on an old dozer doing some welding and mechanical work when a thunderstorm was heard in the distance. We continued working, watching the sky occasionally, when we both saw a bright sphere shape moving in the sky about four to five feet in diameter. It zigged, zagged, then started to come almost straight towards us.

"We dropped everything we were doing and headed straight to the barn, leap-frogging most of the way. When we started to run it was no more than a hundred feet away. Just as we reached the barn, it hit in the area we were working at with a loud clap, just like thunder shaking the barn. It's about as close as I ever want to come to ball lightning."

By Bernard Wieszczyk — bentjess@infoblvd.net

Glenn R. Frazier

"Staying at my Grandfather's small cottage in upstate PA, it was approx 6:00 P.M. There was a large storm that was passing over, I was sitting on a screened-in porch watching the pine trees sway with the wind (a favourite pastime during a storm) both doors to the cottage were open at the time. I remember a brilliant flash of lightning and a large clap of thunder right on its heels. Seconds later my mother screamed. My grandfather and I turned to look in through the doorway and saw what looked like a ball of electricity coming down the hallway from the back door. It was about the size of a basketball and had an off yellow kind of haze. It sounded like a large stream of water coming through a faucet. When it got to the kitchen area it flickered and flashed a little brighter and then was gone. No boom or bang, just faded out like the glow of a TV screen when you shut it off in a dark room. I can still see this as clear as day!"

By Glenn R.Frazier — glennf@loxinfo.co.th

Ruth Parker

"A cop in a car shouted, 'Everyone off the street,' and we went inside a building and looked out of the window, and out on the street bright balls suddenly appeared from golf ball sizes to several beach ball sizes. They rolled back and forth along the street, over the tops of cars and up and down balconies.

"Other people in the building stayed away from the windows, and we moved away as a huge brilliant ball smashed up by the window. We stayed inside for about fifteen minutes too afraid to go outside.

"The whole experience of the lightning lasted about ten minutes. The plants in the courtyards were all burnt black. Many people saw this. The year could have been 1956. The only thing that I could find out was it was ball lightning and that it was rare."

By Ruth Parker — jmreed@sunset.net

Bruce Carrubba

"It was summer. I was twelve years old. It started raining. My father sent me to the basement to make sure the bulkhead doors were closed and latched.

"I got about four feet from the door when I heard an enormous cracking sound. It was lightning hitting the outside pipe the oil heater was attached to. Next thing I knew, three balls of lightning came out of the heating vent next to the door. They were about the size of a softball, very bright, made a crackling sound, and to me, strangest of all had backspin on them.

"They came out of the vent and bounced their way across the room until they hit the wall. They bounced off the wall a couple of times and disappeared, leaving only little burn marks on the floor.

"It happened a long time ago, but I still remember it like it was yesterday. It made quite a lasting impression on me."

By Bruce Carrubba — deejavu@inreach.com

Bill Hale

"Late one evening in July 1995 I was driving an 18 wheeler east on Interstate 40 somewhere in Arkansas. My wife was with me and we were travelling through an area of heavy thunderstorm activity. Suddenly in front of me were what looked like balls of lightning rolling down the road. They looked to be six or eight inches in diameter. I saw several of them, but this phenomenon lasted less than a minute or two. When we stopped to spend the night I asked the local people what it was, but they had never seen it before. I thought it may be something that happened there occasionally. I did not know until today that this sighting was a rare occasion. I was driving for USA Truck at the time."

By Bill Hale — MOAtruck@aol.com

Ian Bateman

"I was driving towards London on the M4 motorway at 17:40 and was a couple of miles from the first exit to Reading. I and many other vehicles were driving through a very large and ferocious thunderstorm. There were frequent serious bolts of lightning striking the ground in all directions around me. Some of the more distant lightning appeared reddish in colour. The sky turned from blue and sunny to black. The whole scene was beautiful.

"Up on an embankment to my left my attention was immediately taken by an intense ball of light. It had a halogen-type of blueness to it for a second then it was white. Nothing I know of shines that brightly. It couldn't have been a vehicle headlight, no vehicle could have climbed this embankment and it would have been committing an offence by facing the wrong way. It lasted for a couple of seconds.

"As I drove by the mound I noticed thin smoke rising from the spot where I saw this light. I couldn't have heard an explosion over the engine/motorway noise and the heavy rain so I cannot report if this happened."

By Ian Bateman — ian@complete-internet.co.uk

The foregoing accounts are very impressive. It seems without a shadow of a doubt that the phenomenon described as ball lightning really exists. The authors are inclined to suggest that research into the area might well lead to valuable new discoveries in energy generation and maintenance. Oddly enough, the ball lightning phenomenon could just possibly link with the curious quest for perpetual motion dealt with in the Orffyreus chapter.

CHAPTER TWELVE:
Strange Steeples

When we take things for granted, we sometimes omit to ask interesting questions. It was Socrates, or his faithful follower, Plato, who said, "The unexamined life is not worth living." Even the most thoughtful of the classical Greeks needed to be reminded of that. They and the Romans did not adorn their temples with steeples; portico and colonnade were their usual architecture. The great Temple of Solomon had two pillars: Jachin and Boaz. Egyptians favoured obelisks with perhaps whole avenues of sphinxes. The beautiful and delicate eastern pagodas often reached a considerable height, but none of these used either a spire or tower as its peak. A beautiful Mohammedan mosque frequently has minarets, but the stateliest minaret is hardly a steeple. Could it be something to do with the Christian church's fondness for bells? As bells and belfries developed, church architects were faced with the problem of creating a structure that would be sturdy enough to sustain the weight and movement, while at the same time being tall enough to make the bells audible over a long distance. Even those churches that were designed along severely classical lines still had to find space somewhere for a belfry well away from the ground. These can be seen in the quasi-classical spires that Sir Christopher Wren loved so much. When some Christian groups abandoned the bells, or, in some instances, were forbidden to use them, the steeples went with them. Many strange tales are told of how the devil tried his hardest to prevent steeples from being erected. Many of the oldest exorcisms — techniques for driving out demons and evil spirits — incorporate bells, so the more bells a church had, the more loudly they rang, and the greater the distance over which they could be heard, the less likely it was that evil forces would trouble the parish.

There grew around this particular belief a number of fascinating myths and legends about the devil preventing — or at least *trying* to prevent — the building of a steeple. At Towednack, in Cornwall, the devil was supposed to have prevented the tower of the church from being completed. Everything that the masons put up during the day was destroyed by demons during the following night. At the village of West Walton, in Norfolk, the devil allowed the masons to build the tower but then carried it away and stood it where it now stands at a considerable distance from the church. Those who disliked the people of West Walton and district proclaimed darkly that it was only because of their wickedness that the devil had been allowed to remove their church tower. There are other legends of saintly assistance to counteract demonic interference. In the parish of Probus, which is named after Saint Probus, the church was built by the saint himself. Like many another man, holy or otherwise, Probus was very short of money and did not know how he was going to be able to afford to erect the tower. Finally he asked Saint Grace for help, and as a result of her intervention the money was found, the church was finished, and the tower was erected. The legend goes on to tell how Probus falsely claimed all the credit for building the church and the tower, whereupon a mysterious spirit voice sang from the tower, "Saint Probus and Saint Grace: not the first but the last." Credit was finally given where it was apparently due.

A wonderful story — so strange it is almost demands to be true — is attached to the tower at Ashton-under-Lyme. A local woman came upon a group of church workmen who were playing cards instead of getting on with the building. Being a sport and a gambler she laughed and told them that if they could turn up an ace with the next card she would be willing to do a share of the building to make up for the time that they had lost. The next card in the pack was the ace of spades. The lady kept her word and being both strong and skilful built several feet of masonry in a very professional manner. It is said that the ace of spades was carved on to the tower in memory of her intervention. Certainly an escutcheon on the tower does look remarkably similar to the ace of spades, but in all probability it was placed there for a completely different reason. Ormskirk has very strange legend attached to it as well. The church there has a spire and a tower. The story told to explain it concerns two sisters, both from the locality, who undertook the building work and then quarrelled about the completion of it. One said it must have only a tower and the other that it must have only a spire. As each was paying a share towards the building costs, they had to compromise, so the

The steeple on the mysterious old church of St. Laurent in Salon, Provence,
France, where Nostradamus is buried in the wall.

church had a spire *and* a tower. It's an interesting story and possibly a
true one, but if the quarrelsome sisters are pure myth, it may be suggested historically and architecturally that the tower, the larger of the
two structures, was erected to hold a larger set of bells than the earlier
structure, which is capped by the spire, was able to contain.

At Prestwich church there is a series of very curious carvings. On one
of the high parapets facing south there is a goose defending her goslings
from a fox, a swan sailing serenely among her cygnets, medieval musicians
playing various old church wind instruments, another man holding a
muzzled dog, and a number of militant angels holding their shields.

Occasionally steeples have been used for purposes other than
strictly religious ones. In 1553, when old St. Paul's was still standing, a
Dutchman climbed the spire and waved a flag. He was paid the sum of
£16 — a fortune in those days. Pilkington, who was bishop of Durham
around that time, preached a sermon in which the central text was that
lightning had struck St. Paul's on June 3, 1561, because various
"wickednesses" used to be committed there. He was particularly unhappy because various performers — forerunners of the modern bungee
jumpers — would throw themselves down attached to a rope in the

hope of surviving when they got to the bottom. Many of them sadly died in the attempt. When Philip of Spain paid a visit in 1555, the entertainment at St. Paul's consisted of a fearless acrobat who slid down a cord from the highest point as fast as an arrow from a bow and landed on what was described as a great sort of feather bed.

George III, despite the reputation of not being the wisest or most mentally stable of kings, was very brusque with a man who had tried to entertain him with a similar performance at Salisbury. What George actually said was, "As the father of my people it is my duty to reward those who save life and not those who put it at risk." Another daredevil rope slider went to All Saints, Derby in 1732 and slid down a rope that stretched from the highest point of All Saints to the step at St. Michael's. On that occasion he was successful. When he tried to repeat the stunt at Shrewsbury in 1740 he died in the attempt. Another rope acrobat performed in Derby in 1734, again using All Saints tower as the highest point. He aimed for the bottom of St. Mary's gate, holding on to a wheelbarrow in which a thirteen-year-old boy hung on for dear life. He got down safely. The next part of the trick was to send a donkey down the same rope. Sadly, when the poor beast was twenty yards from the end of its journey the rope broke at the top. The tumbling donkey knocked people in all directions, chimneys were brought down as the rope fell, and there was general panic and confusion. Miraculously, no lives were lost, but there have been no acrobatic performances on All Saints tower since. In 1600, a fearless performer by the name of Banks (with an equally famous horse called Morocco) somehow got to the top of St. Paul's steeple and stood astride the weather vane. He and the horse survived. A much earlier performer in 1237 did not. This man was giving an acrobatic display on a rope that stretched between the two towers of Durham Cathedral. He fell, broke his neck, and died. The Prior was deprived of his rights for permitting the performance to take place.

In the spire of St. Cuthbert's church in Elsdon a small sinister chamber was discovered containing the skulls of three horses. These were almost certainly a relic of the old horse-worshipping cult. At St. Mary Redcliffe in Bristol there was once a truly remarkable relic. It was said in olden days to have been the rib of a monstrous cow, a benign beast that centuries before had supplied the whole of Bristol with free milk. When the rib came to be scientifically examined it was found to be part of a whale.

It was in this same tower that several old chests were lodged, the chests from which the unfortunate Thomas Chatterton later alleged he had retrieved Rowley's poems. Chatterton was the son of a lay clerk and schoolmaster from Bristol. He went to school at Colston's Hospital, and even during his time there began writing verses. One of his earliest, "Apostate Will," is a satire that he composed at the age of twelve in 1764. Only fourteen when he left, he obtained an apprenticeship in a lawyer's office. At sixteen, he published in *Felix Farley's Bristol Journey* an extract of what he claimed was an ancient work written by someone called Rowley that he had discovered in a chest in the church of St. Mary Redcliffe. Once *Felix Farley's Bristol Journey* was published, it attracted the attention of numerous scholars and antiquarians. Sixteen-year-old Thomas obligingly provided them with forged documents, pedigrees, and deeds, all of which he claimed came from the mysterious chests in St. Mary's.

During the fifteenth century, William Canynge was a perfectly genuine historical Bristol merchant. Young Thomas Chatterton created for him an imaginary friend, a monk named Thomas Rowley, who was a man of letters and a poet as well as a man of God. Not to be defeated by shortage of documentary proof, young Thomas created an entire correspondence between Rowley and Canynge. All the while he was busily writing poems and prose passages in a strange version of fifteenth-century English, which purported to be the work of the holy Mr. Rowley. Some of these forged poems were offered without success to Robert Dodsley in December 1768. Dodsley had begun life as a footman working for a Mrs. Lowther, and while working for her he had written a number of interesting poems. One of these, *The Muse in Livery: or the Footman's Miscellany*, appeared in 1732. Mrs. Lowther had the kindness and good sense to encourage him, as did several of her friends, and in 1735 Robert was able to give up work as a footman and set up as a bookseller. His shop was at Tully's Head in Pall Mall. He went into partnership with his brother, James, and as well as their bookselling enterprises Robert wrote several plays, including *The Blind Beggar of Bethnal Green* and *The Toy Shop*. Although the Dodsleys had published *Percy's Reliques* in 1765, which had greatly encouraged the mid-eighteenth-century interest in primitive poetry and ancient writings, they were not willing to take any of Chatterton's work. In 1769, Chatterton sent a piece of spurious Rowley to Horace Walpole. This particular epic was a short treatise on painting, and for a

A typical spire or broach steeple from an English church.

while even Walpole thought it was genuine. What poor Thomas Chatterton lacked in integrity, he compensated for by productivity. In the same month that he sent the spurious painting article to Walpole, he published the first of seven Ossianic pieces in *Town and Country Magazine*. One of his earliest pieces was *Elinoure and Juga*, supposedly created when he was only twelve. In 1770, at the age of eighteen, driven to despair by hopeless poverty, Chatterton committed suicide. His interesting grave marker in Bristol makes the point that it's God's privilege to judge the boy, not ours: "To the memory of Thomas Chatterton. Reader! Judge not! If thou art a Christian, believe that he shall be judged by a Superior Power. To that Power only is he now answerable."

The Rowley poems were published in 1777 by Thomas Tyrwhitt, but within a year Warton started to raise doubts about whether they were genuine or not. The controversy raged for nearly a century. Forger he may have been, but Chatterton was regarded by both Wordsworth and Keats as a genius and a very talented writer.

There still seems to be room for doubt about the mysterious Rowley poems and some other allegedly "discovered" fifteenth-century works. Is it remotely possible that Chatterton *did* find one or two ancient pieces of literature in those mysterious old chests in St. Mary Redcliffe in Bristol? There seems to be a mass of evidence indicating that much of Rowley's supposed work was a Chatterton forgery — but what if an extract here and there was *genuine*? What were those old parchments doing hidden in that chest in the steeple? The authors' own recent experiences with the mysterious Peplow Chest — described in the next chapter — evoke a certain extra sympathy for Chatterton.

As well as being containers for ancient manuscripts, church towers and steeples have long been recognized as the ideal places for large clocks. In the days before wrist and even pocket watches were affordable, one large, prominent clock was of great value to the parish. These clocks have given rise to a number of strange legends, myths, and superstitions. In Veryan, Cornwall, there lingers a tradition that if the church clock strikes the hour while a hymn is being sung before the sermon on a Sunday morning, or before the third collect at Evensong, someone in the parish will die during the week.

In Shropshire it was believed that if the clock struck during the announcement of the text for the Sunday sermon during the morning, then a parishioner would be called to meet his Maker before the following Sunday. At Baschurch it was considered to be an omen of death if the clock struck during the singing of the final hymn. Various Yorkshire superstitions regard it as very bad luck for the clock to strike while a wedding party is in the church, and some brides and their families living close to the church would refuse to enter until after the hour had struck.

When the battle of Neville's Cross was fought on October 17, 1346, the Durham monks climbed the great tower of their cathedral to watch the progress of the fight, chanting litanies as they watched. When the English were seen to be victorious, the monks broke into a very happy rendering of the Te Deum. That commemoration of the victory went on from 1347 until Cromwell's Puritans put a stop to it. When Charles II was restored, the old custom was revived. Magdalen Tower, Oxford has a choir singing a hymn to the Trinity on May Day.

Occasionally, the great tower of a church could be used as an armoury for military purposes. This was the case at Salkeld, in Cumberland, where there is only one entrance to the tower, which is through the inside of the church. The great door is reinforced with iron and has stout bars fitted on the inside. The tower armour was kept here in case of trouble. Similar fortified towers are found in the Yorkshire towns of Bedale, Melsonby, and Middleham: Bedale even has a portcullis to guard its narrow staircase. This links up with the proud old warrior-priest tradition, which reaches its highest peak in the noble Order of the Templars. Churches that did duty as fortresses were common enough during the Cromwellian civil war. Powderham and Ottery St. Mary were turned into fortresses by the Parliamentarians. The Royalists did the same at Tiverton and Townstall in Devon. The old parish church of Pontefract was used in the same way.

The famous "twisted spire" of Chesterfield has a curious mystery attached to it. Is it really twisted — or is the supposed twisting an optical illusion? The spire was erected some time between 1350 and 1370. It is octagonal and constructed from timber and lead. The way in which the lead was applied gives it its unique appearance. It was put on in a series of diagonal parallelograms, arranged so as to divide each of the eight sides into two distinct and channelled planes. A number of past experts on church architecture gave their considered opinion that the twisting was only an optical illusion caused by the curious way in which the lead had been applied.

Daniel Defoe (of *Robinson Crusoe* fame) described Chesterfield as "a handsome and populous town, with a fair church. The spire of its steeple, being timber and covered with lead, seems to be warped awry. This appearance is a mere *deceptio visus* (optical illusion) owing to the spiral form of the sheets of lead; for if you change your situation, it appears to be bent a different way from what it seemed before."

Rickman's learned tome, *Gothic Architecture,* maintains: "The apparent leaning of the spire arises partly from the curious spiral mode of putting on the lead, and partly from a real inclination of the general lines of the woodwork of the spire." Parker's equally erudite *Glossary of Architecture* maintains: "The lead is so disposed as to give the *appearance* of the spire being twisted."

The Reverend Hall actually measured the twist in the Chesterfield spire in 1818, and found that it was two metres out of the vertical in one direction and a metre and a half in another. Gales and storms damaged it in 1869 and again shortly before 1895, after which Temple Moore, the architect, reported on it and recommended immediate repair work. The twisting seemed to be much more than an optical illusion!

St. John's Church in Davos-Platz in Switzerland also has a twisted spire, very similar to the one in Chesterfield.

Perhaps the most mysterious steeple of all is in the story, brought to light by a researcher working in the Colman Library in Norwich, England, of an apparent UFO sighting in Breckland in East Anglia over three hundred years ago.

As far as flying saucers and other UFOs are concerned, an open-minded attitude is the most prudent one to adopt in these days when the frontiers between science fiction and scientific fact are closing with each other at the speed of an interplanetary rocket.

Quite often a "normal" explanation can be found for many modern sightings; there are so many strange aircraft cruising around our skies anyway that mistakes can easily occur. But what is one to make of UFO reports from a period in the past where modern explanations cannot be applied?

"Upon the one and twentieth day of May, in the afternoone, in this year 1646, there were very strange sights seen, and unwonted sounds heard in the ayre in several places as followeth . . . " Thus begins an extraordinary account, rediscovered almost by chance by a researcher working in the Colman Library in Norwich, an account of a UFO sighting over three hundred years ago, vouched for by "divers and severall persons of credit from Norfolk, Suffolk and Cambridgeshire."

Between Newmarket and Thetford, "a pillar of cloud did ascend from the earth, with the bright hilt of a sword towards the bottom, which pillar did ascend in a pyramidall form, and fashioned itself into the form of a spire or *broach steeple*." (A broach steeple was simply an octagonal one, like the one at Chesterfield.)

At Comberton, soldiers on parade "did behold the form of a spire steeple in the sky, with divers swords set around it." And at Brandon, "the inhabitants came out of their houses to behold so strange a spectacle as a spire steeple ascending up from the earth."

These might all be rather fanciful accounts of a rocket launching at Houston, but the resemblance to US space techniques does not end there. Like ships used by our contemporary astronauts, this strange object rising from the sandy wastes of Breckland had a rendezvous with another craft.

"There descended also out of the sky the form of a pike or lance, with a very sharp head or point, to encounter with it. Also at a distance there appeared another speare or lance, with a very acute point, which was ready to interpose but did not engage itself."

And what about the crews of these mysterious craft? Did they, like the Apollo crew, step out of their space ship on to an alien planet? "About Newmarket, there were seen by divers honest, sober and civill persons, and men of good credit, three men in the ayre, striving, struggling and tugging together, one of them having a drawn sword in his hand."

American scientists designed machines and protective clothing to enable their astronauts to survive in the alien environment of the moon. Surely any visitors to our planet would have done the same?

"In Marshland, within three miles of King's Linne, a captain and a lieutenant, with divers other persons of credit, did hear a sound as of a whole regiment of drums beating a call with perfect notes and stops, much admired by all that heard it. And the like military sound was heard in Suffolk on the same day."

Churches, towers, and steeples — ancient, modern, or extra-terrestrial; twisted or straight; repositories of ancient texts or make-shift fortresses — undoubtedly have strong claims to a place among the world's most mysterious objects.

CHAPTER THIRTEEN:
Mysterious Locks, Keys, and Containers

D r. William Harvey was a medical pioneer who discovered the circulation of the blood. He greatly aided Renaissance anatomy with his brilliant new findings. Harvey rescued the medicine of his day from the strangling grip of traditional Galenic physiology (named after Claudius Galenus, A.D. 129). Harvey advanced the medicine of his time far beyond its contemporary alchemy after he published "Exercitato anatomica de motu cordis et sanguinus in animalibus" ("An Anatomical Essay Concerning the Movement of the Heart and the Blood in Animals").

Born in Folkestone, Kent in 1578, Harvey attended Caius College in Cambridge, then studied at Padua before returning to England two years later. By 1602, he had established himself as a reliable physician, and he was elected Fellow of the College of Physicians in 1607. He later worked at Saint Bartholomew's Hospital, London, a great achievement. Harvey's career leapt to even greater heights when he was appointed by the College of Physicians to be a public dissector and anatomy lecturer. In 1618, he was appointed as a Royal Physician, putting him in the vanguard of medical research. At this time, theories about the blood and its movements were plentiful, so what made Harvey's theories better than others? Among other things concerning the blood, he worked out that the amount of blood pumped through an animal's heart in one hour was much greater than the entire volume of the animal itself!

If only Harvey had used the newly invented microscope, he would have found the tiny blood capillary vessels that he couldn't see with the unaided eye, the absence of which hindered the final and conclusive proof of his outstanding work.

William Harvey died in 1657, a major contributor to the understanding of the cardiovascular system, but the Harvey genius and daring

Ghost Club Secretary Robert Snow with his ancient and mysterious key: note the very curious clasps.

seem to have been an enduring family characteristic. In the days of Elizabeth I, William's close relative, Captain Harvey, developed Drake's habit of raiding the coast of Spain. On one of these expeditions, Harvey captured a massive iron treasure chest from a wealthy Spanish family, several of whom were killed in the accompanying skirmish. Its dying owner cursed Harvey and his victorious seamen as they escaped with their booty — including the chest. The memory of that curse on the Spanish chest lingered in the Harvey family for centuries. The box was of the type popularly known as an Augsburg chest, or an Armada chest, completely hand-forged from raw iron. The locking mechanism had a keyhole in the centre of the lid, and two or three bolts projected into each of the four sides when the lock was operated. Similar chests are to be found in Southwark Cathedral, where one is known as a Nonsuch chest, either because of its unique size and elaborate design, or because it resembles a famous house on Old London Bridge that was called Nonsuch. Another Armada chest is preserved in Warfield Church in Berkshire, and this one has fourteen bolts; strangely, the wards of its key form the number 2233. The *wooden* Armada chest in Woburn Abbey dates from 1550 and stands immediately below a portrait of Elizabeth I painted by George Gower. The Queen is shown as an Empress, with one hand resting imperially on a globe, while other nearby paintings show Drake's fire-ships wreaking havoc on the Armada.

Experts always treat these Armada chests with caution and respect. They are often booby-trapped, and the danger takes one of three forms:

Keys to the Peplow Chest.

The Armada chest in Peplow Hall.

George Olifent, master craftsman and specialist in historic locks, with co-author Lionel Fanthorpe: note the flak jackets in case the Armada chest is booby-trapped.

Co-author Lionel Fanthorpe with key to the Armada chest at Peplow.

a swinging, spring-loaded blade that could scythe fatally through the unwary at waist height; a barbed spearhead that would thrust itself out at high speed and pierce an intruder's ribs at heart level; or a loaded gun (sometimes reduced to an explosive charge) primed to go off when the chest was opened by anyone who did not know its sinister secrets. Conan Doyle, of Sherlock Holmes fame, clearly knew all about Armada chests and used that knowledge to good effect in his short story "The Striped Chest." In Doyle's yarn, the chest once belonged to "Don Ramirez di Leyra, Knight of the Order of St James, Governor and Captain-General of Terra Firma and of the Province of Veraquas." It bore a warning label in both Spanish and English: "You are earnestly requested upon no account to open this box."

A producer friend of the authors working with BBC Wales TV (who knew of their keen interest in researching anything mysterious and of co-author Lionel's willingness to take on daredevil stunts, his gorilla's strength, and his martial artist's total absence of fear) invited them to go with him to Peplow Hall and participate in an attempt to open this same mysterious old Armada chest that Captain Harvey had brought back from Spain almost four centuries earlier.

The titled family to whom it had been bequeathed also wanted co-author Lionel (in his capacity as a non-stipendiary Anglican priest) to bless the chest and those trying to open it, just in case the Spanish Curse was really endowed with some sinister psychic force that needed to be neutralized, rather than merely a mundane mechanical or explosive booby trap. These are the exact words Lionel used:

> "Loving and All-Powerful Heavenly Father, we come before you trusting in the total victory of Good over Evil, of Light over Darkness, and of Love over Hatred. Just as loving families and friends help and protect one another on Earth, so we pray now for the Infinite Protection of Your Absolute Love and Power. Our Lord Jesus taught us that perfect love casteth out fear, and so we believe that God's Perfect Love casts out all fear — and all the causes of fear — and provides us with perfect protection. The protection of God is abundant and eternal. No evil can pierce the Divine Shield which God holds over and around his children.

Lord, as we approach the mystery of this box, with its dark and threatening legends and traditions, keep us safe from any evil or negative forces — real or imagined — which may be associated with it. Angels and Ministers of Grace defend us as we approach this box to investigate it. We ask this prayer in the name of Christ the Lord. Amen."

After employing great skill and many hours of patient effort, the expert locksmiths, George and Val Olifent of Farnsfield near Newark — two of the best craftspeople in the country — finally made the key turn. The lid-bolts sprang back. It was time to try to raise the ponderous iron lid. There was a tense silence. Co-author Lionel (prudently wearing an SAS-style flak jacket) prised up the lid like Samson opening a lion's jaws. No blade scythed across; no gun exploded; no medieval Spanish spearhead bounced off his body armour. The mysterious chest had not been booby-trapped, but it was crammed with a collection of fascinating historic documents, including several sealed papers from the reign of Elizabeth I. Opening the Peplow Chest had definitely been worth all the effort. The huge hoard of valuable old papers it contained is still being analyzed and catalogued by experts, a job that's likely to last years rather than months.

The Armada chest at Peplow finally yielded its secrets to the locksmiths' skill and Lionel's muscle, but the even more mysterious Southwood Chest yielded no more than its handle. Southwood is a very small East Anglian village south of Acle, north of Reedham, east of Hassingham, and west of Freethorpe. Take the A47 towards Great Yarmouth, then strike south on the B1140 through Damgate and Moulton Saint Mary.

The abandoned church at Southwood is close to Callow Pit, and both the ruined village church and the sinister old pit feature prominently in the legendary mystery of the Southwood Chest. A few centuries ago, a village thatcher and his carpenter friend were out of work and desperate for money during a prolonged agricultural recession that was affecting the Southwood area.

There had always been legends in the village that a great chest full of priceless treasure was concealed in the depths of Callow Pit, guarded by the sinister evil spirit, or demon, of the pit, who lurked below the

Callow Pit near Southwood Church in Norfolk, England, where legend says a great treasure box still lies buried.

mud. In traditional treasure folklore of this type, legendary wealth is inevitably guarded by a dragon, an evil spirit, an ogre, or a specific demon like Asmodeus of Rennes-le-Château fame. The thatcher and the carpenter were sufficiently desperate to take on this guardian — whoever, or whatever, he might be. The thatcher brought his longest ladder, which was just big enough to stretch from one side of Callow Pit to the other. Together, he and the carpenter edged it across, then crawled out on it until they were directly over the centre of the notorious pit. Using his long thatcher's roofing hook, the thatcher boldly probed the murky depths beneath them. The ladder flexed alarmingly under their combined weight, but held fast. Then the hook encountered something hard and heavy. A few minutes' manoeuvring engaged the hook in what felt like a handle of some kind, and the two men began to pull excitedly. Inch by inch, something very heavy began to come up on the thatching hook. At last the Callow Pit Chest broke surface, and the thatcher and his friend could see what they'd got. Water and mud were dripping from a large treasure chest.

According to the legend, it was at this point in their adventure that the carpenter shouted, "We've got it now! Not even the Spirit of the Pit can take it from us!" Before he finished speaking, a vast, claw-

The overgrown ruins of Southwood Church in Norfolk; the handle of the Callow Pit treasure chest was once fixed to the door.

Co-author Lionel Fanthorpe at Southwood Church ruins.

like hand arose from the dark water and seized the treasure chest. It says much for their courage — born of hunger and desperation — that the two friends hung on to the ring handle of the chest at their end. Again according to legend, this great ring at their end of the treasure box came away in their hands, and the chest vanished forever into the mud at the bottom of Callow Pit.

The ring handle of the lost treasure chest was secured to the door of Southwood Church, then a flourishing centre of worship. It provided symbolic evidence of human greed and folly, and of misplaced human pride. When the authors went to Southwood to investigate the legend of the great iron ring on the church door at first hand, they found Callow Pit and the ruined church with no difficulty — but not only had the legendary ring handle vanished, there weren't even any doors on the ruined church! There were, however, some sombre old graves whose occupants might well have been contemporaries of the bold thatcher and his carpenter friend.

Robert Snow is Secretary of the Ghost Club, a distinguished and highly respected research group that can trace its roots back over 150 years. Charles Dickens was once a member. Among the many uncanny and mysterious objects that Robert has investigated over the years, few are as tantalizing as one mysterious old key. A well-known author of horror and supernatural stories once remarked that if a ghost is a disembodied spirit, that's unnerving enough — but a body that remained upright and mobile after its soul had gone was infinitely more frightening. The Peplow Chest, with its sinister Spanish curse, was mysterious and intriguing enough, but its tantalizing keys were equally intriguing. A box without a key raises a dozen questions in the minds of the investigators, but a key without a box raises a hundred more. The authors have never seen quite so unusual a key as the one that recently came into Robert's possession. What does it open? A secret door? A mysterious store room? A crypt? A sinister box like an Armada or Augsburg chest? Robert would love to know — and so would the authors!

Yet another singularly mysterious chest, an oaken strongbox dating from the time of Chaucer's pilgrims, is preserved in the church of Saint Beuno at Clynnog Fawr in Caernarvonshire, Wales. A very strange parish custom there was that if a calf was born with oddly shaped ears, it had to be sold and the money placed in this chest as an offering to the church.

CHAPTER FOURTEEN:
Murderers and Mandrakes:
Gallows and Gibbets

The mandrake is one of the world's most sinister and mysterious plants. Its curiously shaped double root, can, in certain growing conditions, resemble a human body with two distinct legs. Because of its vaguely anthropoid form, the mandrake has been associated with magic and superstition for centuries. There may, however, be rather more to the mandrake's "sympathetically magical" powers than its quaint shape. Scientific analysis reveals *hyoscyamine* inside it, enough hyoscyamine, in fact, to induce hallucinations — especially hallucinations of flying. The right dose of mandrake might well have convinced a medieval witch that she was well and truly airborne — with or without her broomstick!

Many useful or beautiful plants have no links with magic, but a few relatively minor plants, such as vervain, are important. Only a very few food plants are thought of as magical, but corn often represented the "magical" return of summer, the end of winter, and the production of essential, life-sustaining food. Cereal crops featured prominently in the rites of Osiris, and the death of Adonis was associated with the anemone because its redness reminded the Adonis worshippers of blood.

Some plants were especially relevant for magic. The humanoid root of the mandrake was popular for associative magic. Mandrake is a narcotic, and as well as providing a flying hallucinogen it was cheerfully administered to the mentally ill to reduce violence and have a general quietening effect on the patients. It was also used to help with convulsions, ease rheumatic aches, and cure toothache. It also had its uses as an anti-depressant and was thought to cure what was popularly called melancholia — although over-large doses caused delirium. As time passed and the medieval witch-hunts worsened, mandrake became known as one of the Devil's plants. A sorcerer, wizard, or

An ominous bird waits on sinister Caxton Gibbet in Cambridgeshire, England.

necromancer who could dig it up with the correct rituals and liturgies could summon Satan to grant his wishes.

Early herbalist-magicians discovered that, like the mandrake, laurel produced strange results in those who chewed it or breathed in its smoke in a confined space. Many an ancient oracle owed its sensational "success" to the chemicals in laurel.

Herbs with genuine healing powers — or those which were strongly believed to have healing powers — soon acquired magical attributes as well. Picking such herbs by moonlight at midnight may have added nothing to their therapeutic biochemical qualities, but it certainly amplified that mysterious psychosomatic element in all healing processes that depends upon the patient's faith in the medicine.

Another example is provided by the five-fingered leaves of cinquefoils, well-known to the ancient Egyptians. These plants were believed to give protection against various manifestations of evil by fighting it off with their five-fingered "hands" extended in permanent gestures of blessing. Garlic is another powerful health-giving plant to which strong and benign magical powers are attributed.

There is a very quaint and curious legend that maintains that garlic originated from Satan's first left footprint when he landed awkwardly after having been thrown out of Heaven. It may well be for this association with Satan that garlic is the traditional vampire repellent. If it's associated with their boss's unfortunate expulsion and clumsy landing, runs the reasoning, it can't be a good omen for his blood-drinking minions!

Herb Paris is better known as *Paris quadrifolia* because of its unusual regular cross-pattern of four leaves and its flower of four inner and four outer divisions. A black berry also grows in the middle of the flower. It was believed to be very useful against sorcery because of its association with the Christian cross. Magic numbers mixed here with magic plants, and the black berries were used in threes, sevens or nines. Some researchers have theorized that the berries were also used in fives, the idea being that if evil spells used *odd* numbers of magic words, and sinister magical gestures and actions, then adding another odd number would produce an even total and so neutralize the harmful effect of the spell.

The piercing scream allegedly uttered by a mandrake being pulled up was often thought to be fatal to those who heard it — so dogs on ropes were used to wrench the plants up from the earth, while their herbalist owners kept out of earshot. The mandrake-scream allegedly killed the innocent dog!

William Turner, who worked as an herbalist in the 1500s, recommended that all a patient needed to do was to smell the "apples of the mandrake" (he meant its berries) as a cure for insomnia. Turner also warned his patients that if they sniffed too many "mandrake apples" for too long they would lose the power of speech.

The hard-working Jewish historian Josephus, who wrote during the first century of the Christian era, was a firm believer in the mandrake's power to drive away demons and evil spirits from the sick and injured, as these negative entities couldn't cope with the mandrake's smell.

In Old Testament times, Leah used the mandrake to persuade her husband, Jacob, to sleep with her, after which she bore him a fifth son; Arab folklore also recommends mandrake as an aphrodisiac.

Mandrakes in Britain were once called "love apples," but were later replaced in that role by tomatoes. Shakespeare himself recognized the aphrodisiac powers of the mandrake when he made Falstaff, in *Henry IV (Part II)*, refer to another character as being "lecherous as a monkey, and the whores call'd him Mandrake." Some believed that the mandrake grew under the gallows from the semen of a hanged man's last

Co-author Lionel Fanthorpe at Caxton Gibbet in Cambridgeshire, England.
(First view)

Co-author Lionel Fanthorpe at Caxton Gibbet in Cambridgeshire, England.
(Second view)

ejaculation, or under gibbets from the fluids that dripped from a murderer's decaying corpse.

Looking at a mandrake was believed to cause blindness, and gathering them was fraught with problems. The herbalist who wanted one for his medicine store had to stand with his back to the wind and draw three concentric circles around the plant with his sword. Next he had to pour a libation into the soil near it, and then use his sword to dig it up while facing the setting sun. The coveted mandrake would mysteriously vanish if this elaborate ritual were not carried out meticulously!

Once pulled up, tradition required any green leaves to be cut off the mandrake and the root to be carefully placed in soil, which had to be *red*. The next few processes were reminiscent of making a snowman or a scarecrow. A red berry was placed on the mandrake to represent its mouth, and two juniper fruits were stuck on it as eyes. It was then kept in a glass jar and placed in sunlight. It was watered each day with human blood — either from the magician who was using the plant, or from one of his victims. It was believed that after three days (echoes of the Christian resurrection narrative) the mandrake would come to life. A day later it was able to speak and forecast the future. It would be kept safely in a coffin or a secret, magical cupboard. Alternatively, it could be worn as a talisman inside a leather pouch around the magician's neck.

The mandrake was believed to be able to make the owner rich, to open all doors, locks, and bolts. It also enjoyed a reputation as a bringer of fertility. These magical, talking mandrakes were regarded as priceless family treasures, and the magician who owned one traditionally left it to his youngest son — whom it would serve and obey as loyally as it had served the old magician before him.

During the medieval witch-hunts, forerunners of the odious Matthew Hopkins and the Holy Inquisitors made certain that possessing mandrake brought charges of witchcraft, followed by torture and death. As late as 1630, for example, three hapless women were executed in Hamburg simply for having mandrakes.

There are numerous other pieces of mandrake folklore that seem to explore the limits of the preposterous: the leaves of the mandrake are supposed to shine in the dark, rather like glow-worms; adventurous souls who attempt to pick a leaf will become airborne; and the mandrake's ultimate aphrodisiac powers extend to elephants, who are reported to mate after eating mandrake — a fact apparently known to very few zookeepers or veterinarians!

Mandrakes are inseparably associated with gallows and gibbets, and one of the best preserved English gibbets can still be seen at Caxton, not far from Cambridge, though whether mandrakes still grow below it is open to conjecture. The authors certainly found none on a recent visit. Caxton Crossroads was a popular spot for highwaymen in the eighteenth century, and it was felt by the local Justices that erecting a gibbet there on which to display their bodies after execution might help to discourage others from taking up the profession. On occasion, live highwaymen were hung from Caxton gibbet inside cages until they starved to death. There is a local Caxton story of one such outlaw who was used for target practice by archers and took three weeks to die in his cage. Not surprisingly, in view of his indescribable sufferings, he uttered a profound curse on all who were in any way associated with his capture, trial, and agonizingly slow execution. Consequently, a number of witnesses have reported a sinister supernatural shape swinging from Caxton gibbet by night.

The famous Tyburn Tree at Marble Arch in London was a notorious gallows for many years. It was a tripodlike structure around which were stands and seats for spectators. The condemned prisoners were brought to Tyburn from Newgate Jail with the nooses already around their necks. The gallows collapsed in 1678, and it was widely believed at the time that the malevolent ghosts of the condemned who had died there had brought the structure down.

The famous W.M. Thackeray, writing in *Sketches and Travels in London* in 1847, gives a detail or two of a hanging that he witnessed there: "On Monday morning at 8 o'clock, this man is placed under a beam, with a rope connecting it and him; a plank disappears from under him, and those who have paid for good places may see the hands of the Government Agent, Jack Ketch, coming up from his black hole and seizing the prisoners' legs, and pulling them, until he is quite dead — strangled."

The bodies of those executed were often taken for medical research by members of the College of Physicians, which was founded in 1518. Unfortunately for some, who had wrongly been pronounced dead below the gallows, they revived during the anatomist's dissection of their bodies. What the rope had failed to accomplish, the pathologist's dissection invariably did.

MURDERERS AND MANDRAKES:
GALLOWS AND GIBBETS

When the infamous Dick Turpin — frequently romanticized after his death on the gallows — was being removed by grave-robbers to be sold to the anatomists, a mob of his supporters took him from the grave-robbers and reburied him in the same plot, this time covered in quicklime to prevent the grave-robbers having a second go at their hero.

Mandrakes, and the gallows and gibbets associated with them in legend, have a macabre niche among the world's most mysterious objects.

CHAPTER FIFTEEN:
Anomalous Codes, Symbols, and Alphabets

L uigi Pernier was working with the Italian Archaeological Mission to Crete in 1908 when he uncovered a mysterious clay tablet in Room 8 of the ancient palace on Phaistos Hill. Known as the Phaistos Disc, it's about the size of a small plate or wide saucer, and both sides are covered with intriguing inscriptions. Current archaeological thinking varies, but it's generally thought that the Phaistos Disc dates from at least three thousand years ago and that the script is probably a syllabic one.

The disc is not perfectly circular: its widest diameter is 165 millimetres and its narrowest only 158 millimetres. Its surfaces are not flat. Side A is convex at the periphery, while Side B is convex in the centre. Close examination of the disc suggests that rather than being made in a mould, the clay was simply squeezed and then pressed flat between the hands of the scribe, or his assistant. The clay itself is of good quality, with small grains finely ground, similar to the clay used in the attractive Minoan "egg-shell" cups. Once the inscription had been made, the disc was fired to give it an attractive, lustrous surface. That golden-yellow surface is in some ways similar to the beautiful surface of Majolica ware, which was originally manufactured in Majorca. The characters that make up the inscription were pressed into the surface while the clay was still soft and moist. The lines between groups of characters — such groups probably representing words or phrases — were cut there with a sharp stylus or a thin, delicate knife blade. The lines defining the spiral along which the characters are placed seem to have been cut with the same instrument. Ancient scribes who created and used the Cretan hieroglyphic systems known as Linear A and Linear B appear to have used similar writing implements.

The spirals that guide and contain the symbols run from their starting point on the circumference towards the centre, as demonstrated by the scribe's occasional problem in spacing some of his characters as he got closer to the centre of the disc.

Scholars attempting to translate ancient records of this kind need first to work out their lisability (the direction in which the script is intended to be read). Dextrograde inscriptions are read from left to right, like almost all contemporary European languages. Sinistrograde inscriptions are read from right to left — like classical Hebrew. Bathograde scripts are read from top to bottom, while an altograde script would be read from the base of the inscription upwards towards the top. One of the most interesting types of lisability is known as boustrophedon — like the backward and forward track that an ox made in the ancient world when it ploughed a field. It simply reversed its direction each time it reached the edge of the field being ploughed. Ferryboats and the shuttles of some ancient looms made similar movements. This type of to-and-fro lisability was frequently used in Greece and Crete until around two and a half millennia ago. When the scribe is using the boustrophedon technique, he reverses some letters to go with the flow: this would make a letter shape like a "b" interchangeable with "d" depending upon which way the line of characters was heading.

So-called serpentine scripts are usually encountered alongside ancient religious illustrations, where the name of a character may well be written around his or her carving.

Although at present the only known example of its kind, the mysterious Phaistos Disc was made with a set of at least forty-five separate printing tools. Each of these had to be very carefully and finely manufactured — the time-consuming work of real craftsmen. Unless it was intended to make *many* such discs, there would have been no point whatever in creating a whole set of forty-five separate stamps (one for each of the different symbols that appear on the Phaistos Disc); yet each one *was* carefully and skilfully made for the industrious scribe to use over and over again — presumably on disc after disc. In all, the symbol-stamps were used 241 times to inscribe both sides of the Phaistos Disc. The most frequently used symbol is the Plumed Head, which occurs 19 times, closely followed by the Helmet, which occurs 18 times. The Shield symbol appears 17 times, and the Hide is there on 15 occasions out of the 241. By contrast with these frequently used symbols, several signs, including the Ram, the Small Axe, and the Bow, appear only once each in the entire inscription.

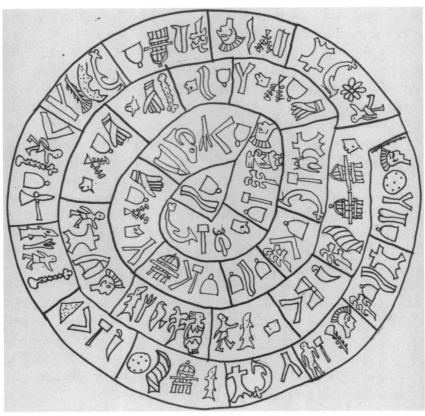

Artist's impression of the ancient and mysterious Phaistos Disc from Knossos in Crete.

The first of the symbols is a man walking briskly. He is either wearing a helmet or has his head shaved. He is unlike the walking men featured in the other scripts found in Minoan Crete, and his costume differs significantly from theirs. The second symbol shows a Plumed Head, similar to depictions of the Sea Peoples shown on the walls of the Temple of Rameses III at Medinet Habu in Upper Egypt, near Luxor. During Egypt's conflicts with these maritime raiders, the Egyptians regarded their attackers as raiders who had come from the Aegean area. The heads of the ethnic groups of Sea Peoples known respectively as Denyen, Peleset, and Tjekker during this early period certainly resemble the Plumed Head on the Phaistos Disc. The Peleset could have come from Crete, and probably developed into the famous biblical Philistines against whom Samson the strong man fought. The Tjekker were thought to have had their original home in Cyprus. Another clue to the *possible* origins of the Plumed Head symbol may link it to the White Goddess fresco in the Palace of Nestor at Pylos. The White Goddess wears a decorated head-band and an elaborate piled-up hairstyle similar to the Plumed Head on the Phaistos Disc. The accompanying sketch shows part of a re-used cross-shaft at Great Urswick in Cumbria, England. The two crested heads face each other on the carving and are very similar indeed to the Plumed Head on the Phaistos Disc.

The third Phaistos character is the Male Head with Tattooed Cheek. Egyptian artwork shows Cretan visitors with very similar facial tattoos bearing gifts. The fourth symbol, the Captive, shows a nude prisoner whose hands are secured behind him. Egyptian art in the Temple of Ammon in Karnak shows prisoners similarly tied. Sign five, the Child, seems to represent a toddler not yet steady on his feet. The Woman, sign six, is very different from the famous firm-breasted Cretan snake goddess, although this disc Woman does resemble the female figurines found in Phaistos. They in turn resemble some early Stone Age carvings of the Earth Mother. The seventh sign arguably represents a bell, a helmet, or a fertility symbol. One archaeologist's view on its identity is neither better nor worse than another's — nor, for that matter, the opinion of any thoughtful reader. Symbol eight is a Glove or Gauntlet of the kind used by early Minoan and Roman boxers. The ninth sign is known as the Tiara, and resembles the characteristic headdress worn by the Hittites. In their great shrine at Yazilikaya, dating from about 1300 B.C., the twelve Hittite gods are shown wearing this kind of head ornament. The tenth sign on the Phaistos Disc is clearly an arrow, ubiquitous throughout Mediterranean civilisation at this time. Other signs and symbols include a shield, a club, manacles, an axe, a saw, and something that looks remarkably like a UFO, although orthodox archaeologists prefer to describe it as a lid! There is also a boomerang and a catapult, although the latter has been interpreted by some students as a sling, or even a carpenter's plane. The remaining characters include a beehive (which also resembles a multi-stage space rocket), a ship, an ox horn, an animal skin, various plants, birds, and fish — plus the ubiquitous wavy-line sign, which is generally thought to represent water, or, more specifically, the sea.

The meaning of the inscription on the Phaistos Disc might be *anything* at all: a prayer, an incantation or spell, an ancient law, a royal edict, an inventory of goods and treasure in a palace, instructions for making something, directions for reaching some special location, a set of passwords — or simply a song or poem.

There are a number of similarities between the unknown symbols on the Phaistos Disc and the ones found on the strange clay tablets in the hole in the field in Glozel, near Vichy in central France. It was here in 1924 that teenager Emile Fradin rescued a cow that had fallen into an unusual hole in one of the Fradin meadows. Having gotten the frightened animal safely back into the meadow, young Emile began to explore the hole that had caused the problem. It was glazed with some sort of vitreous material as though it had once served as a medieval glass kiln. Within these lustrous walls, there were numerous niches and alcoves in which all kinds of Stone Age artifacts were preserved: carved bones and antlers, figurines of the old mother goddess, carvings of animals, and — most curious of all — strange clay tablets covered with an unknown alphabet. Dr. Morlet, a keen amateur archaeologist,

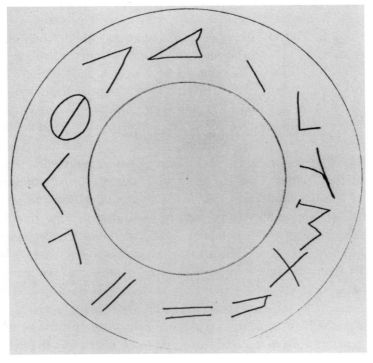

Strange symbols copied from the Glozel Tablets, near Vichy in France, by Lionel and Patricia Fanthorpe. (First view)

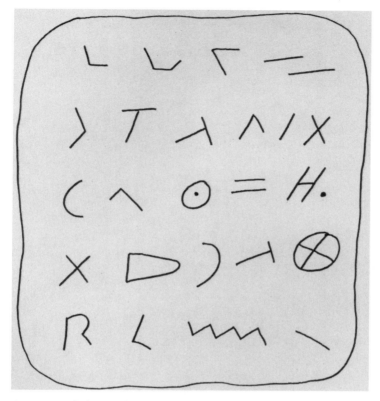

Strange symbols copied from the Glozel Tablets, near Vichy in France, by Lionel and Patricia Fanthorpe. (Second view)

lived in Vichy at the time. He looked at the Fradin finds and was sufficiently impressed to contact the academic archaeological establishment in Paris. Dr. Capitan was widely regarded as a leading expert and was very jealous of his reputation. He duly visited Glozel, spoke to Morlet and the Fradins, and had a quick look at the finds. With great enthusiasm, Capitan declared them genuine and of great archaeological significance. He asked Morlet to write everything up and then send the report to him. Morlet had other ideas: if he was going to do the spadework, he wanted the credit. Accordingly, it was Morlet who published the Glozel Report. All hell broke loose: Capitan was furious and promptly condemned the Glozel material (which had previously impressed him so favourably) as fraudulent. Controversy over the Glozel finds continued to rage despite the intervention of World War II. Morlet and the Fradins maintained that everything was genuine and

Characters from the unknown script on the Phaistos Disc from ancient Crete.

that their story of the cow, the hole, and the weird discoveries was the simple truth. Academic opinion tended to favour Capitan and the establishment view.

The authors met Emile Fradin, then a farmer in his sixties, when they paid a research visit to Glozel in 1975. They toured his museum and his fields. He showed them all the material he had found. They examined the hole where the discoveries had allegedly been made. They saw no reason to doubt the farmer's story. He seemed a very straightforward and honest witness. His whole account had the fundamental ring of truth about it. The authors wrote up their Glozel investigations accordingly, and gave Fradin and Morlet the benefit of the doubt. The question of the genuineness or otherwise of the Glozel tablets with their weird alphabet remained unresolved.

Then came thermo-luminescence. The basis of the technique, which was developed simultaneously in the Universities of Edinburgh and Copenhagen, is that pottery or ceramic ware can be dated by heating it and watching carefully to see what the temperature is when it glows. Modern, recently fired pottery needs a very high temperature to make it glow again. Pottery fired in Roman times — or earlier — glows at relatively low temperatures.

When the Glozel material was subjected to objective, scientific thermo-luminescent testing, it was clearly shown to be ancient — some as much as twenty-five hundred years old. Morlet and the Fradins had told the simple truth and were now fully justified, but the mystery of the origin and meaning of the strange clay tablets grew accordingly. *Who* had made them, *when*, and *why*? What did their weird symbols and characters mean? Did they bear any similarity to the curious inscription on the Phaistos Disc? Had fearless Minoan, or other Mediterranean sea-faring explorers, somehow made their way as far inland as Vichy in central France? If so, what messages had they left? Did the strange symbols on the Glozel tablets bear any significant resemblance to the inscriptions on the Phaistos Disc or the tantalizing *rongo-rongo* symbols from Easter Island with its enigmatic stone guardians?

Ancient Ogham, the coded stone said to have been discovered deep down in the Oak Island Money Pit, the supposed runic inscriptions on the Yarmouth Stone in Nova Scotia, and the inscrutable symbols preserved in the Roswell Museum in New Mexico all pose similar questions: who inscribed them, and what exactly do the unknown signs and alphabetic characters *mean*?

The basic principle of Ogham is a relatively simple one. A line can be marked either vertically or horizontally, and from this foundation line a number of strokes are drawn, cut, or scratched at right angles. The smaller strokes going away from the base line are usually at 90° to it, although a few Ogham lines are at an angle, reminiscent of some twentieth-century shorthand systems. A remarkable and linguistically important fifteenth-century Irish volume, *The Book of Ballymote*,

*Two figures from an ancient stone at Great Urswick, Cumbria, England,
resemble the crested heads on the Phaistos Disc.*

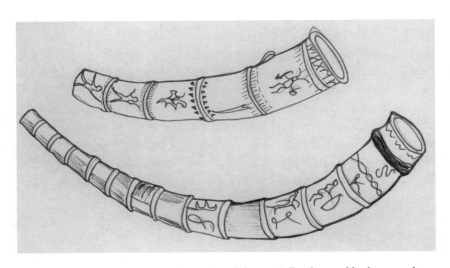

*Symbols from the Lost Battlehorn of Gallehus in Jylland resemble those on the
Phaistos Disc — did the Minoans ever meet the Vikings?*

explains the Ogham system and gives instructions on how to use it for ciphers. This unique volume is kept safely in the Royal Irish Academy in Dublin. There are only twenty letters in the oldest form of Ogham, although later variations and adaptations exist in which the entire English alphabet of twenty-six letters can be represented.

Our friend George Young of Nova Scotia has made a lengthy and detailed study of Ogham inscriptions and has concluded that the manual version of the Ogham alphabet was used by the esoteric seventeenth-century painter Nicholas Poussin. Poussin was apparently involved with the mystery of Rennes-le-Château. One of the coded parchments that was allegedly found in an old Visigoth altar pillar in the Church of Saint Mary Magdalene at Rennes stated that Poussin and another painter named Teniers "guarded the key." By his careful and thorough examinations of many of the Poussin canvases, George Young discovered that the way the painter had depicted the hands of his subjects enabled messages to be read in Ogham. By holding the hand either up or down, or pointing it to the left or right — and using the hand itself as the main base-stroke of the Ogham letter — the number of fingers displayed *could* be used to show the number of strokes forming an Ogham letter. For example, one finger pointing upwards, or to the right, would be the letter B, four fingers plus the thumb would be N, and so on.

The *rongo-rongo* script of Easter Island is only one of its many mysteries. Where did the Easter Islanders come from in the beginning? How and why did they erect the great stone statues that guard their island? What weird secrets are written on the *rongo-rongo* tablets?

A bold Dutch admiral named Ruggewein reached Easter Island in 1722. According to him, the Island then had a population of around six thousand people of different ethnic types. The admiral was impressed by the huge stone statues which he described as "men with long ears . . . wearing red crowns . . ." He saw almost 250 of them on the slopes of the extinct volcano, Rano Raraku, and lining the melancholy road to the island's cemetery. Many other early explorers, including Captain Cook and Gonzales, also visited the island and were equally impressed by the statues, the like of which they had not seen anywhere else.

The statues vary in mass from around twenty tonnes to over sixty tonnes. They have no legs and give the impression that they are weird supernatural beings emerging from the earth itself. Each has the same unusual-looking face: the forehead slopes backwards and the lower jaw juts forward. The mouth gives an impression of cruel, almost disdainful, command and confident social superiority. There is a small odd feature at the tip of the nose, but the most striking facial characteristics are the very long ears that reach down almost to the lower jaw. The great statues seem to be cartoons or caricatures along the lines of the television series *Spitting Image*, rather than accurate portrayals. The Easter Islanders were not unique in their preference for carving heads and torsos. The Olmecs of Mesoamerica also left gigantic stone heads behind them. One particularly striking example from Guadalajara in Mexico has a well-constructed metal helmet and African facial characteristics. If an African adventurer could reach Central America in ancient times, who might have reached Easter Island?

The most frustrating part of the Easter Island mystery is that the answers to its many questions still lie hidden somewhere below the soil of the island. The early inhabitants had their own unique *rongo-rongo* script. Some scholars have recorded a remarkable similarity between it and certain ancient texts from the earliest Indus Valley civilisations.

The present inhabitants of Easter Island are unable to read or understand this ancient written language. When asked about the original texts, they say enigmatically, "They are here but not here." Does this mean that the original *rongo-rongo* tablets are still hidden on the island somewhere?

It's possible that only members of the ethnic group who were distinguishable by their unusually long ears could read the script. It has been suggested that somehow they travelled the great distance from the Indus Valley to Easter Island — could this be in any way connected with the old Indian religious stories of the Vimanas (or flying cars) used in warfare by their ancient gods? It is also interesting to compare the ear-lengths depicted on some of the Indus Valley statues with those on Easter Island. There is also a segment of Korean folk-history in which it was generally accepted that long ears were an indication of very high intelligence. What if a group of early Korean seafarers once made the voyage to Easter Island and became the dominant race? Do the long-eared statues actually depict them? One or two symbols in the Korean alphabet do seem to bear a striking resemblance to the Easter Island *rongo-rongo*.

Thomas Barthel, working in the 1950s, produced an alphanumeric transliteration system for representing the *rongo-rongo* signs and devised six categories for them. First came objects, plants, or natural phenomena; next were anthropomorphic figures or parts of figures; these were followed by miscellaneous figures, some of which resembled birds; anthropoid figures with bird-heads, vaguely reminiscent of Egyptian deities; and, finally, other stylized zoomorphic symbols.

Equally strange zoomorphic symbols are to be found on the Pictish stones preserved in the Meigle Sculptured Stone Museum in Angus, Scotland. Received archaeological dating tends to place these Meigle Stones around the year A.D. 800 , but they could well be much earlier — *or later*.

Curious carvings on the Meigle Stones at Angus in Scotland.

There is considerable mileage in the hypothesis that the legendary Canadian Micmac hero, Glooscap of Nova Scotia, came to Canada by sea long before Columbus crossed the Atlantic. He might well have been the adventurous Sinclair, Lord of Orkney, who befriended a number of gallant Templar Knights after the treacherous and cowardly attack on their noble Order by Philip IV. Philip never succeeded in destroying the Templar fleet, and there is no knowing how far afield such dauntless adventurers might have gone. If Sinclair and a company of Templars did reach Nova Scotia with something priceless that had to be kept safe from the avaricious Philip at all costs, they might well have been responsible for constructing the Oak Island Money Pit with its

Strange zoomorphic symbols on the Pictish stones at Meigle in Scotland.

*Could these peculiar carvings on the Pictish stones of Meigle
have any links with ancient Crete?*

*Does the centaur carved on these Pictish stones at Meigle
indicate Mediterranean connections?*

Glozellian	Cretan	Early Greek	Runic
A Y	V	⅄	
日	ธ	⊐	ﾄ
⅄	ℚ	⌐	⟨ ⅄ ⟩
▷ ▽ △	△	△	⊐ þ
⅄ Ꜫ	ℓ	⅃	ℱ
℘	ʃ	⅂	Ⅴ ℓ
𝔛	𝔛	I	|
⊟	ꓩ	日	N Ⅳ H
⊗ ⊕	⊕ ⊗	⊗ ⊕	Я
⅄	⅂	⟨ ⟨	Ⅹ
⼃ k	Ⅴ	⅄ ⅄	Ⴘ
⅃ ⼃	⟨ ⟩	1 ✓	↑
⧺ ✗	╪	Ⅰ	Π
⊙	⊘ ⊙	o	

Comparative alphabets, including the Glozellian script;
chart compiled by Lionel and Patricia Fanthorpe.

ingenious system of flood tunnels to guard it. Might they have left a cryptic clue to its nature and its whereabouts? Templars were (and are!) masters of intricate codes and ciphers.

When the Onslow Company explored the mysteries of the Nova Scotia Oak Island Money Pit two hundred years ago, one of their strangest finds was an inscribed stone ninety feet below the surface. One theory suggests that the curious symbols carved into the stone were connected with the treasure believed to lie below it; another hypothesis, supported by George Young and Professor Barry Fell, was that the inscription was a religious text left by a group of religious refugees from a North African Coptic Church, who had fled across the Atlantic to escape from religious persecution and had established a new home on Oak Island centuries ago. Templar involvement here is also a matter of conjecture. Their expert knowledge of the southeastern Mediterranean and its people might have led them to assist the North African religious refugees who are central to George Young's and Barry Fell's fascinating theories.

Another of the world's most mysterious objects came to light in Yarmouth, Nova Scotia, when Dr. Richard Fletcher discovered it there in a salt marsh in 1812. The Yarmouth Stone weighs four hundred pounds and carries an inscription consisting of only fourteen characters. Numerous experts have puzzled over it for nearly two centuries. Olaf Strandwold, an eminent Norwegian scholar, believes that the

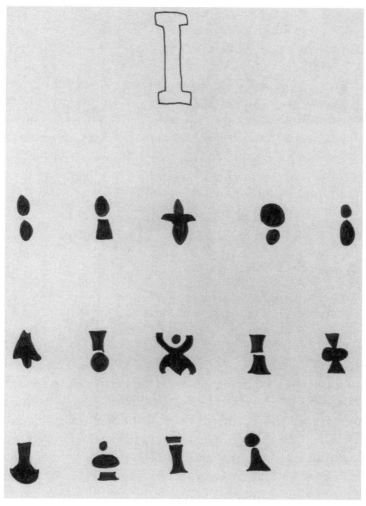

Weird symbols from the controversial "I" beam allegedly seen in the Roswell "UFO" wreckage — do they resemble the Phaistos symbols?

Co-author Patricia Fanthorpe with Eric J. Ruff (museum curator) and the mysterious Runic Stone at the Museum in Yarmouth, Nova Scotia.

characters are runic and can be translated to mean: "Leif to Eric raises (this monument) . . ." The idea of "this monument" following "raises" is understood, rather than inscribed on the stone.

Ancient runic stones similar to the one found by Dr. Fletcher, and the runes themselves, are mysterious and extremely difficult to translate. The unusual angularity of runic characters came about because they were originally designed for ease of carving into wood or stone. They were intended to decorate markers and memorials, rather than to be read as a normal linguistic alphabet is read from clay tablets, codices, or scrolls. Rune masters, who were often believed to control magical powers and to be able to transmit those powers to objects like swords and axes by carving runes on them, would often cut their names into the inscribed artifacts they supplied, so that the rune master's *own power* would be there as well as the magic that he had given to the object. The accompanying illustration shows runic characters.

Other theories about the possible makers of the strange Yarmouth Stone inscription include Japanese or Korean adventurers, Micmac Indians, or Basque fishermen. Those who support the Basque hypothesis suggest that the inscription reads, "The Basque people have conquered this land."

When the authors visited Roswell, New Mexico, researching the famous "Roswell Incident" of 1947 and the supposed UFO crash that allegedly took place there, they were particularly impressed by the curious symbols on the "I" beam. This had allegedly been discovered among the wreckage of the supposed UFO and had been examined by Dr. Jesse Marcel and his father, Jesse Marcel Senior, at the time of the incident. The strange symbols on this beam, shown in the accompanying illustration, also bear a curious resemblance to some of the mysterious characters from the ancient inscriptions examined in this chapter.

If the 1947 Roswell Incident was a genuine UFO crash, is it conceivable that the unknown alphabets on the Phaistos Disc, the Glozel Tablets, and the *rongo-rongo* of Easter Island might have been the work of extraterrestrials making similar visits to Earth long ago? The universe is so vast and its possible planets so numerous that it is statistically close to certainty that many of them will harbour intelligent life forms with technologies — including space flight — millennia ahead of ours.

CHAPTER SIXTEEN:
Crystal Skulls

What may well be the world's most mysterious object bar none is a weird crystal skull with a mass of just over five kilograms. It's carved from pure quartz crystal, and there are those who believe that it's a relic of a long lost and extremely strange civilization — stranger than anything that archaeologists and anthropologists have yet uncovered. The eyes of this weird artifact are prisms, and there are devotees who suggest that the future can be seen in them, or *through* them. Not surprisingly, this awesome object has been called the "Skull of Doom."

The skull supposedly came to light in an ancient ruined South American city, but its real origins are still surrounded by doubt and controversy. Serious, objective, scientific researchers have investigated its origin for years, but results are still inconclusive. Affidavits have been sworn concerning the circumstances in which the skull was found. It's been measured more rigorously and assiduously than all the diamonds in Amsterdam. Callipers have closed over every millimetre of its brilliantly polished surface. Various coloured lights have been projected through it, every test has been applied, but nothing substantive has been discovered — *yet*.

This particular crystal skull is only one of many that have come to light in different localities over the last century or so. One rests in its glass case in the Museum of Mankind (part of the British Museum) near London's Piccadilly Circus, but was not on display when we made a recent research visit. At one time, several of the cleaners found it so disconcerting that they asked for it to be covered when they were working in its vicinity at night in the dim light of the Exhibition Room. A black cloth was duly placed over it for the cleaners' sake. The crystal skull's label is not very specific. It suggests that the skull may be of Aztec origin and from the colonial period. Even this seems to be

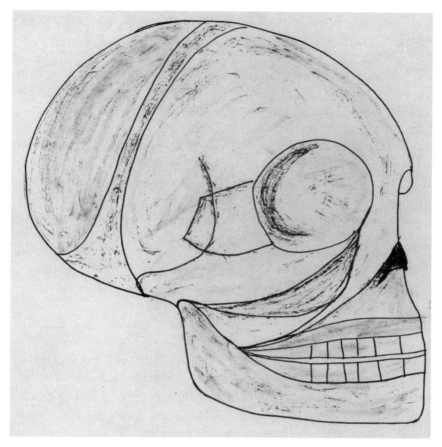

One of the mysterious crystal skulls.

conjecture because there are very few known facts about the skull's real origin. It came from Tiffany's, the New York jewellers, for the sum of £120 in 1898. No one seems to know where it was before it reached Tiffany's, but one theory suggests that it was part of the loot of a nineteenth-century Mexican adventurer.

Another famous crystal "Skull of Doom" is closely associated with Anna Mitchell-Hedges. Anna's father was F.A. ("Mike") Mitchell-Hedges, a British explorer very similar in character to Colonel Fawcett, who did his research in the remoter regions of the Americas in the early decades of the twentieth century. Mike was a gambler, a cowboy, and a soldier with Pancho Villa during the Mexican Revolution. He even shared a room with Trotsky for a while. On one of his trips, Mike encountered a group of men in Ontario. With them was a little ten-year-old orphan girl named Anna le Guillon; Mike adopted her and she later took his surname.

Seven years later, Mitchell-Hedges was excavating the great Mayan city of Lubaantun in the Toledo District of what is now Belize (but was then British Honduras) — a city that Mike believed had once been associated with Atlantis.

The largest Mayan site in Southern Belize, Lubaantun is famous for its rare type of structure. It is situated on a ridge above a valley cut by the Columbia River. Everything is built from limestone blocks, which appear to have no mortar between them. These large stones must have been measured and cut meticulously to fit, and consequently Lubaantun structures have massive strength.

Lubaantun was once a great Mayan ceremonial centre, but the earth on which it stood was vulnerable to subsidence, and some of the blocks collapsed. The name *Lubaantun* actually means "place of the fallen rocks" in the Mayan language.

There are eleven major structures that stand high above five plazas and three courts once used for ball games. The structures have no doorways and rounded corners on the buildings, a feature that doesn't occur in Mayan sites elsewhere. Lubaantun was almost certainly a major administrative, political, and commercial centre, used principally for festivals, games, and religious liturgies and rituals. Many ceramic whistle figurines were discovered at Lubaantun, but only a very few tombs were found.

The visitor centre at Lubaantun today contains a collection of ceramic figurines, pottery, maps, and other information, and the caretakers are local experts on the site. The area is tranquil and serene. Many of the massive stone structures are covered with moss, and vines are anchored to tiny holes and cracks in those structures.

The skull was allegedly discovered on Anna's seventeenth birthday. She suddenly spotted something gleaming below an ancient altar: it was the domed top of the skull. She later found its lower jaw, which had become separated from the rest of the head. Close examination shows that there may once have been a system of wires or subtle hinges connecting the lower jaw to the upper part of the skull. If it was used as an oracle by an unscrupulous priest with the same attitude as Alexander of Abonoteichous, the articulated jaw may have been manipulated to make it look as if the skull was speaking.

According to Anna, her father gave the skull to the local Mayan descendants. "They prayed to it, and said it was their god who could bring healing or death."

Mitchell-Hedges left the ruined Mayan city later in 1927. Anna then recalled, "The Mayan people gave my father back the skull as a parting gift because he had been so good to them, bringing them medicines and clothing."

Ever since Anna allegedly discovered the crystal skull, it's been the centre of more controversy than the clay tablets at Glozel. To start with, no one knows who made it or where it came from. Did Anna really *find* it under the altar at Lubaantun that day — or was it hidden there in advance for her to discover?

It seems a trifle odd that such a priceless and mysterious relic should suddenly just "appear" in the middle of an archaeological dig. Mitchell-Hedges himself was never very forthcoming about the exact circumstance of Anna's find. Although celebrating her seventeenth birthday, she was in low spirits following a bout of malaria. Did Mike put the weird crystal skull there just to cheer her up? If so, where had it really come from? Had Mike acquired it in Mexico, as some researchers suspect, but, if so, from whom and *why*?

Mike died in 1959, but in his autobiography, *Danger My Ally*, published in 1954, he spends relatively few words on the strange crystal skull. Referring to his 1948 African adventure, he says:

> We took with us also the sinister Skull of Doom of which much has been written. How it came into my possession I have reason for not revealing. The Skull of Doom is made of pure rock crystal and according to scientists must have taken 150 years, generation after generation working all the days of their lives, patiently rubbing down with sand an immense block of rock crystal until the perfect skull emerged. It is at least 3,600 years old and according to legend was used by the high priest of the Maya when performing esoteric rites. It is said that when he willed death with the help of the skull, death invariably followed. It has been described as the embodiment of all evil.

Mike was a good and honourable man, but he was also a flamboyant and adventurous extrovert who usually maximized a good story. There has to be some valid reason why such a man says so little about an object with so much potential narrative in it. Anna said that the skull most certainly was *not* deliberately planted — by her father or by anyone else. She argued that he would not have spent a fortune on their Mayan expedition simply to plant a crystal skull there — not even for her benefit! She explained his diffidence by saying that he was a particularly fair and generous man who allocated the right to give an account of the miscellaneous discoveries and adventures during their work at Lubaantun to different members of his team. Anna, a sprightly octogenarian now living in Canada, said that her share was the right to tell the full story of the crystal skull when she felt that the time was right. She has, however, shed some light on one curious episode in the history of the skull, which is now hers. On September 15, 1943, it came up for auction in Sotheby's. Listed as lot 54, it had been sent for sale by London art dealer, Sydney Burney. One version of the story says that it had been left with him by Anna's father as security for a loan. The British Museum tried to buy the skull at the Sotheby's sale, but a note by H. J. Braunholtz, on the British Museum staff at the time, records that when they bid for it up to £340, it was bought back by Burney. The Museum record goes on to say that Burney subsequently sold the mysterious skull to Mitchell-Hedges for £400. This is all very curious, but Anna maintains that the skull was left with Burney simply as security for a loan and later recovered by her father as soon as he realized what Burney was doing at Sotheby's.

The skull then stayed with Mike until he died in 1959, when it passed to Anna.

Only a few crystal skulls have been made from pure quartz, composed almost entirely of silicon dioxide. It's found in many types of rock and its vast crystals can have a mass of as much as eight tonnes. Transparent and colourless in its pure state, when the silicon atoms are replaced with iron, aluminium, manganese, or titanium, the crystal can be superbly tinted: violet, golden-yellow, and grey. Some is green with spots of red. Other forms are known as Tiger's Eye.

Because crystal is ancient, it's impossible to estimate the age of the skulls.

In 1936, Dr. G.M. Morant examined the Mitchell-Hedges skull

and the skull at the London Museum of Mankind together. He thought that they were very similar anatomically and that the one in the London Museum might, perhaps, be an imperfect *copy* of the Mitchell-Hedges skull. Or was it possible that one craftsman had made *both*, and used one as a prototype for the later, more developed version?

The Musée de l'Homme in Paris has a smaller one, which came into their possession at about the same time as the British Museum skull reached London — but details of its true origin are just about as murky. The Smithsonian Institute in Washington has a large *hollow* crystal skull, given to the Institute in the 1990s. It was alleged that this skull's previous owner had killed himself because he thought it was cursed.

Frank Dorland, a crystal expert in the United States, examined the Mitchell-Hedges skull (supposedly from Lubaantun) and concluded that it was older than the Mayan culture. He took it to Hewlett Packard's optical laboratories, where it was examined under very high magnification. The experts there were surprised that there were no tool markings discernible on the skull, and could not decide how it had been made. Other researchers have often wondered about an extraterrestrial or even an extradimensional origin.

The Hewlett Packard team found that the skull had been made from the type of quartz, known as "piezo-electric silicon dioxide," now used extensively in electronics. This type of quartz controls electrical energy and oscillates at a precise and constant frequency. It's a useful asset, technologically. For example, in the official SI Metric System, time is measured in the UK's National Physical Laboratory using a caesium clock, which depends upon similar principles to quartz for its remarkable accuracy. It can measure milliseconds (0.001 seconds) so finely that the Earth's own rotation can be shown to be out by as much as three milliseconds according to the caesium clock.

This special piezo-electric quartz of which the Mitchell-Hedges skull is made can hold electrical energy, potentially a form of *information*, and send out impulses, or "waves of information," as and when required. This is why very similar quartz acts as the "brains" of electronic equipment; most contemporary technology depends upon it.

One of Dorland's other comments was that the Knights Templar had also known this particular crystal skull. Folklore and tradition surrounding their noble and valiant order includes references to a *talking head* from which they received advice and information. This raises another hornet's nest of unanswerable questions. Suppose that Mitchell-Hedges and Anna *had* found the skull in Lubaantun, how did it get from the medieval Middle East of the heroic Templars to Belize? Again, it must be remembered that the despicable Philip IV did not succeed in destroying all of the noble Order in 1307, nor did he capture their fleet — the so-called lost fleet of the Templars. Did fearless Templar navigators take the crystal skull to Belize some time after 1307? If they did, where had the Knights gotten it from in the first place? What strange artifacts were those first few Templar Knights searching for under the mysterious ruins of old Jerusalem?

Sceptics point to another explanation. They suggest that when the crystal quarries in Eder Oberstein in Germany were worked out, so that there was almost no crystal left for the craftsmen to use, several of the expert crystal carvers went to Brazil, where there was still an ample supply of crystal. Along came a rather dubious merchant-adventurer and wheeler-dealer named Eugene Boban, who dealt in antiques and curios in Mexico City towards the end of the nineteenth century. If Boban had contacted crystal-worker refugees from Eder Oberstein who were then setting up in South America, he might have been able to purchase several very authentic-looking skulls from these craftsmen and sell them to explorers like Mitchell-Hedges, wealthy collectors, and museums.

Theories abound; the real origin of the skulls, their powers, and their purposes are still open to conjecture.

CHAPTER SEVENTEEN:
The Lance of Longinus

Although the Grail is far better known as a semi-legendary holy relic, the Lance of Longinus (the Roman soldier's full name was supposedly Gaius Cassius Longinus) also has a place in the mists of religious antiquity. Just as the Grail may well have been far older than the Christian Easter story suggests, actually pre-dating the Christian era by several millennia, so might the Lance. In effect, the ancient legends tell of *two* powerful objects: one is a magical spear, or lance, which guarantees victory to the commander who wields it; the other is a cup, or a dish, perhaps even a cornucopia, which has additional benign magical powers, including healing and longevity. Yet another interpretation views the Grail as a human being metaphorically carrying blood as part of a hereditary bloodline.

The pragmatic medieval Church was always keen for political, social, and economic reasons to take over any well-established popular myths, legends, and traditions and give them Christian meanings. The Spring Renewal Feasts became the Christian Easter; the Mid-Winter Feasts became the Christian Christmas, and so on.

The Christianisation of the legend of the Lance of Victory has its origins in John's Gospel, chapter 19, verses 33–37:

> But when they came to Jesus, and saw that he was dead already, they brake not his legs: but one of the soldiers with a spear pierced his side, and forthwith came there out blood and water. And he that saw it bare record, and his record is true: and he knoweth that he saith true, that ye might believe. For these things were done that the scripture should be fulfilled, a bone of him shall not be broken. And again another scripture saith, they shall look on him whom they pierced.

Ancient Celtic traditions — far older than the Christian era — became entangled with the legends of Arthur and his quest knights and their search for the Grail (whatever the Grail *really* was). Although less widely known, the legendary search for, and use of, the Spear (or Lance) of Victory ran concurrently with the medieval Grail quests.

At least four Holy Lances were thought to exist in Europe at one time. The Vatican had one, although it was never credited with any great supernatural powers. Another was preserved in Paris, where Saint Louis lodged it after his safe return from the Crusades in Palestine. A third was kept in Cracow, Poland, but was even then acknowledged by its keepers to be a mere copy of the fourth spear, held by the ancient Habsburg dynasty. This Habsburg Lance, so it was *claimed*, had been re-discovered during the First Crusade in Antioch, where Helena (mother of the Roman Emperor Constantine) had hidden it many years before. But where had it been in the meantime?

In 570, Saint Antoninus of Piancenza visited the holy places of Jerusalem, and records seeing "The crown of thorns with which Our Lord was crowned and the lance with which He was struck in the side." Antoninus goes on to say that they were then in the Basilica of Mount Sion. In 615, Jerusalem fell to Chosroes, Shah of Persia. The Christian relics were then in Persian hands, but Nicetas was given the head of the Lance, which had broken away from the shaft, and took it to the Church of Saint Sophia in Constantinople. The point was set into a "yeona," or icon.

In 1244 (which by a strange coincidence was the year when the Cathars of Montségur were brutally martyred) the Lance and its icon-setting were presented by Baldwin to Saint Louis, and it was then enshrined in the Sainte Chapelle with what purported to be the Crown of Thorns. During the French Revolution these relics were removed to the Bibliotheque Nationale, but the Lance disappeared from there at some later date.

Meanwhile, Heraclius had restored the larger section of the Lance, and in the year 670, Arculpus reported that he had seen that same larger section in Jerusalem in the Church of the Holy Sepulchre. Curiously, from then onwards there is no mention of it from pilgrims who visited Palestine. Saint Willibald, for example, who was in Jerusalem in 715, says nothing about it. Does this mean that the larger portion had been taken to Constantinople to be with the point? Some early Russian pilgrims, who were characteristically very enthusiastic about holy relics, maintained that it was there.

Sir John Mandeville stated in 1357 that he had seen the blade of the Holy Lance both at Paris and at Constantinople. It appears from some later chroniclers that the Turks later captured the sacred relic. However controversial, entangled, or divergent the various histories of the Holy Lance tend to be, the Crusaders found something in Antioch that they felt to be of great significance.

The tides of medieval religious war ebbed and flowed around the ancient city. The Crusaders had barely gained control of Antioch after a hard battle when Saracen reinforcements arrived and shut them in. Stores were soon running low, and the defenders were hard pressed to prevent the Saracens from re-taking Antioch, when a priest had a vision that led him to recover part of the Holy Lance from its hiding place in Antioch's ancient Church of Saint Peter. The Lance — although only a spearhead — inspired the encircled Crusaders to ride out and shatter the Saracens.

There are, of course, several other versions of the Lance's history and of its many travels and adventures. In some of these accounts the Lance was carried by: Theodosius, Alaric the Visigoth, who had possible Rennes-le-Château connections and sacked Rome in 410, Charles Martel, who defeated the Moslems in 733, and Charlemagne in the ninth century. It saw him safely through forty-seven victorious campaigns, but shortly after accidentally dropping it, Charlemagne died.

The next Lance-bearer was Heinrich the Fowler, an eminent Saxon leader. He drove the Poles back toward the east. Five Saxon monarchs apparently wielded its paranormal powers, and then it passed into the custody of the Swabian Hohenstauffens. The greatest of their line was Frederick Barbarossa, who was born in 1123. After the Lance had supposedly inspired him to a great series of victories, including the conquest of Italy — where he drove the Pope into exile — Barbarossa dropped it when crossing a Sicilian river; he was dead within minutes. Napoleon believed in the Lance and its paranormal military powers. He tried to take it after the Battle of Austerlitz, but the Austrians had smuggled it out of Vienna, and the French Emperor never found it.

More fascinating information regarding the adventures of one of the Holy Lance's adventures can be found in Pastor's *History of the Popes*. This records that the Sultan Bajazet sent one of the Lance relics to Pope Innocent VIII to try to persuade him to release Bajazet's brother Zizim, who was then the Pope's prisoner. This lancelike relic that was sent by Sultan Bajazet is the one that is still in Rome, under the dome of Saint Peter's.

On yet another occasion, Saint Benedict wrote that that he had obtained a precise and accurate drawing of the point of the Lance from Paris. When he compared it with the relic in St. Peter's in Rome, Benedict felt sure that the two had originally been one. In 1904, M. Mély showed an accurate portrayal of the Lance and its conspicuous lost point. Yet another Holy Lance relic is currently preserved at Etschmiadzin in Armenia, although this looks more like part of the head of a standard than a real spear.

Yet another contender for the Holy Lance's title is the Lance of Saint Maurice, which is among the imperial insignia at Vienna. This one is recorded as having been used in 1273 during the Emperor's coronation. It came to Nuremberg in 1424.

William of Malmesbury told a story of how the Lance was given to King Athelstan of England by Hugh Capet, but this is not very likely.

An early use of the Lance is credited to Attila the Hun, who acquired it as he bored his bloodthirsty tunnel of destruction through Europe. His army weakened by hunger and disease, he galloped to the gates of Rome and hurled the lance at the feet of the officers who had been sent out to surrender the city. "Take back your Holy Lance," he said, "it is of no use to me, since I do not know Him that made it holy."

The Holy Lance's powers have been spoken of and written about for centuries. After being used by the Holy Roman Emperors, the Lance was exhibited in the Hofburg Palace in Austria. Hitler gained possession of it in the 1930s and sent it to Nuremberg in October of 1938. It was kept there in Saint Catherine's Church for the next six years until, with the tides of war turning against him, Hitler ordered it to be transferred to the safety of a bomb-proof underground vault. As Germany fell, Lieutenant Walter William Horn (U.S. Army Serial Number 01326328) formally took possession of the Lance on behalf of the American government; it seems a very odd coincidence that within minutes of that historic event in Nuremberg, Hitler shot himself in the head in his Berlin bunker miles away.

The wheel has now turned full cycle, and, as far as is known at the time of writing, the Lance is now back in the Hofburg Museum in Vienna.

CHAPTER EIGHTEEN:
Screaming Skulls

Screaming skulls provide the psychic investigator with a whole genre of paranormal phenomena. The common denominator in all the reports are: a background story that provides some sort of reason — logical or otherwise — to explain why the owner of the skull (while still alive) did not wish to be taken from the location; several abortive attempts to remove it; and resignation to the fact that the skull had to be left in situ or there would be further trouble.

One interesting account of these screaming skulls concerns Burton Agnes Hall near Driffield in North Yorkshire. It was allegedly haunted by the skull of Anne Griffiths, daughter of Sir Henry Griffiths, who built the Hall in 1590. This unfortunate lady was fatally wounded by two robbers. She left instructions that after she died her skull was to be placed in the home that had given her so much pleasure during life. People being what they are, the basic screaming skull pattern soon unfolded itself, and her skull (popularly known as Old Nancy) was taken from the Hall on several occasions. All accounts report that trouble — in the form of piercing screams — started when the skull was removed and continued grimly until it was brought back again. The problem was finally solved in 1900 when it was bricked up in the wall of Burton Agnes Hall, which has been tranquil ever since.

Calgarth Hall, on Lake Windermere in Cumbria, was reputedly haunted for years by *two* skulls belonging to Kraster and Dorothy Cook. A very unpleasant local Justice of the Peace, Miles Phillipson, who wanted Calgarth for himself, falsely accused the Cooks of theft and sentenced them to hang. He seems to have got his idea from the story of Naboth's vineyard in the Bible. Before she died on the scaffold Dorothy foretold that her skull — and her husband's — would haunt Calgarth Hall. Their bodies were still metaphorically warm from the hanging when the gloating Phillipsons took over the Hall. They were

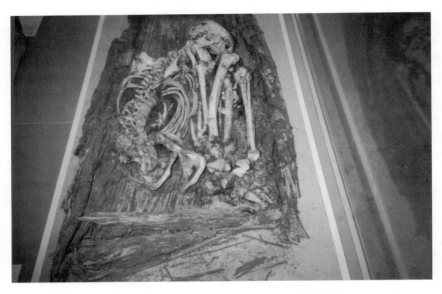

*Old skeletal remains in a primitive woven "coffin" —
do such bones retain strange powers?*

not destined to enjoy it for long! The Cooks' skulls reportedly made life unbearable for the avaricious and murderous Phillipsons, and the hauntings ceased only when they moved out of Calgarth.

Other notorious screaming skull sites in England include Bettiscombe Manor near Sherborne in Dorset. Built mainly in the 1600s, it's a fine structure of white stone and brickwork typical of the period. Parts of it, however, are much older, and there are archaeological traces indicating that the site was occupied in prehistoric times. Bettiscombe was built by the Pinney family, who are still prominent in the are and who treat the weird Bettiscombe skull phenomena with serious respect. One version of the explanation for the skull goes back to 1685. Azariah Pinney of Bettiscombe was rash enough to support the ill-fated Monmouth Rebellion. As Monmouth lost dramatically, Azariah was lucky to escape with simple banishment and exile to the West Indies. There, however, he did well and his wealthy descendants were able to afford to come home in style. One of the returning Pinneys brought with him an Afro-Caribbean slave, who soon became well known in the Bettiscombe area. It was understood that when he died, Pinney would pay for his body to be sent home to Africa for burial. Unfortunately for the slave, Pinney — a generous and kindly

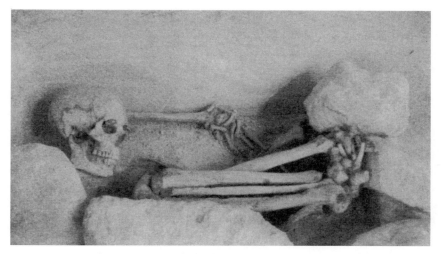

Do bones — particularly skulls — act as focal points for mysterious psychic energy?

employer, and a man of his word — died first, and when the slave finally died, the original promise was not kept, as it had been forgotten. Instead, the family did what they thought was right and appropriate and buried him in the local churchyard close to the grave of the John Frederick Pinney, who had brought him to Dorset and had been more of a friend than a master to him.

Being near his kind old master, however, was no compensation for not being returned to his beloved homeland. All kinds of trouble reportedly followed: crops failed, cattle became ill, heavy and persistent storms battered the Bettiscombe area. In a desperate attempt to placate the restless spirit of the former slave, his body was exhumed and the skull taken back to Bettiscombe Manor. It was laid reverently in a shoebox and placed solemnly in Pinney's study. The traditional legend attached to the skull says that it will cause widespread trouble if removed from Bettiscombe, and will actually bring about the death of the person responsible for moving it.

Scientific examination of the skull has proved controversial, however, and there are reports that it is female and several thousand years old — not from the eighteenth century, but dug up in the vicinity, possibly by a ploughman working for the Pinneys. There have sometimes been understandable conflations of the traditional story of the Bettiscombe skull in Dorset and the story of a complete skeleton of a

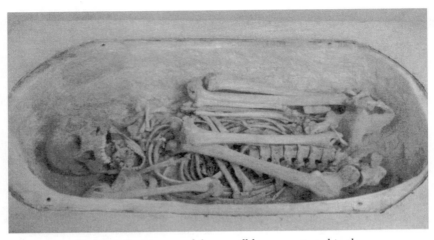

Can weird, paranormal forces still be concentrated in the skeletons of the long dead?

young female said to have been found in Chambercombe Manor, near Ilfracombe in Devon.

The original Chambercombe Manor was built in 1385 and had associations with the tragic young Lady Jane Gray. She was there before the death of young Edward VI and her own very brief reign as Queen of England. A room at Chambercombe is still named after her, but it does not seem to be her ghost that disturbs the ancient house.

Working on a ladder high up near Chambercombe's roof in 1865, an observant repairman spotted a small window, almost invisible from ground level. On being informed of this, the tenant searched hard for a door into the room that that window served; there wasn't one. Determined to solve the mystery, he had a wall broken down. A low-ceilinged, dingy corridor ran from behind the demolished wall. It led to a small room. Inside this room, he found fragile old tapestries and some crumbling Elizabethan furniture. The most striking feature of this hidden chamber was a four-poster bed. Its decaying curtains were still closed around whatever mystery lay within. The yeomen farmers of Devon have much in common with the historical Drake and the fictional but realistic John Ridd — they fear nothing. The decaying bed-curtains came down in the farmer's hand, and there on the rotting bed lay the skeleton of what was later pronounced to have been a young woman. Three explanations are offered for the girl's tragic death. All feature a brutal villain named William Oatway, who was a notorious Ilfracombe wrecker

*Victims of the Chambercombe wreckers plunge to their deaths
on the jagged Ilfracombe rocks.*

and smuggler in the relatively lawless 1600s. In the first version, his daughter, Kate, found out about the wrecking and smuggling and threatened to inform the authorities. Oatway dealt with the threat by bricking her up in her room and letting her die of thirst there.

In version two, Kate was returning from Ireland, and hadn't told her father what ship she was on. It was lured on to the Ilfracombe rocks by Oatway and his heartless wreckers, who later found Kate's drowned body on the beach. Her heartbroken father carried her home, laid her reverently in her room, and bricked up the corridor. Overcome with grief, Oatway gave up his life of crime, went abroad, and died there.

Version three includes a detail missing from versions one and two: in this final version the young girl's skeleton was *chained to the bed*. The skeleton was *not* Oatway's daughter, Kate, but a girl passenger who had survived one of their earlier wrecking exploits and, instead of being murdered on the beach as she struggled ashore, had been white-slaved by the wrecking and smuggling gang and left to die in the upper room when they had no further use for her.

Kate Oatway — or the kidnapped girl's ghost — has never been seen, but light female footsteps have been heard regularly ever since the discovery of the skeleton. She seems to walk in the vicinity of the bricked-up chamber where her bones were discovered on the bed. Footsteps are also heard near the chapel and in the courtyard, which is cobbled.

Tunstead Farm is situated near Chapel-en-le-Frith in Derbyshire. A screaming skull, affectionately called Dickie's Skull, allegedly haunts the farmhouse, although it could be the skull of a woman! According to one version, the skull is all that remains of farmer Ned Dickson, who abandoned his hill farm in Derbyshire to go adventuring as a soldier of fortune. While fighting for the King of Navarre, Ned was badly hurt in 1590 during the Battle of Ivry. Having had more than his fill of danger and adventure, Ned came back to resume his life as a Derbyshire farmer. However, the story goes on to relate that his misfortunes at Ivry had been exaggerated in the telling. The story that reached Chapel-en-le-Frith was that Ned had been killed in action at Ivry. His opportunistic cousin had promptly moved in and assumed ownership of Ned's farm. He was understandably less than delighted when Ned reappeared — and Ned's sudden death in suspicious circumstances on his first night home was no surprise to those who knew the background. Salacious stories may also have circulated to the effect that the enterprising cousin had taken over Ned's attractive young "widow" Dickson as well as her "late" husband's land! An unexpectedly resurrected Ned was just too much of an inconvenience, whichever way his cousin looked at it.

Another version relates that the skull belonged to a female Dickson killed at the farm. She loved the place so much that, before dying, she begged that her earthly remains might always be kept there. Certainly, stories of hauntings at the farmhouse have always featured a female ghost.

Lomas, a tenant farmer in Tunstead towards the end of the nineteenth century, was caring for his very sick infant daughter, who was in a cradle beside him. The farmer reported seeing a ghostly woman gliding across the kitchen from the stairway. The spectre stooped tenderly and sympathetically over the desperately ill child, like a gentle, loving nurse who had come to help. As Lomas tried to speak to the phantom, it disappeared. The sick child died during the night.

Is it Ned Dickson's skull, or the girl's?

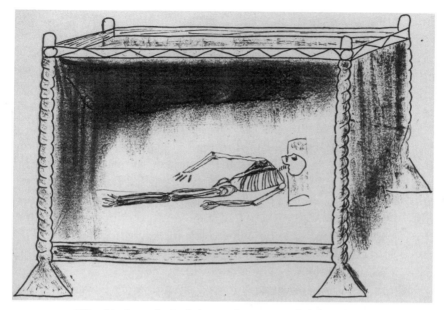

Was this the pathetic skeleton of a young girl abducted and white-slaved by the brutal Chambercombe wreckers?

Whoever its original owner was, there's a long, impressive history of trouble and bad luck following its removal from Tunstead Farm. Things continued to go wrong until the skull was returned. Once when it was away from Tunstead, the barn roof collapsed. On other occasions when it was absent, farm animals died mysteriously. Its absence was invariably accompanied by inexplicable ghostly thuds and bangs, as if a particularly energetic poltergeist was at work in the farmhouse. Various disposal contingencies for the skull were tried over the years: it was buried in the nearby graveyard, dropped in the river, stolen and taken as far as Disley in Cheshire, but it caused so much disturbance there that the thieves swiftly brought it back to Tunstead!

The skull was allegedly responsible for driving several burly labourers away from the farm. Three itinerant Irish workers refused to stay on the farm any longer after the weird noises had kept them awake all night in the hayloft where they were sheltering. Two other casual labourers helping with the haymaking left early because of the paranormal sounds apparently emanating from the skull. In the mid-nineteenth-century railway expansion, the London and North Western Railway Company was planning an extension of the Stockport-to-

Buxton line across part of Tunstead Farm. The skull apparently disapproved! One landslide after another made the track-laying impossible. The line was re-routed. Expert railway engineers said that the land was just naturally too unstable to be suitable for track-laying. Those who knew the story of the Tunstead skull had other theories about the causes of the LNWR's insurmountable difficulties.

Although reputedly the bringer of trouble and bad luck if disturbed, the screaming skull of Tunstead also acted benevolently on occasion. When animals were ill or injured, unmistakable knocks sounded on the kitchen window, and this signalled the farmer or one of his family to go out and put things right. At the period in the farm's history when there were several live-in servants, the sounds emanating from the skull acted like an alarm clock for any who overslept. The mysterious knocks also served on at least one occasion to warn the family that a burglar was prowling around the farmhouse.

Skulls, skeletons, or whole corpses that retain their power to protest and to influence events in the world of the living go back at least as far as the medieval records left by Gervase of Tilbury around the year 1210.

Gervase was an Anglo-Latin author, a priest, a scholar, and an adventurer who was related to Patrick, Earl of Salisbury. Shortly before 1200, Gervase was employed by Otto IV, who promoted him to be Marshall of the Kingdom of Arles, where, in spite of being a priest, Gervase had the good sense to marry a rich and beautiful young heiress. It is from Gervase's text *Otia Imperialia*, Decisio iii, c.90, that this strange story of Arles Cemetery comes:

> . . . the majority of the corpses borne downstream on the River Rhône, were brought to the cemetery of the Elysian Field. It is quite astonishing that no dead person placed in a coffin ever overshot the outer boundary of the city of Arles (which they called Rocheta), driven by whatever force of wind or tempest, but remaining close to the shore, the coffin circles in the water until it lands, or else is borne into the sacred cemetery by the direct current of the river. Marvels succeed to marvels which we have seen with our own eyes in the case of innumerable multitudes of people of either sex. As we have said, the dead are usually sent in vessels of bitu-

men and in coffins from distant reaches of the River
Rhône, with figured coinage, which is offered as alms to
so sacred a cemetery. On one occasion, less than ten
years ago, a vessel with its corpse came down stream
into that strait which is overlooked on one side by the
camp of the Tarasconians and on the other by that of
the Belliquadri. Some youths of Belliquadri jumped out
and dragged the vessel to shore, and, leaving the dead
body, seized the money laid within the boat. The vessel
having been pushed out again into the river stood still
amidst its fierce currents, and neither the force of the
headlong flood, nor the thrusts of the young men could
make it go downstream. Turning and turning about on
itself, it circled those same waves of the stream . . . At
last, when the whole sum of money was restored, the
body forthwith pursued its way without the help of anyone impelling it, and within a short space of time, landing at Arles, was given an honourable burial.

These medieval accounts of corpses being miraculously conveyed
by water are strangely echoed in Tennyson's mysterious Arthurian story
The Lady of Shalott:

> Down she came and found a boat
> Beneath a willow left afloat,
> And round about the prow she wrote
> *The Lady of Shalott.*
>
> And down the river's dim expanse —
> Like some bold seer in a trance,
> Seeing all his own mischance —
> With a glassy countenance
> Did she look to Camelot.
>
> And at the closing of the day
> She loosed the chain, and down she lay;
> The broad stream bore her far away,
> The Lady of Shalott.

. . . For ere she reach'd upon the tide
The first house by the water-side,
Singing in her song she died,
The Lady of Shalott.

In Wardley Hall near Manchester is the skull of a Roman Catholic priest who was executed for treason in 1641. His contemptuous accusers arranged for the priest's skull to be exhibited on the tower of a church in Manchester, where it remained — defying the elements — until a devout Catholic family rescued it and transported it to a place of honour in Wardley Hall. In true screaming skull tradition, the Wardley priest's skull makes horrendous noises if removed from the premises. It is also believed to be the cause of violent local thunderstorms if tampered with. Renowned psychical researcher Eric Maple once related that the skull persistently made its way back to Wardley after every attempt to remove it.

Closely allied to the screaming skull phenomena are the mysterious mummified cats that are found in scores of locations throughout the United Kingdom. While lecturing on *The Psychology and Sociology of Unexplained Phenomena* for Cambridge University's E-M Board, in East Anglia in the UK, the authors were invited to visit an old hotel in Sudbury, Suffolk. The management related how a curious mummified cat had been found under the floor during renovation work, and how a whole sequence of problems followed its removal. The cat was brought back, laid reverently in a beautiful miniature coffin of brass with a thick glass lid, which was then incorporated into the hotel floor. The cat's casket is so arranged that a corner of the carpet can be raised for viewing. The accompanying photograph of the cat in its tiny sarcophagus was taken by the authors during their research visit to the hotel.

Similar examples of cats interred in houses or hotels can be found in the Coventry Arms at Corfe Mullen near Wimborne Minster in Dorset, UK. Unlike the Sudbury cat in the hotel floor, this one was originally found nailed to the rafters, and was later displayed in a glass case over the bar. In Whitecliff Mill Street in Blandford Forum, the mummified body of another cat was discovered in a standing position on a ledge between an old lath and plaster partition and the solid, heavy bricks of the wall. There was no way it could have gotten in by itself, or by accident. Clearly,

The sinister mummified cat that guards a hotel near Sudbury in Suffolk, England.

someone had placed it there deliberately after it had died. A black-covered book, resembling a Bible — but actually a volume of poems published in 1851 — had been buried with the cat. Some researchers have suggested that if the person responsible had been unable to read, that poetry anthology could easily have been mistaken for a Bible.

What sort of explanation — if any — can tentatively be put forward to account for this category of mysterious objects? Perhaps the tried and tested theory that certain psychic manifestations, though by no means all, are the result of paranormal recordings may be of some use here. If thought, particularly strong emotion, is a form of energy like heat, light, and electromagnetic waves, then the skull itself, being in such close proximity to the brain that is experiencing and generating those emotions, may be an especially sensitive recording medium. A skull thus saturated with emotional energy could then — according to this hypothesis — perhaps redirect that psychic force and change the energy-form into sound or kinetic poltergeist-type activities, including generating electrical storms. Similarly, a mummified cat could become a cult focus, or centre, for the thought-energy of an individual or group. But this is only one hypothesis.

The evidence for survival is also persuasive. In almost all the screaming skull cases, there are understandable reasons in the accompanying narratives for the owner of the skull to have an unfulfilled purpose. Do such owners then return periodically to activate the skull as a paranormal implement for their psychic energy?

CHAPTER NINETEEN:
Holy Waters and Holy Wells

Water has always ranked among humanity's most treasured possessions, especially in areas where it's in short supply and where whole agricultural populations risk death by starvation if the rains fail to fall. Several important wells are recorded in the Bible, and there are also references to special pools like the one at Siloam. Life-giving water and purifying water have been associated in the human mind with the sacred and with healing since earliest times.

Water is often seen as the mysterious, primordial element associated with many of the worldwide creation myths. In the varied accounts of the flood, Noah and his equivalent heroes avoid destruction by water, after which the survivors are instrumental in bringing about the new creation, or renewal and refurbishment, of the planet.

Assyrio-Babylonian mythology teaches that life arose from the union of salt water and sweet water. Hindu holy books tell of the first living things emerging from the seas. In Genesis, the Spirit of God "moved upon the face of the deep."

Not surprisingly, there were water deities of many types in almost every mythology, ranging from the terrifying Finno-Ugric giant frogs named *Vodyanoi* to the harmless little water sprites similar to Kingsley's fictional *Water Babies*.

The Rivers Jordan and Ganges have been regarded as holy for many centuries. Lourdes is famous for its healing properties because of its association with Saint Bernadette's visions of the Virgin Mary, and Chalice Well at Glastonbury is associated with Saint Joseph of Arimathea — although it was almost certainly a sacred site in pagan times long before the Christian era.

In addition to their healing powers, some sacred wells and pools were thought to go much further, even conveying eternal youth, great longevity, or immortality. The water of the fountain at Pon Lai in China was said to confer a thousand lifetimes upon those who drank from it.

Mysterious and beautiful Ishtar, the Babylonian moon goddess, was closely associated with water, largely because of the moonlight reflected from it. Her temples were frequently situated in locations where water flowed naturally from the earth.

One of the most interesting and mysterious of these holy healing water locations is in the graveyard attached to St. Nicholas's Church in Dereham, Norfolk, UK. In the seventh century, a beautiful and pious Anglo-Saxon princess named Withburga, who was the youngest daughter of Annas, King of East Anglia, settled there and founded a nunnery. She and the holy sisters who followed her depended for their subsistence upon the milk of the neats, which later gave their name to the Neatherd Moor and Neatherd Road in Dereham.

An unpleasant local lord disapproved of this nunnery and tried to destroy it by hunting down the animals on which the sisters depended, but his sinister plans were miraculously thwarted, and the nunnery continued to flourish.

The mysterious tomb of St. Withburga of Dereham in Norfolk, England.

Healing water in the tomb of St. Withburga in Dereham, Norfolk, England.

Saint Withburga died in 654 and was buried in Dereham. Her elder sisters, also famous holy women, were buried in Ely. Withburga's tomb soon became a centre of pilgrimage, and pilgrims were always welcome because they spent money. The monks of Ely felt that it would be financially desirable to transfer Withburga to their holy place and re-inter her there beside her three royal sisters. A row of *four* holy women might, they hoped, become a world-famous (and highly lucrative) pilgrim attraction!

According to local historical traditions, the rascally monks laid on a great feast for the men of Dereham, and when the men were too full of wine and venison to take part successfully in a hectic pursuit, the monks stole Withburga's sacred body and set off with it down the river to Ely. The sturdy lads of Dereham recovered quickly from the after-effects of that huge feast and did their best to retrieve Withburga, but they never quite succeeded in overtaking the crafty monks.

The story, however, did not end there. From the spot where the saint's holy body had lain, a spring of water bubbled up after the heavy sarcophagus was removed. This water turned out to have remarkable healing powers, and more pilgrims came for the sake of the sacred spring than had previously come to see Withburga's tomb.

Saint Winifride's Well is located in Treffynnon, otherwise known as Holywell. It lies in a region of the Welsh-English border country known as the Marches. Ruthless savagery and fanatical religion lived side by side during the Middle Ages, and nowhere more so than in the Welsh Marches.

Saint Winifride's shrine has historical connections with two of the redoubtable fortified border towns, Chester and Shrewsbury, and is in easy reach of both. Winifride was also known as Gwenffrewi, and her holy well can be found below the town that is named in its honour. The well is situated beside the road that descends from Holywell to Maes Glas (also known as Greenfield) on the coast. The great tower of the Church of Saint James stands above the shrine, and the Pilgrims' Rest marks one side of it. A little lower down, there's an old, disused textile mill. The shrine itself is entered via a gate beside the gatehouse.

Although Winifride's seventh-century story is now almost fifteen hundred years old, it was preserved in the oral tradition for centuries before being written down in the 1100s. The *Life of St. Winifride* was one of William Caxton's works in 1485.

The basic story concerns a lovely young princess belonging to the family of Tewyth, a local prince. Winifride's uncle Beuno was a monk who later became one of the greatest Welsh saints, and his church was close to Tewyth's home.

A band of armed men led by Prince Caradog of Penarlag called at the house to ask for rest and refreshments while Winifride's parents were at church. Caradog repaid the girl's kindness and generosity by trying to seduce or rape her. She broke free and ran to Beuno's church nearby. The powerful Caradog, frustrated and furious with her for refusing him, cut off her head with a single blow from his mighty sword. Just as the murder took place, Beuno ran out from his church and picked up Winifride's severed head. He prayed for a miracle, and, according to the ancient story, God restored Winifride to life in answer to her holy uncle's prayer. Caradog's fate varies from one version of the story to another — but it was certainly nothing he enjoyed! Most accounts agree that he died on the spot in great agony and his corpse sank into the ground — taking the most direct route to hell!

Meanwhile, just as with the saintly Withburga of Dereham, a spring arose. In Winifride's case, the spring burst forth exactly where her head had originally fallen. As a direct consequence of Uncle

Beuno's prayers, Winifride was none the worse for being decapitated, apart from an almost imperceptible white scar encircling her neck.

There are three major elements in Winifride's story: the miracle of her resurrection after being decapitated, the grim fate of the passionate and hot-tempered war-leader Caradog, and, finally, the magical creation of Saint Winifride's miraculous healing spring, like the one that sprang up as Withburga's sarcophagus started its journey to Ely.

Another fascinating holy well is Saint Ann's Well, also known as the Virtuous Well, near Trellech in Wales. Its twin titles suggest that it may have been regarded as having remarkable healing powers long before the early Christians took it over. The remarkable thing about the mysterious Virtuous Well is that it is supposedly fed by four separate springs, three of which bring water that is rich in iron. Contemporary medical knowledge leads to the idea that the Virtuous Well did indeed have remarkable healing properties at a time when people were often likely to suffer from dietary iron deficiency and the anaemia that it caused. To drink regularly from iron-rich water at the Virtuous Well might have had a parallel effect to taking lime-juice on board an eighteenth-century sailing ship to prevent scurvy, another deficiency disease. In the vicinity of the Virtuous

The Virtuous Well near Trellech in Wales; also called St. Ann's Well.

Co-author Lionel Fanthorpe at St. Ann's Well, also known as the Virtuous Well.

Well, those who wished to optimize its healing powers would hang ribbons and garlands; sometimes these were requests for healing, at other times they were tokens of gratitude either to the spirit of the well or to Saint Ann, after the site was Christianized.

Another famous holy well is associated with Saint Cuthbert, who was a seventh-century contemporary of Winifride and Uncle Beuno. He lived up near Weem in the Tay region of Scotland, where he did missionary work among the Picts. Living in his hermit's cave in the great Weem Rock, Cuthbert allegedly had the devil as a neighbour in the cave immediately below his own; the difference in the elevations of their respective caves indicated the saint's supremacy over Satan. Cuthbert's cave later

*Co-author
Lionel Fanthorpe examining
the mysterious garlands
above St. Ann's Well.*

The mysterious well of St. David Weem, Tay Forest Park, Scotland. (First view)

The mysterious well of St. David Weem, Tay Forest Park, Scotland. (Second view)

became the hermitage of Sir David Menzies, a fifteenth-century landowner in the district. He decided to give up his wealth and power and devote himself to the religious life instead. The holy well that supplied all his needs is fed not by an underground source but by water seeping out of the rock above. There are strong local religious traditions that Saint David's well never runs dry, but just occasionally meteorologists and geologists have shown otherwise.

The Chalice Well in Glastonbury is very ancient and deservedly world famous. The healing powers in its reddish-tinged waters may again be due to the richness of the essential minerals dissolved in them — like the waters of Saint Ann's Virtuous Well — or to something more miraculous. Standing as it does at the foot of Glastonbury Tor, Chalice Well was believed to have been the place where Saint Joseph of Arimathea originally hid the Holy Grail. Many different legends are attached to the ancient and mysterious Grail, and it may well have pre-Christian origins to which the story of Christ and the cup used at the Last Supper were simply later Christian additions. What can be said from the authors' own first-hand knowledge and experience is that an ancient wooden cup, now known as the Nanteos Cup, was allegedly

*The Glastonbury Thorn associated with Joseph of Arimathea
and the mystery of Chalice Well nearby.*

brought from Glastonbury (where it could have been hidden at one time in the Chalice Well) when Henry VIII turned his attentions to the monastery there. There is a strong and plausible tradition that this ancient cup reached Strata Florida in Wales and was then taken over by the powerful Powell family of Nanteos. They looked after it for centuries, and one of their butlers kept a faithful record of the many healings that were credited to that Nanteos Cup. Could it have been the *real* Holy Grail, which Saint Joseph of Arimathea had brought to Glastonbury?

When the last of the Powell family of Nanteos died about half a century ago, the Cup passed into the custody of a niece, and when she died it passed to one of her daughters, the present guardian. The authors, and a few of the guardian's other close friends, know where to find her, and from time to time the authors have been able to obtain small quantities of holy healing water, which have passed through the mysterious old Nanteos Cup.

In certain circumstances water seems to be a very powerful and mysterious substance indeed — and the persistence of so many holy healing wells over the centuries provides evidence, not only of the apparent power of holy water, but of the healing power of the mind and the power of faith.

CHAPTER TWENTY:
Ymir and the Derby Ram

When our ancestors first came across the bones of extinct giant reptiles, or of mammoths and mastodons, they were convinced that they'd found the remains of giants. After all, giants were mentioned in the Bible, and not merely in the form of Goliath the Philistine champion: "There were giants in the Earth in those days."

The giants of popular and relatively bowdlerized nursery tales and children's pantomimes — including the scholarly C.S. Lewis's Narnian giants — tend to be stupid, avaricious, and cannibalistic, but in a semi-humorous way, setting their anthropophagous predilections to music:

> Fee, fi, fo, fum!
> I smell the blood of an Englishman!
> Be he alive — or be he dead —
> I'll grind his bones
> To make my bread!

The heroes of these yarns were frequently called Jack (indicative of universalism and reminiscent of *Everyman*). They were as resourceful as Ulysses and invariably overcame their enormous opponents.

The ancient giants of early mythology may have personified the enormous forces of nature to our forebears, and were frequently seen in their stories and legends as dangerous and evil. The Irish Fomorians, for example, were the enemies of humanity and fought against the benign Irish gods, who did their best to assist people. The vast Greek Titans were also frequently involved in combat against Zeus and his formidable Olympic pantheon. The Norse giants of Jotunheim in the Viking sagas and legends were also hostile, aggressive, and dangerous.

Co-author Patricia Fanthorpe with the mysterious Derby Ram.

Giants often featured prominently in creation myths — usually they were here even before the gods appeared, and they often pre-dated humanity by countless eons. When the gods duly arrived, one popular scenario was for them to fight and kill the giants and then create Heaven and Earth from a giant's corpse. The stories of Ymir and Tiamat illustrate this effectively — and the mysterious folk memory of Ymir seems somehow to have been preserved against all the odds in the strange old folk-song about the Derby Ram.

In the oldest Norse mythology, Ymir is the first of the giants, and the founder of the whole race of awesome Frost Giants. He himself had come into being when the hot air from Muspell had encountered the melting ice of Niflheim. While Ymir slept, his monstrous legs became parents in their own right and produced a son, while a human male and female emerged from one of his great armpits, like troglodytes emerging from a cave. Ice continued to melt and soon gave rise to the magical cow called Audumla. (Is this where the idea of the cow came from in *Jack and the Beanstalk*, and could the celestial Audumla be the same cow that jumped over the moon in the "*cat and fiddle*" nursery rhyme?) Audumla provided four great torrents of milk, on which Ymir depended for food. As the sacred cow licked the ice for her own sustenance, she uncovered Buri, who went on to become the grandfather of Odin, ruler of the Norse gods. Odin finally slew Ymir, and there was so much blood that most of the giants were drowned in it. Ymir's flesh was used as filler for the huge *Ginnungagap*; his blood became seas, oceans and lakes; his bones turned into mountains; his teeth became rocks and boulders; his hair was fashioned into trees; and his thoughts and brain drifted as clouds in a sky made from the dome of his vast skull.

One traditional version of "The Derby Ram"

As I was going to Derby, Sir,
All on a market day,
I met the finest Ram, Sir,
That ever was fed on hay,

This Ram was fat behind, Sir,
This Ram was fat before.
This Ram was ten yards high, Sir,
And perhaps a little more.

The Wool upon his back, Sir,
Reached up unto the sky,
The Eagles made their nests there, Sir,
For I heard the young ones cry.

The Wool upon his belly, Sir,
It dragged upon the ground,
It was sold in Darby town, Sir,
For forty thousand pound.

The space between the horns, Sir,
Was as far as a man could reach,
And there they built a pulpit
For the Parson there to preach.

The teeth that were in his mouth, Sir,
Were like a regiment of men;

And the tongue that hung between them, Sir,
Would have dined them twice and again.

The Ram jumped o'er the wall, Sir.
His tail caught on a briar,
It reached from Darby town, Sir,
All into Leicestershire.

And of this tail so long, Sir,
'Twas ten miles long an ell,
They made a goodly rope, Sir,
To toll the market bell.

This Ram had four legs to walk on, Sir,
This Ram had four legs to stand,
And every leg he had, Sir,
Stood on an acre of land.

The Butcher that killed this Ram, Sir,
Was drowned in the blood,
And the boy that held the pail, Sir,
Was carried away in the flood.

All the maids in Darby, Sir,
Came begging for his horns,
To take them to coopers,
To make them milking gawns.

The little boys of Darby, Sir,
They came to beg his eyes,
To kick about the streets, Sir,
For they were football size.

The tanner that tanned its hide, Sir,
Would never be poor any more,
For when he had tanned and stretched it, Sir,
It covered all Sinfin Moor.

The Jaws that were in his head, Sir,
They were so fine and thin,
They were sold to another Parson,
For a pulpit to preach in.

Indeed, Sir, this is true, Sir,
I was never taught to lie,
And had you been to Darby, Sir,
You'd have seen it as well as I!

The similarities with Ymir's story as a creation myth are significant — especially the drowning in blood.

Ymir was not by any means the only mysterious giant, or gigantic mythical creature, to be used as the raw material of creation. Babylonian myths refer to a huge female dragon called Tiamat. Originally the personification of the primeval Ocean of Chaos, this Tiamat the dragon became the universal mother. Apsu, her consort, represents the mysterious "waters below the Earth." From their union, the first two gods — Lachmu and Lachamu — were born. They were the parents of Ansar and Kisar, grandparents of Anu and Ea.

The Derby Ram, famed in song and story: was it really the giant Ymir?

In this four- to five-thousand-year-old Babylonian creation epic, the Enuma *elish*, their descendants, angered Tiamat and Apsu, who decided to destroy their own children. Ea found out about the plan and killed Apsu as he slept. Tiamat, bent on revenge, created an army of monsters led by her son Kingu, who was also her new consort.

Marduk, the young god who defeated Tiamat and her monsters, had come, very significantly, from somewhere deep in *freshwater* sea. This immediately links with Oannes and the theory of highly intelligent extraterrestrial amphibians. It also raises the equally interesting possibility that Oannes and his aquatic amphibian colleagues *might* have been Atlanteans from a technologically advanced submarine culture, rather than aliens from outer space.

Marduk cut Tiamat's body in half. He used the upper half to make the sky, the lower half to fashion the Earth. The water that had been in the great dragon's body formed the clouds. Her flowing tears started both the Tigris and the Euphrates. Kingu, her evil son, the erstwhile leader of her cohorts of monsters, was also killed in their wild battle against the mighty Marduk, and from Kingu's blood, Marduk made the first human beings.

It is especially interesting to note the linguistic link between "The Deep" (Hebrew *tehom*) at the beginning of Genesis and the name of Tiamat the dragon. So much for rams and giants within the creation myths. Rams have several other elements of religious significance, which are practically ubiquitous.

Unlike their significance in Egyptian and Indo-European symbolism, rams are chthonic in Celtic culture. Horned gods accompany them in the iconography, and the ram brings both life and death. War gods are associated with rams, while geese, serpents, and human beings are sometimes shown with rams' heads.

Celtic folklore abounds with strange stories of weird, paranormal rams, which later manage to infiltrate the wilder legends of early Celtic Christian saints. Rams were associated with the cheerfulness and security of the fireside, as well as with the grim portal to the world of the dead. Gaulish tombs often had rams' heads on them, and the same motif featured prominently on statuary raised to honour subterranean Gallic gods.

The major god of the Gauls was, in fact, Belin the Ram; his sister-wife Bélisama accompanied him (a relationship similar to that of Pharaoh and his sister-queen, and to the biblical Abraham and Sarah). The ram, in

*Co-author Lionel Fanthorpe with the mysterious giant ram
famed in Derbyshire legends.*

spite of — or, perhaps, *because* of — its religious importance was a sacrificial animal to the Gauls and Celts, just as it was for Abraham.

In a widely separated cultural context, Ba — the ram — was revered by Banebdjedet himself, the ram-god of Mendes. Khnum, a skilful craftsman and the potter-god who created men from clay on his wheel (rather like Adam being made from the red earth in Genesis), was also a divine patron of the ram. The god Amun could appear in the form of a ram. Rams were a universally popular and vigorous symbol of fertility, so it was natural that the fertility god, Heryshef, was frequently shown as a ram or as a powerful, muscular man with a ram's head.

The ram represented mostly male fertility, although it was also linked with various sun gods, storm gods, and thunder gods. The Sacred Ram of Mendes embodied not only the souls of Ra and Osiris, but of Kephera and Shu as well. At the Feast of Optet, Amon's boat was actually decorated with rams' heads.

Baal/Hamon, the Phoenician sun god, is endowed with rams' horns. The Babylonian Ea/Oannes, god of the deeps, also has a ram's horns.

Oannes has frequently occupied the minds of many thoughtful and open-minded researchers as a possible extraterrestrial from a world in which he and his kind were used to an aquatic environment. If that turns out to be the case, the mystery of the widespread worship of ram-headed gods would be partially resolved. If the benign Oannes and his followers spread knowledge and culture wherever they went on Earth in the remote past, dim folk memories of them would perhaps have included their ram associations.

Rams were also sacred to Zeus, Dionysus, and Pan. Followers of Attis were bathed in ram's blood during their initiation ceremonies. Does this link back yet again with the profuse bleeding of the giant Ymir and the legendary blood of the Derby Ram, which drowned its butcher and carried away the boy who held his basin?

Phrixus and Helle were carried away across the sea by a ram with a golden fleece. Many miles away, and in a totally different religious culture, Agni, the Vedic god of fire, has a ram that symbolizes the sacred fires of the Hindu faith.

The simple but mysterious statue of the legendary ram in modern Derby is only a relatively recent link in a curious chain of sacred mythology stretching back for many thousands of years and touching almost every culture in the world.

CHAPTER TWENTY-ONE:
The Mysterious Golem of Prague

Abba Ben Rav Hamma, also known as Rava, was a fourth-century merchant who lived and worked in Mehoza, on the Tigris, and was a friend of the Persian royal family. He and Rav Abaye were among the most notable scholars of the Babylonian Talmud. Their work is still highly revered and studied by religious mystics.

Rava was especially famous for his knowledge of the mystical Sefer Yetzirah (the Book of Creation) and his application of its ancient wisdom to create a Golem. The ancient and mysterious text of the Sefer Yetzirah is thought by its dedicated students to enshrine the forbidden secrets of creation itself, the power by which God brought the universe into being and gave it life. Traditionally, Abraham wrote the Sefer Yetzirah — and its devotees believe that the wise old patriarch was actually able to create souls. Some Sefer Yetzirah students believe that the Hebrew word translated as *dependants* in modern versions of Genesis, chapter 12, verse 5 actually refers to *souls,* the word preferred by earlier translators. They also believe that Abraham himself created souls when he left Haran accompanied by his sister-wife, Sarah, and his nephew, Lot.

According to a Midrashic account written by Yehuda Barceloni, Abraham worked with Shem, Noah's son, who survived the Flood along with his family. Barceloni wrote: "They meditated on the Sefer Yetzirah until they understood the means by which the world was created." Barceloni also emphasized the need for *two* scholars to work on the Sefer Yetzirah as a team: "Meditate on it with a companion if you want to understand it." Accordingly, Rava worked on it for three years with his learned friend and fellow scholar, Rabbi Zera. It was alleged that they were then able to produce a living calf. Weird and wonderful as this seems to the modern scientific mind, is it so very far removed from the contemporary mysteries of genetic engineering, DNA analysis, and cloning?

Rava apparently pursued his studies relating to ancient Golem tradition to a level where he was able to use the Sefer Yetzirah by himself, without Rabbi Zera. The Talmud itself records that Rava created a Golem and despatched it to Zera. The good Rabbi tried to initiate a polite conversation with it, but failing to receive any answers, he recognized it as a Golem and used his own considerable powers to return it to the clay from which it had allegedly been made. Rashi's commentary on the Talmud suggests that Rava had made it by using the Sefer Yetzirah, although the Talmudic text itself doesn't give any *details* of the Golem manufacturing process that he was supposed to have used.

In fact, this is the only mention of making an anthropoid Golem in the whole of the Talmud, and the absence of information on the details of the technique is in itself interesting. Cabbalistic literature, as already noted, invariably refers to *two* scholars being involved together in Golem-making. Does that indicate that the heart of the theory was to project the astral body of one partner into the man-of-clay to animate it, while his companion acted as guardian and guide?

The Cabbala records, for instance, that Rabbis Hanina and Hoshia studied the Sefer Yetzirah to create a calf, which they then proceeded to consume for their Sabbath meal. Their choice of a Friday for the creation of the calf was significant because the creation story, in Genesis, chapter 1, verse 24, places the creation of cattle on the Friday of Creation Week.

According to the old Cabbalistic lore, Golems were usually manufactured merely to show that the students had mastered the mysteries of the Sefer Yetzirah — rather like an apprentice during the Middle Ages producing his master-piece in order to satisfy his Guild's Examiners that he was now a skilled master craftsman in his own right.

Rabbi Loeb of Prague, in the most famous and challenging of all the Golem stories, was part of a triumvirate. He worked with his son-in-law, Rabbi Isaac Cohen, and his disciple, Rabbi Levi. These three scholars created a Golem — not as a craftsmen's test-piece, but to defend the Prague Jews from persecution and death.

This Prague episode is the best known of all the many Golem legends. Many brilliant Jewish scholars and students of mysticism lived in Prague, and Rabbi Loeb was among the very greatest of these distinguished medieval academics. Born in 1513, he lived to be ninety-six years old, not dying until 1609. During his long, fulfilled life, he was a fearless defender of his people against their many enemies. Consequently, they revered him as the Exalted One.

Curiously, it was often felt by devout religious enthusiasts that any attempt to create life was wrong. This probably tied in with the old Greek religious idea of *hubris* — the type of forbidden pride that led some tragic Greek heroes to think of themselves as equal to the gods and to compete with them. The Greek pantheon — being notoriously moody and jealous — would then send Nemesis to deal with the human rival, whom they regarded as an impertinent upstart, rather than a welcome companion. Tragically, this curious ethical attitude still survives in some contemporary cultures, where it frequently hinders the advancement of medical science.

Because of the massive dangers threatening the Jewish community in Prague in the sixteenth century, Rabbi Loeb was prepared to use his great intelligence, courage, and initiative to break free of the quaint "don't-create-life" prohibitions.

In the accounts of the Golem of Prague, the brave old Rabbi had divine help and made his Golem by using Cabbalistic secrets, which came to him in dreams.

This is particularly interesting. It's reminiscent of the case of a mathematician who failed to solve a problem while lecturing to his students, but later that night dreamed a geometrical solution to it that came to him as bright green animated lines against a black background. He scribbled down what he'd seen in the dream, examined it closely in the morning, and found that it worked.

The common-sense explanation is that his subconscious — full of mathematical data — had provided him with the dream answer. Some mystics, however, might suggest that he could have been inspired by a benign and helpful external Power. Did wise old Rabbi Loeb's subconscious provide the mysterious Golem formulas — or were they given to him by a Power outside himself? Would Jung, perhaps, have hypothesized that the Rabbi was in touch with the Global Subconscious? Was the Golem concept, perhaps, associated with one or more of the Jungian archetypes?

In considering the whole Golem concept, the idea of a thought form, the Tibetan *tulpa*, cannot be ignored. The uncanny experiences of Madame Alexandra David-Neel are relevant here. During her travels in Tibet in the early part of the twentieth century, this former

French opera star — a contemporary of the famous Emma Calvé who was involved with Saunière in the Rennes-le-Château mystery — reported her very strange experience in creating a *tulpa*, which later turned nasty and refused to go away!

In her account, by dint of much meditation and mental concentration, such as the Cabbalistic Golem-makers always had to employ, Alexandra succeeded in materializing the thought-form figure of a monk. From being a plump, happy, smiling, and innocuous little companion, he gradually became leaner, meaner, and more real, until he was actually able to *touch* her. He was also visible to other pilgrims who were travelling with her.

In her book *Psychic Self-Defence*, written in 1930, Dion Fortune describes how she inadvertently created a terrifying werewolf thought form because she was full of anger and hatred against someone who had wronged her. Just as in the case of Alexandra's monk *tulpa*, Dion's materialized lupine mind-entity was very difficult to dispose of.

The common denominator between these strange accounts of materializing thought forms and making Golems is the very demanding mental effort and intense concentration of the creators.

In the various accounts of the Golem of Prague, Rabbi Loeb went through great dangers and put in countless hours of intensive research. Although the formulas themselves allegedly came to him in dreams, he had to do the arduous work of deciphering them. Again, according to the various accounts of the process, it was essential to use the awesome *Shem Hameforash*, the true and secret Name of God known only to a very few holy men. Traditionally, there were great dangers inherent in pronouncing it because its unimaginable power could all too easily destroy the user.

In addition to describing the work of *one* scholar instead of the normal *two*, the specific account of the Golem of Prague is unusual in that it is supposed to have happened in one identifiable year: 1580. Numerologically, 1580 is significant. Adding the digits gives fourteen (twice the sacred number seven). Adding one and four then gives five. This five in its turn links with the *five*-lettered name, Moses, the traditional author of the *five* books of the Pentateuch: Genesis, Exodus, Leviticus, Numbers, and Deuteronomy. Finally the word *Golem* itself has *five* letters. To Cabbalists the year 1580 was, therefore, an ideal time to create a Golem. In that year, too, the Jewish community in

Prague was exposed to additional danger from a singularly noxious priest named Taddeush, who was levelling vile propaganda against them. Similar lies had been used against the noble and honourable Templar Order prior to the treacherous attack launched against it by the venomous Philip la Belle of France in 1307. In response to the threat from Taddeush, Rabbi Loeb prayed for divine guidance to help him protect the Jewish community in Prague. According to the old, traditional accounts, the good Rabbi received an answer, which has alphabetical significance in Hebrew: "Ata Bra Golem Devuk Hakhomer Ve Tigzar Zedim Chevel Torfe Yisroel." A basic translation is: "Create from clay a Golem and you will defeat all who make problems for the Children of Israel."

The secret *hidden* meaning also had to be understood. Wise old Rabbi Loeb extracted this arcane message using Cabbalistic formulas known as *Zirufim*.

According to some versions of the legend, Rabbi Loeb *did* call on two trusted colleagues to help in the work of creating the Golem. One was his son-in-law, a Cohen, descended from the ancient order of Jewish priests; this son-in-law brought his pupil, a Levite, descended from the ancient servants of the Great Hebrew Temple. Loeb believed that they needed the four classical alchemical elements: fire, water, air, and earth.

At this juncture, the Golem of Prague accounts are paralleled by the Rennes-le-Château mystery. Just inside the door of Saunière's ancient church of Saint Mary Magdalene is a group of very strange statuary: a hideous demon or earth spirit, probably Asmodeus, the traditional demon guardian of treasure, comes first; above the demon's head is a bowl of water; above that are two salamanders, creatures of fire; and right at the top are four angels, beings of air, or spirit, and those four angels are together making the sign of the cross.

In the Golem of Prague account, Rabbi Loeb's two assistants represented fire and water; Loeb himself stood for the air, while the Golem (made of clay) was earth. The three participants put themselves through lengthy purification rituals that lasted an entire day. They followed this with readings from the Sefer Yetzirah and then went down to the Moldau River. Here they used clay from the riverbed to build a gigantic Golem. The huge clay anthropoid lay on its back, while its builders stood at its feet.

Rabbi Cohen walked seven times counterclockwise around the clay model, reciting *Zirufim*. The clay glowed a fiery red. Then Cohen's Levite disciple walked another seven times around the body, clockwise this time, reciting additional *Zirufim*. The fiery red tint faded and water flowed over the clay. The Golem grew nails and hair. Finally, Rabbi Loeb walked once around the body. Very solemnly he placed a scrap of parchment into the great clay mouth: that parchment had the *Shem Hameforash* written on it.

According to tradition, the three Golem-makers then bowed to the four cardinal points of the compass and recited together: "And He breathed into his nostrils the breath of life; and man became a living soul." At this point in the ceremony the Golem opened his eyes and looked at his creators. He was then led to the synagogue, where he began his work of defending the Jewish community of Prague.

When his work was completed, the Golem was turned back into inert clay by the removal of the *Shem Hameforash*. The huge clay figure, now no more than a statue, was concealed in the attic of the synagogue. Some nineteenth-century researchers reported that they had visited Prague and actually *seen* the outline of the Golem on the attic floor.

According to the old documents and traditions, Golems can allegedly be created using many different methods over and above the techniques used by Loeb, Cohen, and Levi. Certain sets of instructions say that combinations of letters called *gates* are needed. Different Cabbalistic schools recommend different numbers of gates, from 231 up to 271, depending upon the secret methods by which the letters are brought together. Other ancient experts considered that a Golem was activated by using several of the Divine Names. Talmudic teaching proclaims that there are 12-, 42-, or 72-letter Names of God that might have been used.

The Hasidim, however, had a different technique. They taught that the Hebrew word "emet," meaning truth, should be cut into the clay forehead of the Golem, which could then be deactivated when necessary by crossing out the *aleph*, the first letter of emet. The remaining word, "met," meaning dead, denatures the Golem.

Magic is forbidden in the Hebrew Bible, but the Talmud permits some paranormal work in certain desperate circumstances, such as the sixteenth-century anti-Semitism in Prague.

Materials used by Golem-makers have to be of the highest possible quality, but their motivation must also be beyond reproach. According to the ancient traditions and lists of instructions, Golems should never be made for any evil purpose. The theological argument runs that as the Golem has no soul, any sin that it commits is accorded to its builder, not to the amoral Golem itself. It is also considered wrong — and possibly hazardous — to exploit a Golem for routine, servile jobs, like the legendary zombies of Haiti.

The Golem of Prague remains one of the most mysterious objects in the world — indeed, one of the most mysterious objects of all time.

CHAPTER TWENTY-TWO:
The Philosophers' Stone

L
ike most other fields of study, alchemy exists at a number of levels. At its foundation, the simplest — and perhaps the greediest — students of alchemy are interested only in discovering the elixir of life and the philosophers' stone, a remarkable chemical that is alleged to have the power of changing base metal into gold. At higher levels of alchemical study, it is suggested that the elixir of life and the philosophers' stone are not real, in the sense that they can do what their primitive hunters claim they can. The higher alchemists see them as being philosophical rather than physical. The elixir of life is then interpreted as arriving at an understanding of the *meaning* of life, which is so deep and profound that those who have mastered it will live lives of such quality and enjoyment that they *feel* as if they have achieved immortality. For them, too, the philosophers' stone, which changes base metals into gold, is not a simple physical transmutation intended to make a man rich. They regard it as part of this same mastery of true wisdom and knowledge, which — once a person possesses it — makes the world seem so joyful a place that it is *as if* the ordinary ingredients of everyday life had metaphorically changed to gold. So then, is alchemy symbolic, or can it be taken literally as an art which will indefinitely extend the human life span and change lead into gold? Does it merely refer to an allegedly superior existence of such high quality that its commonest components seem rarer and richer than the purest gold? The word alchemy may mean "art of the land of Khem, the dark land." (Khem was a very old Arabian name for Egypt.) Certainly, an ancient Theban papyrus dating back some five thousand years had within it a formula for changing the *colour* of metals, if not the nature and character of the metals themselves. The writer confidently asserted that the metals whose colours were so altered would cheerfully pass what were the then-known tests for gold and silver, so perhaps this is the soil in

which alchemy and the legend of the Philosophers' Stone first grew. Other etymologists suggest that the word came from the ancient Greek *chymia*, which referred to metalwork. Greek "chemistry," based on Aristotle's four-element theory of earth, air, fire, and water, was dominant until the seventeenth century — and even then it refused to lie down and die quietly. There was also a theory that each of the four basic elements contained two of the four primal "humours": hot, cold, wet, and dry. Fire was a combination of heat and dryness, water was made up of wetness and cold, air was seen as a combination of heat and wetness, while earth was the result of combining coldness and dryness.

The early alchemists believed that if *one* of the essential qualities — hot, cold, wet, or dry — was changed, a different element would be formed. For example, if cold, wet *water* was heated, it would turn into hot, wet *air*.

Jabir ibn Hayyan, a brilliant philosopher and imaginative researcher, made an important contribution to alchemy. Jabir was well aware that Aristotle thought that any smoke produced by burning was a particularly earthy substance, while the vapour given off as a result of heating water was something qualitatively different.

He also had the idea that stones, which weren't changed by combustion, were made from what he identified as *earthy smoke*, while metals, by contrast, turned into liquid when they were heated. He argued that they must be produced from the different *watery vapour*. Jabir suggested, therefore, that steam might be a sort of halfway house in the transformation process. Jabir also had the idea — quite a logical one in view of the profound absence of any real scientific chemical data — that this vapour could be transformed into mercury, which combined metallic lustre and fluidity. He also argued that *earthy smoke* was a transitional stage in the process of turning earth into air. Jabir also worked out — in accordance with the evidence available to him — that this earthy smoke could also be turned into *sulphur*, which he regarded as simultaneously earthy *and* fiery. Various metals and minerals, according to Jabir, were necessarily combinations of sulphur and mercury. He merrily distilled various organic materials and convinced himself and his contemporaries that he had successfully isolated the four primal humors. He had great fun distilling water seven hundred times, which resulted in a white crystalline substance. Jabir announced that this was the actual quality of coldness in its purified form! He hoped ultimately to isolate pure moisture, pure dryness, and pure heat — and that's one of the clues to the real nature and origin of the Philosophers' Stone. With perfect logic, based on this primitive data, Jabir said that the essence of purified heat would be brilliant, lustrous, and red — just like the Philosophers' Stone in the account relating to James Price, old Dr. Irish, and the mysterious visitor to Guildford.

When the Arabs lost Toledo in Spain, Christian academics translated the learned Arab manuscripts that were left there. Consequently, European scholars began to experiment with alchemy. Famous names involved in these studies included Albertus Magnus, Roger Bacon, and Paracelsus, who put forward the idea of something called *alkahest*, a universal solvent that would convert anything to prime matter. Alchemists at that time had a theory that everything had come from something called the First Matter, the building blocks from which the world was first constructed.

The heart of alchemical theory was that any material could be reduced to its rudimentary element of First Matter, and the busy, practical alchemist could then add whatever was needed to create gold.

Albertus Magnus, granted the status of saint by the Roman Church during the twentieth century, was one of the finest minds of the thirteenth century and included alchemy among his wide range of interests. In the fourteenth century, Geoffrey Chaucer was not especially impressed with the alchemists he had encountered, and made that clear in his writings. Paracelsus, in the fifteenth century, used his explorations of alchemy to develop several useful new medicines.

Another alchemist well worth studying in depth was a seventeenth-century doctor from Holland: Johann Friedrich Schweitzer. William of Orange, who became William III of England, was one of Schweitzer's patients. In 1666, when Johann was in his early forties, a mysterious stranger arrived at his house — possibly the same man of mystery who turned up years later in England and called at Guildford near Stoke, with tragic consequences for James Price several decades afterward. It was a cold December day, just after Christmas. Like other savants and proto-scientists of the time, Schweitzer had adopted the Latin name Helvetius, and it was as Helvetius that the mysterious stranger had heard of the Dutch doctor's work. Schweitzer described his strange visitor as a small, dark man, with unusually black hair that had no trace of a curl or wave in it. One of Helvetius's recent publications had been highly critical of an English medical researcher who claimed to have created a universal medicine — an almost magical panacea. Schweitzer and his guest discussed it at length — the stranger being on the side of the Englishman. As their debate continued, the visitor showed Helvetius a curiously carved ivory casket from which he produced three mysterious nuggets — each one about the size of a pigeon's egg and a pale golden colour. Helvetius reported that they were heavy for their size, as if the material was unusually dense. The mysterious visitor declared that this was the Philosophers' Stone and that there was enough of it there to turn several cartloads of lead into gold. When the stranger refused to leave a sample with Helvetius, the wily doctor secretly scraped off a tiny piece under his thumbnail. As soon as his weird guest had gone, Helvetius impatiently tried out the minute sample. All that happened was that the lead seemed to disintegrate suddenly, leaving only a few disappointing ashes behind.

The mysterious stranger paid Helvetius a second visit and left him a minute speck of the Philosophers' Stone for a second experiment, explaining that Helvetius's failure with the stolen piece had resulted from its not being wrapped in wax before being placed into the molten lead.

After their strange visitor had left again — having promised to return, although he never did — Helvetius and his wife performed a second experiment, and this time (according to the records he left) it worked perfectly and turned half an ounce of lead into gold. Spinoza the philosopher examined the "transmuted" gold, as did Porelius, who was an assay official, and both were convinced that it was genuine. The great unanswered question hovers over Helvetius, as it later hovered over Dr. Irish and James Price: did the mysterious stranger ever exist? Did the curious stone ever exist? Or were Helvetius and Price both hopelessly self-deluded, victims of an obsessive, alchemical fantasy?

The weird proto-science of alchemy was not confined to those early experiments. As recently as 1782, young James Price, a fellow of the Royal Society, fell victim to the lure of alchemical gold. Insofar as a human being could have the best lifestyle that this world offers, young James Price seemed to be a fortunate man. Engaged to a loving and beautiful woman, possessed of a large fortune and a fine scientific brain, Price seemed as though he had a great future ahead of him.

His tragedy began when he bought an estate at Stoke, not far from Guildford. The previous owner had been another scientist, an old man known locally as "Dr. Irish," although that may well have been a pseudonym. It appeared that Irish had been something of a hermit, and local gossip suggested that his death had not been from natural causes. His body, it was said, had been found in his laboratory.

One fateful spring day in 1782, Price and his fiancée were exploring their future home. Almost all of Dr. Irish's furniture and other possessions had been left there after the old recluse's death. It appears that among the things Dr. Irish had left behind was a strange manuscript giving an account of how he had come by a weird secret. Some thirty years earlier, according to this document, old Dr. Irish had welcomed a strange traveller who had brought him a sample of the Philosophers' Stone. This weird stranger, according to the manuscript that Price and his fiancée allegedly found among Dr. Irish's possessions, had left a small sample of a substance rather like bright red glass. Following the mysterious stranger's instructions, Irish supposedly recorded in the tantalizing manuscript that he had succeeded in transmuting base metal into gold. Irish's manuscript also stated that the alchemical process and the mysterious red substance were both injurious to health — and deadly dangerous.

If the stories about what happened to Price are reasonably accurate at this point, he then found a small packet attached to old Dr. Irish's remarkable manuscript. This packet supposedly contained a curious red powder. By this time, the unfortunate James Price was well and truly hooked on alchemy and transmutation.

Leaving his beautiful young fiancée waiting in the adjoining room (she regarded anything redolent of magic as satanic, and therefore to be avoided at all costs) James went to what remained of old Dr. Irish's laboratory and began trying to reproduce the weird experiment described in the strange manuscript. In his opinion, if in nobody else's, it worked.

He and his fiancée quarrelled bitterly over his decision to explore the strange mysteries of alchemy, and she left him.

Price's scientific curiosity was now working in two incompatible directions simultaneously. The honest, objective scientist with the open, questioning attitude wanted to test out the powder simply to ascertain whether it really *did* work as he *thought* it had done during his first experiment. The other, darker side of his interest in the powder seems to have been tainted with a feverish desire for wealth and power beyond the dreams of avarice.

After his fiancée left him, Price crossed his personal Rubicon. He changed from an objective, open-minded scientist to a fanatical, obsessive alchemist. Price went on and on with his strange experiments in the lonely old house at Stoke, like a man possessed.

For several months things seemed to go amazingly well with his odd experiments. On some occasions, he would entertain groups of friends and fellow scientists and invite members of the audience to carry out the actual process while he directed them. This was apparently done in order to avoid any suspicion of conjuring, trickery, or prestidigitation. Samples of the gold, which Price seemed to believe that he was making, were examined by goldsmiths and metallurgists who pronounced in its favour. They were sure that it was gold and they were equally sure that it was pure.

The response of the Royal Society, however, was predictable. In the eighteenth century, pioneering scientists had to fight hard to preserve their objective scientific methods. When a brilliant member of the society, who had seemed to have a great future before him as a research chemist, suddenly deserted the ranks of science and went to join the alchemists, the Royal Society had to protect itself.

On the third day of August in 1783, Sir Philip Clark and Dr. Spence went to visit Dr. James Price. They were more than a little disturbed by stories circulating in the district of Price's irrational behaviour. He was said to be acting like someone who was clinically insane: roaming over the fields by night, ranting and raving like a maniac. Not at all sure of what would meet them when they knocked at Price's door, they were more than a little relieved to find that Price seemed to have recovered his sanity.

He looked gaunt and very pale and was obviously seriously ill. He told his two distinguished visitors that he had been successful in manufacturing a further quantity of the mysterious red powder and invited them to watch a demonstration. The three men entered Price's laboratory and — according to most accounts of the grim tragedy — before the night was over Price was dead.

Something had gone horrendously wrong with the transmutation experiment: it had failed dismally and totally, whereupon Price had snatched at a flask of prussic acid, downed a lethal dose, and died on the floor of the ill-fated laboratory that had once belonged to strange old Dr. Irish.

What was the secret of the mysterious red powder? Had an itinerant scientist, magician, or alchemist *really* called on Dr. Irish in 1753, or was all of that simply a figment of the lonely old recluse's distorted imagination? Did the alchemical manuscript really *exist* when Price and his fiancée entered the house or had they quarrelled about something else that caused the girl to leave in distress? Was it the mentally disturbed Price himself who had fabricated the entire story of the Irish manuscript and the weird rubylike substance, which the itinerant alchemist had supposedly left for Dr. Irish? *Why* had the experiments apparently worked at first and then gone so disastrously wrong?

It has been said by some historians of science, medicine, and technology that samples of mercury — which was often used medicinally in the Middle Ages — were mixed with a minute amount of dissolved gold, which was thought to help preserve the mercury.

It is both odd and interesting to recall that Sir Francis Bacon, in his book *Silva Silvarum*, described experiments for preserving manuscripts in a bath of mercury. One of the many theories attached to the Oak Island Mystery is that at the bottom of the Money Pit there may have been a number of manuscripts lodged there by a servant of Sir Francis Bacon. Among the many curious objects discovered on Oak Island over the years were some early storage flasks containing a few traces of mercury. They could have dated from the seventeenth century. Mercury certainly fascinated and intrigued many of the pioneering scientists of that time — just as much as it did the alchemists.

One of the theories put forward to explain James Price's tragedy was that he had at last realized that he was not *making* gold at all — merely extracting a little of it from the mercury that he was using as part of his experiment. Was it one of the brilliant Royal Society chemists who gently pointed out to him that this was what was really happening? Was the sudden realization of his error the final straw as far as James Price's overwrought mind was concerned? Was it in an agonizing moment of truth that the once brilliant young chemist realized he had thrown away a beautiful fiancée, his reputation, and much of his fortune on something that was a fallacy? Stronger men than Price have committed suicide with far less reason than that. The element of mystery, however, must not be overlooked. It is remotely possible — contrary to the understanding of modern physics and chemistry — that the Philosophers' Stone might really have existed and might really have worked. Some things that appear to fly in the face both of science and commonsense are nevertheless remarkably persistent. Given the billion-to-one chance that the seemingly impossible transmutation *could* be made to work — what was the price? The old proverb "mad as a hatter" came about because the early hatters' trade used a great deal of mercury in the preparation of their material. This mercury, which the hatters worked with for long periods in close proximity, caused brain damage. If young James Price had persistently conducted experiments involving the use of mercury, it is small wonder that he deteriorated rapidly both mentally and physically.

The red powder, which may or may not have come to James Price via old Dr. Irish from Stoke near Guildford, remains an unsolved mystery and, as such, qualifies as one of the world's most mysterious objects.

CHAPTER TWENTY-THREE:
Mysterious Mazes and Labyrinths

The mysteries of labyrinths and mazes can be examined under seven main headings:

- Religious locales, inducing altered states of consciousness and deep meditation.
- Sacred places where a god or goddess may be found.
- Gateways and vortices leading to other dimensions — tesseracts, for example.
- Places of imprisonment for people and spirit beings.
- Defensive creations against physical or psychic opponents.
- Aspects of courtship and marriage practices, e.g. the "virgin-in-the-maze" rituals.
- Tests of aptitude or intelligence.

The induction of altered states of consciousness by using mazes and labyrinths seems to have been effected in two main ways: a small maze or labyrinth pattern is cut into a portable piece of stone such as a sheet of slate and kept at home by the user; or a maze pattern is carved into a large rock, or cliff face, which the users then have to visit — perhaps at particular times such as the full moon, new moon, solstices, or equinoxes. Whether the stone is portable or fixed, the users seeking an altered state of consciousness close their eyes and trace the labyrinth pattern with their fingertips. A low chanting or singing can accompany this ritual. Once the desired state of trance has been achieved, much depends upon the belief system of the particular labyrinth user. Some may think that they are in communication with the cosmic Consciousness. Others believe that they are in touch with the spirits of dead ancestors — or different psychic entities. Other users may simply feel that they are in contact with the vast powers stored in the depths of their own subconscious minds.

Rocky Valley is a unique and spectacularly beautiful spot near Tintagel in Cornwall. Carved into one of its steep sides is an ancient maze design that has defied the passage of time. At the Boscastle Museum of Witchcraft, not far from Tintagel, there is another stone that is closely connected with the Rocky Valley carving. This one is a sheet of slate forty-five centimetres long and fifteen centimetres wide carrying a typical labyrinth design very similar to the one at Rocky Valley. This fascinating old slate came from a field in Michaelstow, south of Boscastle. It had for many years done duty as a ritual object and been used by several local wise-women. The stone was actually donated to the museum in the 1950s by the daughter of Kate "The Seagull" Turner, who had enjoyed a great reputation as a local wise-woman during the first half of the twentieth century. Kate Turner, herself, had received it from Nan Wade, the Manx wise-woman. Sarah Quiller from Ballaveare, Port Soderick, Isle of Man, had given it to Nan. But Sarah was far from being its maker: she had simply received it from an *older* wise-woman. It appeared to have been handed down over many generations.

This type of stone, carved with a maze or labyrinth design, is popularly known as a Troy stone and is traditionally used to facilitate an altered state of consciousness. The myths and legends associated with the ancient city of Troy — and with the far older capital city of Atlantis — described

Maze carved on the cliff wall at Rocky Valley in Tintagel, Cornwall, U.K.

Co-authors Lionel and Patricia Fanthorpe at the centre after exploring Hampton Court Maze in 1956.

the basic layout and plan of the city as *seven concentric circles*. If, as some researchers have suggested, Troy was modelled on Atlantis, then the maze carved onto a Troy stone (traditionally credited with so many strange, magical powers) has very ancient and mysterious origins.

The old Egyptian labyrinth at Harawa in the Fayum district, built on the orders of Pharaoh Amenemhet four thousand years ago, may also have been constructed on this basic Troy pattern, but using the grand scale. The famous Cretan Labyrinth was said to have been modelled on the one at Harawa. Although very little now remains of the original grandeur of the Harawa labyrinth, it was visited by Herodotus while it was still in pristine condition. The prolific ancient historian credited it with three thousand rooms and antechambers. Even allow-

Co-author Patricia Fanthorpe at Hampton Court,
site of the famous maze, in 1956.

ing for the colourful exaggerations and occasional inaccuracies for which Herodotus is well known, he undoubtedly saw a very impressive structure: a huge complex that involved storage, burial chambers, shrines, and rooms for religious observances and initiations.

All this long historical tradition lay behind the Troy stones. The user would trace the labyrinth design with a fingertip in both directions — to the centre and out again — and often sing or chant at the same time, until a state of trance was reached.

In 1958, another famous old Troy stone was deliberately destroyed on the instructions of the previous owner, who left orders to that effect in her will. It was duly smashed and the pieces hurled to the four winds.

Undoubtedly, among a small, surreptitious group of the initiated, some venerable old Troy stones are secretly still in use today.

In Indian women's magic, something very like a Troy stone, but called a *yantra*, is used to help women in labour. One of their priests consecrates the yantra and tells the expectant mother to travel through

Bull dancer statuette from the Minoan Palace at Knossos, Crete.

The ancient Cretan Bull — did the legendary Minotaur look like this?

it in her mind. This has the effect of providing her with an altered state of consciousness, which is similar to the benefits of giving birth under mild hypnosis instead of anaesthetics.

After making her mental journey to the centre of the miniature stone labyrinth, the young mother is told to find her own way out again — thus coming slowly and gently out of the mild analgesic trance. It is interesting to note in this connection that until comparatively recent times in the United Kingdom, the local wise-woman was also the midwife.

In addition to its uses in altering states of consciousness, the labyrinth's religious symbolism was connected with the traditional Seven Heavens. To start with, seven is regarded as a benevolently propitious and powerful magic number. The Babylonians believed in seven heavens, and according to their legend of Etemenanki, the biblical Tower of Babel, there were also seven labyrinthine layers *below* the tower, representing the seven concentric circles of hell, as in Dante's *Inferno* many centuries later.

In the Welsh Arthurian tradition, these seven concentric rings are also highly significant. The poem *The Spoils of Annwm* tells how King Arthur and his warriors visited a faerie underworld, and only seven returned. The Canadian Oak Island legend maintains that the fabulous treasure deep below the island will not be recovered *until seven men are dead*. The Welsh legends also refer to *Caer Sidi*, meaning Spiral Castle, and to *Caer Droia*, meaning Turning Castle.

The early Church was deeply involved with the idea of mazes and labyrinths. One of the oldest so far discovered is in Algeria, where walking the labyrinth became an important ritual for the early Christians. This one is laid out as a marble pavement, the idea being that the worshipper can tread its length without thinking about where to place his feet. The journey becomes monotonously rhythmic and tranquilizing so that the worshipper's mind can concentrate on immaterial things and the eternal verities.

The idea of a labyrinth representing the circuitous path of life and of spiritual development is interwoven with religious theory. The seeker after God and Truth has to metaphorically — and literally, in some old cathedrals like Chartres —pursue a difficult and winding route. There was also a sense in which by walking the labyrinth in church and giving money generously to the church, the "pilgrim" could complete a religious journey without running all the grave risks

Co-author Patricia Fanthorpe with the giant ceremonial axes of ancient
Heraklion in Crete.

A typical section of a Roman mosaic labyrinth.

of death, injury, and disease by making a real, physical pilgrimage to the danger-fraught Middle East.

The second mystery of the mazes and labyrinths was their role as a sacred place where a god or goddess might be found. Reaching from the everyday life of earth to the sphere of the divine was no undertaking for the faint-hearted or for those who lacked courage and stamina. The symbol of the sacred maze was a constant reminder to the worshipper that any worthwhile spiritual quest was an arduous undertaking. The gods did not choose to reveal themselves lightly. The mortals who sought them must prove themselves worthy of their divine favour. Mind, body, and spirit had to be committed totally to the quest. The maze was also a warning of danger. Some of its strange, convoluted pathways could lead to death and destruction. It offered a choice at every turning, an option at every branching of its ways. The right choice led to the heart of the labyrinth, to victory, to rich rewards and fulfilment. The wrong choice led to defeat, to failure, and to suffering.

The third set of theories is that mazes and labyrinths are gateways, entrances, portals, and vortexes leading through hyperspace, opening into other dimensions, other times, or other probability tracks. Certainly the idea of the tesseract (a four-dimensional hypercube) in association with mazes and labyrinths is an intriguing one. A thirteenth-century Catalonian numerologist, who was also a mystic, was alleged either to have drawn a two-dimensional sketch of a tesseract, or, more likely, to have built a three-dimensional model of one. According to the account, he acquired an altered state of mind by meditating on it fixedly, and this significantly enhanced his psychic abilities. Modern scientific research into the link between tesseracts and psi-powers has suggested that contemplation of a tesseract by psychic sensitives and mediums may increase their powers.

A fourth group of theories concerning mazes and labyrinths suggests that they may have been designed to imprison either people or animals — or, more bizarrely, demons, genies, elemental spirits, or ghosts. According to this hypothesis, the design of the labyrinth worked like an old-fashioned wasp or slug trap: bait was placed inside (usually sugared water or sweet ale) and a funnel-shaped device led into it. The unsuspecting victim entered the trap and died (blissfully!) wallowing in the bait. The maze (because of its religious associations) lured the lost earthbound soul — or the curious demon, elemental, or genie — inside,

*View of the Cretan Labyrinth at Knossos associated with the
Minotaur legend. (First view)*

*View of the Cretan Labyrinth at Knossos associated with the
Minotaur legend. (Second view)*

*View of the Cretan Labyrinth at Knossos associated with the
Minotaur legend. (Third view)*

*View of the Cretan Labyrinth at Knossos associated with the
Minotaur legend. (Fourth view)*

*View of the Cretan Labyrinth at Knossos associated with the
Minotaur legend. (Fifth view)*

*View of the Cretan Labyrinth at Knossos associated with the
Minotaur legend. (Sixth view)*

View of the Cretan Labyrinth at Knossos associated with the Minotaur legend.
(Seventh and last view)

and once trapped within the coils of the maze, the prisoner was unable to escape. This theory has some elements in common with the stories of King Solomon the Wise imprisoning evil spirits in brazen vessels, sealing them with his Great Seal, and then hurling the brazen vessel into the sea, where the occupant had to wait for Judgement Day. The labyrinth design was considered to be an effective psychic seal, though a genie who could perform all the mighty deeds that Aladdin's slave of the lamp performed wouldn't find it too difficult to get out of a maze!

One of the wilder speculations about the real purpose of the Oak Island Money Pit in Nova Scotia was that the mysterious labyrinth below the shaft, reached via Borehole 10X, was not to guard a treasure but to keep something unimaginably dangerous safely imprisoned. This hypothesis takes into account the numerous layers of oak found within the original Money Pit two hundred years ago, and suggests that oak had magical as well as physical properties — being sacred to the wise and ancient Celtic druids. The underwater television camera showed what looked like parts of a deep and complex labyrinth that was an artifact rather than a work of nature.

Ramifications of this hypothesis examine legendary and mythical beings like Ea, otherwise called Oannes, the Phoenician water deity.

He was at one time a god of the Akkadians, to the north of Babylon, and his cult was absorbed from there. Records date him from as far back as 5000 B.C. The nineteenth-century archaeologist, Paul Emil Botta, found a carving of Oannes dating from almost three thousand years ago in the palace of Assyrian King Sargon II at Khorabad near Mosul. The suggestion is that these strange, amphibian beings with godlike powers were actually aliens from a distant world with an aquatic environment. The scenario then develops into a plot in which one of the aliens is held prisoner and kept alive in his labyrinthine, submarine prison in return for technological secrets: a classic stand-off situation. If the prisoner gives his captors all the information they want, there is no more need for them to keep so dangerous an entity alive. They won't kill him until they believe that they have all the advanced secrets of his alien technology. He won't give them that data because he still cherishes the hope of eventual escape. The Oannes legends have much in common with later mermaid legends — both hint at strange, intelligent beings who are adapted to life in the water.

One such legend, for example, relates to the disappearance of Mathy Trewhella of Zennor in Cornwall, England. He was supposed to have been abducted by a mermaid. Years after Mathy had gone missing, a sea captain came back with the story that while anchored off Pendower Cave, he had seen a mermaid who had begged him to weigh anchor as it was blocking the cave entrance and preventing Mathy and their children from getting out!

The fifth set of theories concerning mazes and labyrinths relates to their possible uses as means of defence — both against physical and psychic foes. Hereward the Wake, the Anglo-Saxon hero of the East Anglian Fenlands in the United Kingdom, depended upon his secret knowledge of the safe paths through the dangerous marshes around the Isle of Ely, not far from Cambridge and Huntingdon. While his heavily armoured Norman pursuers floundered and drowned in the swamps — like Pharaoh's charioteers crossing the Red Sea in pursuit of Moses and the Israelites — the agile Hereward ran boldly along firm, safe, secret ways that he had known since childhood.

Secret defensive mazes and labyrinths in this category can also be invisible and conceptual — referring to a vital sequence, like the lines in a computer program. If a certain lever is not pulled, or a particular stone is not rotated, the lethal booby-trap will be activated. Those who know the secret order of this sequential labyrinth — similar in some ways to numbers or letters on a combination lock — will be able to enter safely; intruders will fall victim to the trap.

The sixth group of maze and labyrinth theories is connected with courtship rituals — or older, more primitive mating customs. There are numerous aspects of Scandinavian folklore and legend in which — more or less as a game — the most beautiful of the village girls stands in the centre of a maze while the village boys trace the difficult, circuitous pathways to reach her. In some versions, the girl represents the prisoner of a dragon, demon, or ogre, and the boys are running to her rescue, much as Perseus rescued the lovely Andromeda from the sacrificial rock and the savage teeth of the sea monster.

In Finland, certain mazes and labyrinths where these games are played are referred to as *Jungfrudanser*, meaning the dances of the virgins. In a church at Sibbo in Nyland, Finland, there is a six-hundred-year-old painting showing a woman in the centre of a labyrinth.

The early Church connection with the girl-in-the-labyrinth theme *may* contain some oblique references to the temptation of Eve, the talking serpent, and the forbidden fruit of Genesis; beautiful young Rahab, who entertained her clients in the house on the labyrinthine walls of Jericho; Mary Magdalene, who was, perhaps, the same girl as Mary of Bethany; the woman whom Christ saved from the stoning party; and the "woman-who-was-a-sinner," who poured the precious ointment over Christ's feet. The labyrinth in that case could possibly refer to the symbolic maze of temptations, and the spiritual and mental struggles of the girls and their rescuers. Adam was with Eve; the Hebrew spies rescued the lovely Rahab; and Christ himself saved Mary Magdalene and the others.

From the village of Munsala, near Vasa in Finland, as recently as the 1980s, an elderly inhabitant recalled how, as a young girl, she had actually participated in the girl-in-the-maze ritual. She said that the young people taking part kept it all very secret from their parents and guardians. In her account of the ceremony, the boy had to reach the girl without making any mistakes as he trod the convoluted pathway. If he was successful, he carried her out of the maze — and she then became his.

The seventh and final set of theories refers to mazes and labyrinths as aptitude tests. Ancient kings, emperors, and warlords needed two great qualities in their generals and statesmen: courage and high intelligence. A brave commander is no asset if the enemy can out-think him. A brilliant commander is equally useless if he lacks the courage to get out on the field and put his first-rate strategy into action.

The legend of the world-famous Cretan Labyrinth at Knossos has this aptitude-test element. The courage required to tackle the vast and powerful bull-headed Minotaur made up one component of the test. The ingenuity needed to find a way out of the labyrinth again — if successful — was the second component. If Theseus had the strength and courage, it was Ariadne who had the intellectual power. Theseus was more than a match for the Minotaur in straight hand-to-horn combat, but it was Ariadne's powerful mind that devised a way out of the labyrinth by following the thread. Between them, therefore, they provided an ideal team and met all the requirements.

In less important aptitude testing situations, one of the main requirements was memory. Monastic life, the priesthood, the work of a storyteller, a druid, a bard, or a minstrel — all required phenomenal powers of memory in the days when literacy was the jealously guarded privilege of a small elite. To remember a maze, perhaps well enough to walk it blindfolded or in the dark, was a fair indication that the candidate had a promising memory.

The power, persistence, and purpose of the ancient mazes and labyrinths may be assessed by considering how many of them still survive and attract as much interest today as when they were first fashioned.

The maze at Hampton Court — which the authors first explored in 1956 — is probably the oldest hedge maze in the United Kingdom. It is unusual because it is based on a rudimentary trapezium pattern, perhaps signifying the plinth of a statue, suggesting that the royal owner of the maze deserved to be raised on such a platform.

Other fascinating mazes can be found in the parish church of St. Mary Redcliffe in Bristol; the village green at Hilton in Cambridgeshire; Saffron Walden in Essex; Mizmaze Hill in Breamore in Hampshire; Tor Hill in Glastonbury in Somerset; the ruined church of Rathmore in Meath in Ireland; and at Caerleon in South Wales.

CHAPTER TWENTY-FOUR:
Miscellaneous Mysterious Objects

In this final chapter, we're making a panoramic sweep of the outlines and summaries of many more mysterious objects that definitely deserve to be mentioned. Witchcraft, magic, and the Old Religion abound with them: broomsticks for witches who thought they were able to fly; cauldrons in which they mixed their bizarre ingredients; talismans and charms in a thousand different shapes and sizes designed to promote anything from love to violent death.

What is the real mystery of Joanna Southcott and her box of sealed writings? Joanna's exact date of birth is a mystery. Her followers believe it was April 26, 1750, but the records show that she was baptized in Ottery Saint Mary on June 6, 1750. Her parents, Hannah and William Southcott, were married on February 6, 1739. Her father had many financial problems and was evicted from a small farm once leased by his wife's parents. The family, then suffering desperate poverty, moved out to Gittisham, where the local squire (Thomas Putt, of whom all the villagers were terrified) befriended them. It is important to understand this abject poverty and dependence on charity during her formative years in order to understand the motivation that later drove her to convince herself — and her fourteen thousand disciples — that she was a divinely inspired prophetess. It did nothing to help her dubious mental state when her mother told Joanna that she was a very special child who had a mission from God.

Reading through Joanna's sad and troubled history, it becomes clearer with every piece of research that she was obsessive about escaping from poverty and becoming *someone*. She longed for respect and status in the community. She wanted to build a reputation. She worked in every way she could think of to establish an image of herself as someone mysterious and powerful. The downside of her responsiveness to encouragement was her bitter hatred and vengefulness towards any who criticized or opposed

Co-author Lionel Fanthorpe with a weird witches' cauldron.
What horrors might it once have brewed?

her in any way. She convinced herself and many of her followers that she was directly responsible — by virtue of her special divine powers — for using paranormal means to bring about the deaths of two members of the Bruce family (Basil and his son) after Basil Bruce had crossed her. When King George III failed to answer her letters, she immediately claimed that she had caused the mental illness that had brought him down and led to the Regency. In fact, she had embroidered a quilt with the date of his mental illness on it: 1811.

Witches' broomsticks and cauldron.

This opportunism in claiming responsibility for tragedies and disasters seems to be a common factor in cases of similar personality disorders. When co-author Lionel was Deputy Headmaster at Hellesdon Comprehensive High School near Norwich, Norfolk, England, he had to deal with the unusual problem of a small and rather inadequate third year pupil who was successfully terrorizing a group of burly sixteen year olds far bigger and stronger than he was. The younger boy was seriously in need of professional psychiatric help, which became apparent later.

He was suffering from the delusion that an evil spirit manifesting itself as an Egyptian mummy was standing beside him and telling him to curse people. A parent collecting his daughter from a village disco skidded and ran into a tree. Immediately the young man with the delusion told other pupils that he had *caused* the accident. On a later occasion a pupil had a collision with a glass door, which involved emergency treatment and stitches. Once again, the sadly deluded boy claimed that he had done it using the powers of his ghostly Egyptian mentor. So powerful was his delusion that he actually visited the Castle Museum in Norwich and laboriously copied out Egyptian hieroglyphics from a mummy case on display there. He also bought bandages and carried these around with him, intending to wrap himself in them to resemble his ethereal companion.

Egyptian sarcophagi — what strange secret knowledge
did the ancient Egyptians possess?

Lionel decided that the best way to remove the terror that the older pupils were experiencing was to confront them with their tormentor and demonstrate that there was nothing to it except the "post hoc ergo propter hoc" fallacy ("after this, therefore because of this"). As soon as the sad little boy demonstrated that he actually *believed* in his Egyptian curse delusion, and that help from a mental health specialist was urgently needed, Lionel asked him where he thought the Egyptian mummy was standing. The boy pointed out a spot in the office, and Lionel addressed the non-existent being: "I think you are the ugliest and stupidest spook I've ever encountered. Now then, sunshine, if you're that powerful, have a go at me. Come on, where's the lightning? Why hasn't the ceiling dropped on me?" Of course, nothing happened.

The previously terrified older pupils began to laugh. The mummy's reign of terror was over. Lionel sent for the boy's family to arrange the necessary professional medical help for him.

There is an epilogue. When Lionel was reporting the incident to the Headmaster, he looked a little anxious. "Whatever you do, Mr. Fanthorpe," he said, "don't have an accident on the way home!" It demonstrated that an intelligent and well-qualified professional man could have misgivings about the supposed power of a "curse"! It also demonstrates just how far Joanna's curses might have affected the minds of her eighteenth-century listeners and readers.

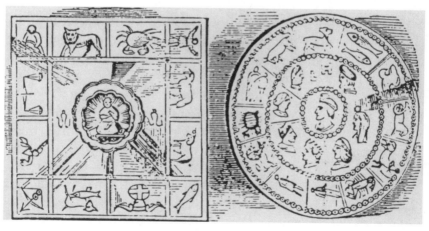

Strange representations of ancient zodiacs.

The mysterious object associated with Joanna is the Box of Sealed Writings. This purported to contain various eschatological prophecies, the signs of the imminent end of the world, Christ's second coming, and so on. After Joanna's death, following her tragic phantom pregnancy with a divine child (who was to have been called Shiloh, had he ever appeared), the box was in the custody of numerous guardians. These included William Sharp, James Townley, Thomas Foley, Richard Foley, Cecil Jowett, and Annie Stitt. Its present whereabouts is uncertain, but the British Museum Library apparently accepted it from Annie Stitt, went through its contents, and bound anything they considered of any significance. According to Southcottian tradition, it is supposed to be opened and its contents studied by seven bishops, up to twenty-four additional clergy, and twenty-four virgins clad in white raiment. There is a cynical joke circulating to the effect that there's no problem in finding the bishops and clerics — but it may be difficult to locate the necessary virgins! Perhaps they're still in the middle of the mazes in chapter twenty-three.

With the present major skin-health problems all over the world following the depletion of the ozone layer, and the dramatic decrease of its former vital protection from ultra violet radiation, one of the amazing inventions of the brilliant and mysterious electrical scientist Nikola Tesla is more relevant today than it was in the nineteenth century when Tesla patented it. The device is a perfectly feasible ozone generator. It carries patent number 568177 and was registered on September 22, 1896. Instead of concentrating solely on reducing fluoro-carbon emissions that damage ozone, the use of large-scale Tesla ozone generators could patch up the holes in the ozone layer. The project would not be cheap — but human life and health are priceless. Which superpower government or international agency would be prepared to study Tesla's amazing ozone machine and put the vast, life-saving project into operation?

Shrouded in the mists of prehistory, the Emerald Tablets of Hermes Trismegistus still gleam triumphantly. If they are what some researchers believe them to be, they could well qualify as the most mysterious objects of all. Among the myths and legends of ancient Egypt, Hermes Trismegistus was otherwise known as Thoth, the scribe of the gods. His mysterious Emerald Tablets contained all the secret knowledge from which the arcane Egyptian pantheon drew its miraculous powers. But

Thoth also seems to have enjoyed a *third* identity as yet another super-being: Melchizedek, Priest-King of Salem, and friend of Abraham the patriarch. This Melchizedek was regarded as having no birth and no mortal origins, neither beginning of days nor end of time. Among the nomadic patriarchs of his era, Abraham was a very wealthy and powerful man indeed, yet Abraham himself acknowledged the superior status and honour of Melchizedek. In order to make any sort of sequential historic sense of the interwoven myths and legends associated with Hermes, Thoth, and Melchizedek, it is necessary first to revisit the theories appertaining to the legends of Lemuria, Mu, Lyonesse (off the coast of Cornwall), and submerged Atlantis. Interwoven with the Atlantis tradition is the question of the origin of the people or beings who may once have inhabited that great sunken continent. If they were in any way connected with legends of wise and powerful amphibian beings like Oannes, or Ea, of the Middle East, is it possible to consider that they came originally from a distant aquatic world? If so, how

Could an ancient craft like this one have carried Atlantean survivors to Egypt ten thousand years ago?

much of their advanced alien technology did they bring with them, and how much of it survived the cataclysm that overtook Atlantis?

Consider, then, a scenario in which a group of intelligent and technically advanced semi-humanoid amphibians reach Earth in the remote past and establish a base in what subsequently became known as Atlantis. The submergence may even have been by design rather than by accident; perhaps the sea-bed was a welcome environment as far as they were concerned. Does this ancient Egyptian scene represent the arrival of the Atlanteans in Egypt millennia ago?

If the theory is correct, from Atlantis they spread to the Middle East, to Babylon, to Egypt, to South America — even to Easter Island. Wherever they went they established their reputations for super-human powers, longevity, and great wisdom. A group of them could have been responsible for the dramatic leap forward in Egyptian knowledge and culture. A leading light among this group would have been the one they called Hermes Trismegistus or Thoth. He was their chief scientist, their consultant, their computer expert. He was the man with the Emerald Tablets (the computer chips?) on which all their vital knowledge was stored. Where did he get those emeralds from? Were they available in the Egypt of that period? How did the ancient Egyptians come to have this special knowledge of emeralds unless it was brought in from outside? The emerald is found in Upper Egypt, which was probably the first known source in the entire world. Emerald mines occur in the mountain ranges bordering the west coast of the Red Sea, and the French explorer Caillaud discovered the ruins of these ancient emerald mines about 1820. He found the mining plant and tools intact, just as the workmen had abandoned them millennia before. The mines date back at least to the period of Sesostris, almost four thousand years ago, and are possibly much older. The emerald that Moses affixed to the breastplate of the high priest *may* have come from these mines. Did Urim and Thummim come from there as well, and were they once part of the mysterious Emerald Tablets of Thoth? As a development of these hypotheses, did Thoth and the Atlantean technocrats bring with them the *knowledge* of how to use the mysterious crystal powers inherent in emeralds, rather than the emeralds themselves? In other words, were the Emerald Tablets of Hermes Trismegistus actually constructed and programmed in Egypt with knowledge brought from somewhere far older and stranger?

Did these weird hybrid Egyptian deities originate in Atlantis? (First view)

Did these weird hybrid Egyptian deities originate in Atlantis? (Second view)

It is clear, for example, from the carved emerald scarabs recovered from Egyptian and Etruscan tombs, and now in the British Museum, that emeralds were known and engraved in very ancient times. Who showed the earliest Egyptian jewellers how to do it? Did the skilled and specialized knowledge of emerald carving and engraving come from the hypothetical Atlanteans who reached Egypt in the very remote past? The famous engraved emerald presented to Cleopatra almost certainly came from these Egyptian mines, as did the emeralds that early historians record as being used by Nero as glasses through which to watch the Roman gladiatorial games. Spaniards allegedly received gifts of emeralds from the indigenous inhabitants of South and Central America in the sixteenth century. This immediately raises the question of Atlanteans once more. Was it Atlanteans who took the crystal technology of emeralds to Muzo, in Colombia, South America — which still supplies many emeralds today?

Although benign and highly intelligent, these hypothetical Atlantean extraterrestrials were not perfect. They had rivalries and disagreements. One of them, identified in the literature as Set, was particularly negative and uncooperative, and he and Thoth were rivals. Their enmity caused problems for the group as a whole and for the human beings whom they were trying to help, educate, and *develop*. Why, for example, were their prime candidates, the Pharaohs, encouraged to *interbreed* with their sisters? Could that be part of a genetic engineering experiment with which the aliens were trying to produce superior human beings? Perhaps part of their godlike longevity was dependent on periods of hibernation and rest. Frogs hibernate. Do extraterrestrial amphibians occasionally need to go into suspended animation while their internal processes rebuild and refurbish themselves?

The Bible records that Sarah and Abraham visited Egypt during their travels, and, as she was so beautiful, Pharaoh sent for her. Abraham, afraid that he would be killed if Pharaoh thought Sarah was his wife (so that Pharaoh could then take her legally as a widow) told her to say that she was his sister.

There is a fascinating ancient legend that this same Sarah, the beautiful sister-wife of Abraham, had gone into a cave for some essential personal privacy and found Hermes Trismegistus already concealed there in a state of suspended animation. His famous Emerald Tablets lay beside him. Versions of the story vary, but in essence Sarah was said to have picked up two of the fascinating emeralds. The moment she touched them, Hermes began to stir. She fled from the cave still clutching the powerful and mysterious gems.

Did those stones eventually find their way into the hands of the Hebrew high priests and so become the powerful and mysterious Urim and Thummim?

There are several references to these strange, precious and awesome oracles in the Old Testament:

Thou shalt put in the breastplate of judgment the Urim and the Thummim: and they shall be upon Aaron's heart, when he goeth in unto the holy place: and Aaron shall bear the judgment of the children of Israel upon his heart before the Lord continually.

Exodus 28:30

And he put the breastplate upon him; also he put in the breastplate the Urim and the Thummim.

Leviticus 8:8

And he [Joshua] shall stand before Eleazar the Priest, who shall ask counsel for him after the judgement of Urim before the Lord: at his word shall they go out, and at his word shall they come in.

Numbers 27:21

And of Levi he [Moses] said, Let thy Thummim and thy Urim be with thy holy one.

Deuteronomy 33:8

And when Saul inquired of the Lord, the Lord answered him not, neither by dreams, nor by Urim, nor by prophets.

I Samuel 28:6

And the Tirshatha [governor] said unto them, that they should not eat of the most holy things till there stood up a priest with Urim and with Thummim.

Ezra 2:63 and
Nehemiah 7:65

With a holy garment, with gold and blue and purple, the work of the embroiderer, with an oracle of judgement, even with Urim and Thummim.

Ecclesiasticus 45:10

Urim and Thummim are referred to first in Exodus, chapter 28, verse 30, but there are no directions for *making* them, nor instructions on how to *use* them. This may suggest that in the mind of the writer they had some very special origin indeed. Either they were believed to have been engraved supernaturally — just as an account of the giving of the Tablets of the Law says that they were actually inscribed by God — or they were known to have been brought from Egypt when the Israelites left. An interesting sub-plot here refers back to Sarah's adventures with Pharaoh, when he believed her to be Abraham's sister. What if his fury with Abraham for that deception was mollified when Sarah offered him the two Emerald Tablets that she had taken from the cave where Hermes Trismegistus was sleeping? And what if those precious Emerald Tablets left Egypt with Moses many centuries later?

It is perfectly possibly that the Emerald Tablets that were destined to become the Urim and Thummim were among the treasures that left Egypt at the Exodus, and that, along with other irreplaceable artifacts, they were carried in an Egyptian ark. The famous Ark of the Covenant, in which the most sacred and holy Hebrew treasures were carried, may, in fact, have originated in Egypt. It has to be remembered that Moses was raised as an Egyptian prince, and as such would have had access to all Pharaoh's royal secrets. Perhaps Pharaoh's costly change of mind about letting the Israelites go came about when a white-faced palace treasury official ran into the royal throne room gasping that Moses had taken the Egyptian ark containing the Emerald Tablets and other unique objects that had come originally from Atlantis. Small wonder that a distraught and desperate Pharaoh launched the flower of his charioteers on a mission so suicidal that it made the charge of the Light Brigade at Balaclava look like a master stroke of military tactics and strategy.

If Moses was, in fact, well aware of the true nature and potential power of the contents of the royal Egyptian treasure ark, he may also have been well aware of the practices of other contemporary cultures. How, for example, did the priests of Babylon and Assyria, of the Minoans, the Akkadians, and the Chaldeans use such things — always assuming that the Atlantean culture really had spread that far?

Another essential line to explore is the *precise* meaning of the two vital Hebrew words—Urim and Thummim.

Dr. Harold Browne says of Urim, "Hebrew scholars, with hardly an exception, regard it as a plural word for 'or,' meaning Light or Fire." It is the same word as used in Genesis, chapter 1, verse 3, "Let there be light, and there was light."

In the Septuagint version the corresponding Greek words are *delosis*, meaning "manifestation," and *deloi*, meaning "visible" or "clear"; *photizein*, meaning "to shine or give light," is also used. The Latin Vulgate gives a much wider interpretation: *doctrina*, meaning "teaching" or "instruction." In other locations, the word *urim* is paraphrased as if meaning "endowed with truth." Thus the Vulgate rendering of the word implies that it was a method endowed with truth and used for giving instruction.

Thummim is a derivative from the Hebrew *tom*, meaning "perfection, completeness." On other occasions *aletheia* (meaning "truth") is used. Most modern Latin, Greek, and Hebrew scholars would probably settle for "light" and "perfection" as being about the closest we can get.

Contemporary technology enables mobile phone users to get in touch with their main computers at home and pick up their e-mails. What if the Urim and Thummim were an Atlantean equivalent based on an advanced crystal technology? Perhaps even the symbolic casting of the emeralds energized them sufficiently to receive the messages, which the knowledgeable priest then translated for the enquiring king or general.

The mythology and legends of bees go back many millennia. The Egyptians believed them to be the tears of Ra, the sun god. Wherever his tears fell on to the earth, bees were created. Virgil, the Latin poet, told the story of Aristaeus, son of the Greek god Apollo, and his beehive. Aristaeus had tried to seduce Eurydice, wife of Orpheus, and, in revenge, Orpheus had destroyed Aristaeus's cherished beehive. Aristaeus promptly sacrificed a number of cattle to the gods, who rewarded him by creating more bees out of the bodies of the sacrificed animals. There's an interesting parallel here with Samson in the Old Testament finding honey in the body of the lion he'd killed earlier. Aristaeus went on to teach the skills of bee-keeping to human beings. This Greek association with bees and bee-keeping is very much alive in Crete today, where the symbol of the golden bees is greatly respected and highly prized. A superb piece of golden artwork in the shape of two bees — like mirror images of one another — was discovered among the treasures in the four-thousand-year-old Minoan palace of Malia.

Another element of bee folklore regards them as the hard working organizers and administrators of that part of the biosphere that lies between earth and sky. The bees symbolize vitality and are thought to encapsulate the soul itself. They were associated with the goddess of crops and agriculture, Demeter. The sacred bee tradition is very widespread indeed. Siberia, Central Asia, and even indigenous South Americans think of the bee as symbolizing the soul when it leaves the body. When an ancient traditional belief is spread as widely as that, there are reasons for wondering whether it spread originally from some central point of culture, a role that Atlantis could have fulfilled.

Bees traditionally symbolize imperialism and royalty. Questions are sometimes posed by avant-garde psychologists, zoologists, and entomologists as to the possible existence of a hive-mind, or group-mind, governing and controlling a swarm of bees or a colony of ants. If such a mind does exist, is there a sense in which each individual bee is rather like a cell in a human body? Is a hive-mind conscious in the same way that we are? Is it able to communicate? Does the place of the bee in religious traditions and history have anything to do with hive-minds and group consciousness? If bees represent royalty and imperialism, to what extent is there a form of consensus among the units that share this ethereal hive-mind? It might also be asked whether such a group mind can exist as a form of pure energy, as something immaterial that *transcends* the hive as well as controlling all that goes on there.

On May 27, 1653, a stonemason named Adrien Quinquin was working on the church of Saint Brice in Tournai when he found the Merovingian tomb of Childeric I, father of Clovis. Among the treasures buried with Childeric were three hundred gold bees. These passed into the hands of Archduke Leopold William, who took them to Vienna. When he died they passed to Leopold, Emperor of Austria. The bees were given to the French Sun King, Louis XIV, in 1665, passing eventually to the Louvre and the Bibliotheque National, where they were stolen in 1831. In 1832, the police recovered two of the stolen bees from the Seine.

The Emperor Napoleon — never a man to suffer from modesty — knew about the Childeric tomb and the symbolism of the Royal Merovingian golden bees. He caused them to become an integral part of his heraldry, even including bees in the motif of his carpets. Members of Napoleon's Imperial Family wore mantles adorned with heraldic bees because of the Merovingian connection.

Numerous early genealogists tried to please their royal masters by tracing back their ancestral lines to great Greek or Roman heroes such as Romulus, Horatius, Achilles, Hector, or even one of the ancient gods. Various attempts of that kind were made to link the Habsburg Dynasty, for example, with great semi-legendary heroes from the distant classical past.

Those genealogists and heralds who knew about the tomb of the Merovingian King Childeric I and the three hundred symbolic royal bees buried with him did their best to link that ancient house with a strange mystery concerning the birth of Merovee, founder of the dynasty. According to this particular tale, Merovee's mother — already pregnant with him — was either seduced or raped while swimming and so obtained a further genetic input from a weird and mysterious sea-creature called a quinotaur.

One of the most probable theories surrounding the mystery of Bérenger Saunière, the priest of Rennes-le-Château who became inexplicably rich in 1885, is that his parents had told him that the Saunières were secretly descended from the "lost" Merovingians via King Dagobert II, controversially regarded as the last of the Merovingian line. Feeling that he had a dynastic right to any Merovingian treasure that might have been concealed at Rennes, young Bérenger went through years of abject misery in a Jesuit seminary to qualify for the priesthood and then applied for the incumbency at Rennes — the ideal vantage point for a man who was searching for a treasure cached below the ancient church of St. Mary Magdalene. Having obtained his mysterious wealth — from whatever source — he treated his parishioners with great generosity, and was, in the best sense, paternalistic to them. Consequently, when he died, a very strange ceremony took place. Bérenger's body was propped up in a chair — like the corpse of a king on a throne — and dressed in a thick, regal, cloaklike garment from which many villagers plucked a tassel the *size and shape of a bee*. Saunière might have been posthumously proclaiming, "I was the Merovingian lord of this village. The bees are my symbols."

From whichever direction we regard bees, they are strange creatures, and they have often played significant, if symbolic, roles in human history.

From the mysteries of medieval royalty to the mysteries of the Knights Templar is a comparatively short step — and Templarism (still very much alive today) abounds in mysteries. Many volumes could be filled with the gallant deeds and secret arcane knowledge of the noble

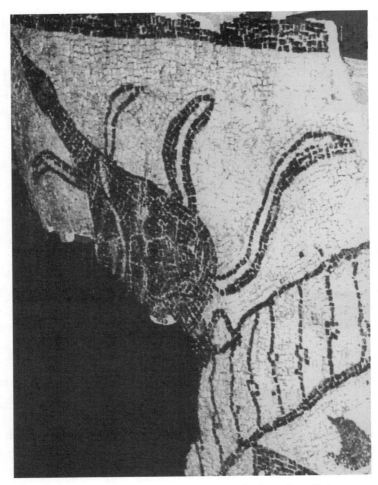

*Could this ancient Roman mosaic represent the legendary Quinotaur,
the amphibian demi-ancestor of mysterious King Merovée?*

Order of the Temple, and the full story of Templar courage and
Templar wisdom would still not have been told.

Both authors are members of the Templar Order via the Magistral
Priory of Saint Mary Magdalene: Lionel as Magistral Chaplain General
with the rank of Knight Commander, Patricia with the rank of Dame.

First, it is very simple and easy to dismiss the lies and foul propagan-
da directed against the Templars by their arch-enemy, the odious Philip
IV of France, prior to his treacherous and cowardly attack on their great
Order in 1307. Nothing that Philip and his minions alleged against the

Templars was true.

The outline facts are that the Order began as a handful of valiant knights led by Hugues de Payns and Godfroi de Saint Omer in 1119. Their purpose was to defend the pilgrims visiting Jerusalem and the other shrines in the Holy Land, a task that needed all their strength, skill, and stamina in a region plagued by brutal thieves and brigands.

Baldwin II, King of Jerusalem from 1118 to 1131, gave them part of his palace for their headquarters. This section was adjacent to the al-Aksa Mosque, known locally as Solomon's Temple. Their Jerusalem headquarters were also very close to what had once been the stables of Solomon's Palace many centuries previously. The Templars were an outstanding evangelical and redemptive order. They sought out former knights who had been excommunicated for one reason or another (during an age when excommunication actually *meant* something to such people) and brought them back into the fold, thus welding a miscellaneous collection of former outcasts into a disciplined fighting force that was second to none. The Templars enjoyed many important privileges, including exemption from excommunication by mere parish priests or petulant local bishops. With the

John the Baptist baptizing Jesus — did the Templar Knights have John's preserved head as a holy relic?

powerful backing of the formidable Bernard of Clairvaux, the Order was recognized officially at the Council of Troyes in 1128. For many years, the great Order progressed from strength to strength, acquiring lands and gold, and serving as bankers to many kings and princes.

The downfall of the Templars was the work of an inadequate, insolvent, profligate, and jealous king: Philip IV of France. Having used up Jewish and Lombard wealth, Philip exiled the Jews and Lombards. He then turned his greedy eyes in the direction of the Templars, but was shrewd enough to know that if he dared to attack them, he would have to be totally successful in bringing them down — or suffer the direst consequences. The great Order was neither to be trifled with nor provoked.

Among the slanderous and libellous accusations included in Philip's anti-Templar propaganda was the story that the Templars were devil-worshippers who possessed a demonic "talking head" — said in some versions to be a strange metallic object — from which they took their orders. This was reported by their accusers to be a fiend named Baphomet, an entity close to Lucifer in the demonic hierarchy.

It is remotely possible, however, that the Templars possessed the head of John the Baptist, executed by King Herod after the infamous episode involving his step-daughter, Salome, the exotic dancer. The biblical records show that John's disciples were allowed to collect John's body (Mark 6:29). If his head had eventually passed into Templar hands, they apparently preserved it in gold leaf, covered it with bronze, and venerated it as a holy relic. John the Baptist, fearless and outspoken, a challenger of corrupt royalty, would be exactly the kind of robust saint who would appeal especially to the dauntless Templar spirit.

Whatever ridiculous claptrap their enemies might insinuate against them, the sacred head of the Templars "spoke" only in an inspirational and spiritual sense, in so far as it reminded them of John's courage and fortitude when persecuted by Herod.

The great mystery of this unique holy relic is how it came into their possession in the first place — if, indeed, it ever did. When the original group of nine Templars were exploring beneath the ancient ruins of twelfth-century Jerusalem, there were whispers that they found not one priceless holy relic but several: the Grail, the Lance, and the Ark of the Covenant have all been mentioned in that connection. There is also a great deal of informed conjecture about where they hid whatever they found to keep it as far as possible from Philip IV. The Lost Fleet of the Templars, which Philip's men failed to apprehend, might even have reached Nova Scotia — which is what makes the mystery of the Oak Island Money Pit so intriguing.

There are also theories that suggest the Templars had an ancient and mysterious crystal skull, with which they were able to communicate. If the strange crystal skulls really are ancient arcane objects, rather than nineteenth-century forgeries, then it is just possible that the fearless Templars had obtained one and had fathomed some of its timeless mysteries. Their characteristic courage extended to intellectual exploration as well as to prowess on the battlefield.

From the possibility that the Templars possessed a crystal skull or that they had preserved and venerated the head of John the Baptist as a holy relic, it is germane to move to another mysterious head: a *conehead* from South America. As shown in the accompanying illustration, various skulls of this distorted type exist. They have been reported from ancient

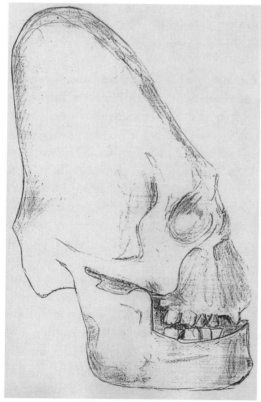

Nubia, Egypt, and other ancient civilisations where it was sometimes the practice to bind skulls in order to create weird, conical head shapes. There are intriguing problems of cranial capacity, however, when the skulls are examined in detail. Modern cranial capacity caters for a brain size of approximately fifteen hundred cubic centimetres, and if it is a modern type of human

Were these strange coneheads aliens from a distant planet, victims of skull binding, an unknown quasi-human subrace — or Atlanteans?

skull that has been bound to deform it conically, the capacity is not significantly altered. Much as we modern human beings may like to pride ourselves on our brain size compared to our earliest cave-dwelling fore-bears, Cro-Magnon and Neanderthal people both had skulls with brain capacities of around seventeen hundred cubic centimetres — two hundred cubic centimetres bigger than ours! When researcher Robert Connolly was on a recent world trip looking into ancient civilizations for his CD-ROM *The Search for Ancient Wisdom* (Cambrix, 1-800-992-8781) he came across conehead skull samples with brain capacities in excess of twenty-two hundred cubic centimetres. This is not easily explained, but it is interesting to bear in mind that some conehead skulls were located in Paracas in Peru, and Peru has been the site of much reported UFO activity in recent years — even though such activity now seems to be on hold. For example, as recently as Wednesday, March 3, 1999, flying silver discs were reported over Lima and remained in sight for over half an hour. In the small town of Chilca, about forty miles from Lima, residents are convinced that UFO-riding aliens have done something miraculous to the local mudflats so that they now have amazing healing powers. If the coneheads are extraterrestrials, they seem to be medically efficient and very benign!

While considering the cranial capacities of our ancestors — even though brain size is not necessarily positively correlated with intelligence — it's interesting to look at the Antikythera Machine, sometimes referred to as an ancient Greek "computer." It isn't quite that, but it's nevertheless ingenious and well worth considering among the world's most mysterious objects. As the accompanying illustration reveals, many beautiful artifacts have been recovered from the wrecks of Greek merchant ships, which traded all over the Mediterranean millennia ago. Like the vase in the illustration, when they are recovered they are thickly encrusted with marine material, seashells, and similar sedimentary debris.

While working at Easter over a century ago, a sponge diver found an ancient Greek wreck containing an amazing piece of engineering work that a contemporary Swiss watchmaker would have been proud to design and build. It contained 40 or 50 cogwheels altogether, and had a central cog with nearly 250 beautifully precise teeth cut into it. After long and painstaking restoration work, it was clear that the exquisitely made device was an astronomical calendar designed to

Like this beautiful Greek vase, the weird Antikythera Machine was covered with shells and marine deposits when it was recovered.

show the movements of the sun in the zodiac as well as the risings and settings of bright stars and constellations.

A device such as that links with the many theories of the vital importance of the Great Pyramid and the Riddle of the Sphinx. In the minds of many theorists, those amazing structures have their own very special astronomical and astrological significances, which are widely known to researchers of the paranormal. What is rather less well known — and richly deserves a great deal more study — is the link between the Great Seal of the United States and the symbolic mysteries of the ancient pyramid itself. A brilliant academic study by Dr. Bob Hieronimus entitled *America's Secret Destiny* traces links between great founding fathers, like George Washington, Benjamin Franklin, and Thomas Jefferson on one hand and mysterious orders such as the Rosicrucians and the Illuminati on the other. As far as Dr. Hieronimus is concerned, the lesser known side of America's Great Seal (with the pyramid and the eye in the triangle above it) certainly qualifies as one of the world's most mysterious objects. Dr. Bob's fascinating theories make it clear that if the Great Seal's full significance was understood and applied today, it would be especially relevant to the current tense and critical international political situation.

Does the riddle of the Sphinx go back ten thousand years?

If Jefferson, Washington, and Franklin were really aware of strange secrets and mysteries older than the Sphinx and the Great Pyramid — via organisations such as the Templars, Freemasons, Illuminati, and Rosicrucians — then it is very probable that one earlier, powerful personality involved in the acquisition and transmission of such arcane knowledge was Francis Bacon, a contender for the real authorship of the plays attributed to Shakespeare.

Bacon and his Elizabethan contemporaries — including his secretive, undercover brother, Anthony, who was a member of the Elizabethan secret service — almost certainly communicated by means of a cleverly concealed watermark code.

The world's most mysterious objects often seem to be independent of time. A modern mystery, like the true meaning behind the Great Seal, has intriguing roots that go back to the American founding fathers. Then they penetrate even further beyond them to men like Sir Francis Bacon, the Templars, the Illuminati, the Rosicrucians, and the Freemasons. At their deepest, those roots drink from the same water that may once have lapped around the Sphinx and the lost towers of ancient Atlantis.

Today's news items and those of half a century ago can both inadvertently refer to the same mysterious object — or to something remarkably like it. In 1953, an Australian diver was working in the South Pacific. He reported that a five metre shark was circling around him and looking curious rather than hungry. The diver went on descending and wondered just how far the shark would continue to come down with him. The diver reached a ledge, below which he described a vast black chasm of awesome unknown depth. It was not safe to attempt it, so he rested on the ledge for a few moments. The shark was hovering about seven metres above him. Even through his suit, the diver felt a sudden significant drop in temperature. He observed a great, dark brown mass — about half a hectare in area — rising slowly from the vast abyss below him. It seemed to be pulsating, and he was convinced that the enormous thing was alive. The shark was motionless — possibly, the diver thought, overcome by fear, or else by the intense cold. The great, brown blob reached the shark and touched it. The shark convulsed just once and then sank into the body of the monster. The diver never saw it again. He waited motionless on the ledge until the huge blob had vanished again into the darkness below him, and then slowly returned to the welcome light and human company on the surface.

That strange story ties in with a report dated April 2, 2002. A huge blob of *something* mysterious and sinister has been reported in the ocean drifting towards the coast of Florida. Some scientists think it's a huge bloom of algae. It was noted, however, that marine life seemed to be trying to avoid it, and one official's report contained the very natural and human comment: "It's scary looking, and we really don't know what it is." Is it remotely possibly that it could be the same strange *thing* that paralysed and absorbed a shark in the South Pacific half a century ago, while an amazed diver stood watching it from his ledge above the chasm?

Another fabulous underwater mystery may have been found in April 2002, just off the coast of India. Researcher Graham Hancock and a team of divers from the Dorset-based Scientific Exploration Society have found what looks very much like the ruins of the ancient city of Mahabalipuram, which could date from ten thousand years ago — *or even more*. These latest findings would seem to suggest that the Atlantean theories have a solid base in fact, and that the survivors of Atlantis — whether terrestrial or extraterrestrial — went on to found other great and enduring cities much further back in time than is generally realized.

BIBLIOGRAPHY

Adkins, Lesley and Roy. *Abandoned Places*. London: A Quantum Book, 1990.

Andrews, William. *Curiosities of the Church*. London: Methuen & Co, 1890.

————. *Curious Church Customs*. London: Simpkin, Marshall, Hamilton, Kent, & Co. Ltd., 1895.

————. *Old Church Life*. London: William Andrews & Co., 1900.

————. *Old Church Lore*. London: Simpkin, Marshall, Hamilton, Kent, & Co. Ltd., 1891.

————. *Antiquities and Curiosities of the Church*. London: William Andrews & Co., 1897.

————. *The Church Treasury*. London: William Andrews & Co., 1898.

Arscott, David. *Curiosities of East Sussex*. East Sussex: S.B.Publications, 1995.

Bell, Walter George. *Unknown London*. London: Spring Books, 1966.

Berlitz, Charles. *World of Strange Phenomena*. London: Sphere Books Limited, 1989.

Blashford-Snell, John. *Mysteries: Encounters with the Unexplained*. London: Bodley Head, 1983.

Blundell, Nigel and Roger Boar. *The World's Greatest Ghosts*. London: Octopus Books Ltd., 1984.

Bord, Janet and Colin. *Mysterious Britain*. London: Granada, 1974.

Boudet, Henri. *La Vraie Langue Celtique et le Cromleck de Rennes-les-Bains*, reprint. Nice: Belisane, 1984.

Briggs, Katharine M. *British Folk Tales and Legend: A Sampler*. London: Paladin, 1977.

Camilleri, George. *Realms of Fantasy: Folk Tales from Gozo*. Victoria, Gozo: Camilleri, 1992.

Cavendish, Richard, (Ed.). *Encyclopaedia of the Unexplained*. London:

Routledge & Kegan Paul, 1974.

Chamber, Aidan. *Ghosts and Hauntings*. England: Puffin Books, 1973.

Clark, Jerome. *Unexplained*. United States: Gale Research Inc., 1993.

Cohen, Daniel. *Encyclopaedia of Ghosts*. London: Guild Publishing, 1989.

Cooper, Rev. Chas W. *The Precious Stones of the Bible*. London: H.R. Allenson Ltd.

Cruz, Joan Carroll. *Relics*. Huntington, Indiana: Our Sunday Visitor, Inc., 1983.

Dixon, G. M. *Folktales and Legends of Norfolk*. Minimax, 1983.

Doyle, Arthur Conan. *The Conan Doyle Stories*. England: Blitz Editions, 1993.

Dunford, Barry. *The Holy Land of Scotland*. Scotland: Brigadoon Books, 1996.

Dyall, Valentine. *Unsolved Mysteries*. London: Hutchinson & Co. Ltd., 1954.

Eysenck, H.J and Carl Sargent. *Explaining the Unexplained*. London: BCA, 1993.

Encyclopaedia Britannica. Britannica Online: http://www.eb.com

Fanthorpe, Patricia and Lionel. *The Holy Grail Revealed*. California: Newcastle Publishing Co. Inc., 1982.

————. *The Oak Island Mystery*. Toronto: Hounslow Press, 1995.

————. *Secrets of Rennes le Château*. Maine: Samuel Weiser Inc., 1992.

————. *The World's Greatest Unsolved Mysteries*. Toronto: Hounslow Press, 1997.

————. *The World's Most Mysterious People*. Toronto: Hounslow Press, 1998.

————. *The World's Most Mysterious Places*. Toronto: Hounslow Press, 1999.

————. *Mysteries of the Bible*. Toronto: Hounslow Press, 1999.

Forman, Joan. *Haunted East Anglia*. Great Britain: Fontana, 1976.

Fowke, Edith. *Canadian Folklore*. Ontario: Oxford University Press, 1988.

Godart, Louis. *The Phaistos Disc*. Itanos Publications, 1995

Graves, Robert. "Introduction." *Larousse Encyclopaedia of Mythology*. London: Paul Hamlyn, 1959.

Green, Jim. *Holy Ways of Wales*. Y Lolfa Cyf.: Talybont, Ceredigion, 2000.

Guerber, H.A. *Myths and Legends of the Middle Ages*. London: Studio Editions Ltd., 1994.

Guirdham, Arthur. *The Lake & The Castle*. Wales: Cygnus Books, 1992.

————. *We Are One Another*. Wales: Cygnus Books, 1992.

————. *The Cathars and Reincarnation*.

Hieronimus, Dr. Robert. *America's Secret Destiny*. Vermont: Destiny Books, 1989.

Lambert, R.S. *Exploring the Supernatural*. London: Arthur Barker Ltd., 1955.

Lampitt, L.F., (Ed.). *The World's Strangest Stories*. London: Associated Newspapers Group Ltd., 1955.

Lewis, Val. *Satan's Mistress*. Middlesex, England: Nauticalia Ltd., 1997.

Mack, Lorrie, et al, (Ed.). *The Unexplained*. London: Orbis, 1984.

Massingham, Huge and Pauline. *The London Anthology*. London: Spring Books.

Maziére, Francis. *Mysteries of Easter Island*. England: Wm. Collins Sons & Co Ltd., 1968.

Michell, John and Robert J.M. Rickard. *Phenomena: A Book of Wonders*. London: Thames & Hudson, 1977.

Morton, H.V. *Ghosts of London*. London: Methuen & Co Ltd., 1939.

Moss, Peter. *Ghosts Over Britain*. Great Britain: Sphere Books Ltd., 1979.

Owen, George, and Victor Sims. *Science and the Spook*. London: Dennis Dobson, 1971.

Page, R.I. *Reading the Runes*. London: Trustees of the British Museum, 1987.

Pennick, Nigel. *Mazes and Labyrinths*. London: Robert Hale, 1998.

Playfair, G.L. *The Unknown Power*. London: Granada, 1977.

Poole, Keith B. *Ghosts of Wessex*. Canada: Douglas David & Charles Ltd., 1976.

Porter, Enid. *The Folklore of East Anglia*. London: B.T. Batsford Ltd., 1974.

Pott, Mrs Henry. *Francis Bacon and His Secret Society*. London: Sampson Low, Marston & Company, 1891.

Rawcliffe, D.H. *Illusions and Delusions of the Supernatural and the Occult*. New York: 1959.

Reader's Digest. *Folklore, Myths and Legends of Britain*. London: The Reader's Digest Ass. Ltd., 1973.

————. *Strange Stories, Amazing Facts*. London: The Reader's Digest Ass. Ltd., 1975.

Rolleston, T.W. *Celtic Myths and Legends*. London: Studio Editions Ltd., 1994.

Russell, Eric Frank. *Great World Mysteries*. London: Mayflower, 1967.

Saltzman, Pauline. *The Strange and the Supernormal*. New York: Paperback Library, Inc., 1968.

Scott, Michael. *Irish Ghosts & Hauntings*. Great Britain: Warner Book, 1994.

Sharper Knowlson, T. *The Origins of Popular Superstitions and Customs*. London: Studio Editions Ltd., 1995.

Snow, Edward Rowe. *Strange Tales from Nova Scotia to Cape Hatteras*. USA: Dodd, Mead & Company, 1946.

Spencer, John and Anne. *The Encyclopaedia of the World's Greatest Unsolved Mysteries*. London: Headline Book Publishing, 1995.

Target, George. *Holy Ground*. London: Bishopsgate Press, 1986.

Tyack, Rev. Geo S. *Lore and Legend of the English Church*. London: William Andrews & Co., 1899.

Van Buren, Elizabeth. *The Dragon of Rennes-le-Château*. Vogels: 1998.

Warren, T. Herbert. "Introduction." *Poems of Tennyson*. London: Humphrey Milford Oxford University Press, 1940.

Welfare, Simon and John Fairley. *Arthur C. Clarke's Mysterious World*. England: William Collins Sons & Company Ltd., 1980.

Whitehead, Ruth Holmes. *Stories from the Six Worlds*. Nova Scotia: Nimbus Publishing Ltd., 1988

Wilson, Colin. *The Psychic Detectives*. London: Pan Books, 1984.

Wilson, Colin and Damon Wilson. *Unsolved Mysteries Past and Present*. London: Headline Book Publishing, 1993.

Wilson, Colin, Damon Wilson, and Rowan Wilson. *World Famous True Ghost Stories*. London: Robinson Publishing, 1996.

Wilson, Colin and Dr. Christopher Evans, (Eds.). *The Book of Great Mysteries*. London: Robinson Publishing, 1986.

Young, George. *Ghosts in Nova Scotia*. Nova Scotia: George Young, 1991.